Dr Jan-Wim Wesselius is Senior Lecturer and Head of the Department of Semitic Studies in the Theological University of Kampen, Netherlands.

JOURNAL FOR THE STUDY OF THE OLD TESTAMENT SUPPLEMENT SERIES
345

Sheffield Academic Press
A Continuum imprint

The Origin of the History of Israel

Herodotus's *Histories* as Blueprint for the First Books of the Bible

Jan-Wim Wesselius

Journal for the Study of the Old Testament
Supplement Series 345

Copyright © 2002 Sheffield Academic Press
A Continuum imprint

Published by Sheffield Academic Press Ltd
The Tower Building, 11 York Road, London SE1 7NX
370 Lexington Avenue, New York NY 10017-6550

www.SheffieldAcademicPress.com
www.continuumbooks.com

British Library Cataloguing-in-Publication Data

A catalogue record for this book is available from the British Library

Typeset by Sheffield Academic Press
Printed on acid-free paper in Great Britain by Bookcraft Ltd, Midsomer Norton, Bath

ISBN 1-84127-267-1

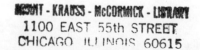

CONTENTS

PREFACE

Few works have had more influence on the course of human history, religion and culture than the books of the Old Testament or Hebrew Bible, yet strangely their origin has hitherto remained shrouded in mystery. Mainly describing episodes in the history of the kingdoms of Judah and Israel and of the Jews in the Persian empire in the tenth to fifth centuries BCE, the collection now known as the Hebrew canon emerges into the light of history nearly complete (at first with the important omission of books such as Ezra, Esther and Daniel) in the writings of Jesus ben Sira around 250 BCE and a little later in the earliest of the Dead Sea Scrolls. Unfortunately, our information about the formative period of the Hebrew Bible is scanty at best, and of the actual writing of its books we know next to nothing. Our only way to get to know the literary world in which the Hebrew Bible originated is through the works themselves. True, we know or suspect that certain texts were known before they entered into the collection, and we have extraneous information about the historical situation underlying the books of Kings, as well as about various biblical figures outside this historical framework, such as David and even Balaam, but we have no external evidence whatsoever about the books' writing, redaction and being collected into the Hebrew Bible.

Nearly all the supposed information about their time of origin, original form and collecting in the canon therefore rests on internal analysis of the works in combination with analogies with better-known situations and with extrapolation into the past of later conditions. Thus the complex textual situation of the biblical text in the Dead Sea Scrolls is taken to be representative of an earlier period also, providing us with some insight into the way in which the biblical literature may have originated,[1] and the

1. See, for example, the essays in E. Ulrich, *The Dead Sea Scrolls and the Origins of the Bible: Studies in the Dead Sea Scrolls and Related Literature* (Grand Rapids, MI: Eerdmans, 1999).

various ways in which other canonical collections have come into being are applied to the biblical canon also.[2]

The internal analysis has mainly used two approaches, the first being the recognition of discontinuities in books and episodes, which are supposed to be reflexes of redactional processes, and the second the contrasting attempt to identify coherent works and episodes in larger units and to isolate them. These two approaches are usually associated with historical criticism (and related methods) and with literary study, respectively. Although they are completely separate approaches, to a degree they appear to need each other in order to reach a complete picture of the origin and nature of the books of the Hebrew Bible. Even the most hardened adherents of historical criticism and related types of historical analysis of the text of the Hebrew Bible must pay some lip service to the final form of the parts that are distinguished in the texts, otherwise they can hardly defend the basic thesis that the present text was amalgamated from various layers of writing and redaction. By contrast, most literary scholars have been very reticent to attach their observations to historical situations, but on the whole somewhat reluctantly endorse the idea that the text is the result of a historical process also, even when they defend the primacy of the text as we now have it.

Some scholars tend towards the position that the text is most usefully studied entirely in its present form. Although this eliminates the dichotomy sketched above, and turns out to be a remarkably useful and productive hypothesis, it does not solve the problem of the origin of the texts, nor can it provide a model that explains why they look the way they do.

The information that is supposedly gained by means of internal analysis is often used to fit the constituent parts of the literature of the Hebrew Bible in reconstructed literary and religious histories of the period of about 1200–165 BCE. It should be noted, however, that there are relatively few issues where there is complete agreement among researchers, usually trivial matters such as the priority of the books of Samuel and Kings over Chronicles.[3]

All this presupposes that most of these books are multi-layered works with a complicated history, and we would have no choice but to accept

---

2.   A good recent example is P.R. Davies, *Scribes and Schools: The Canonization of the Hebrew Scriptures* (Louisville, KY: Westminster/John Knox Press, 1998).

3.   A very complete critical survey of different approaches to the study of the Pentateuch is found in C. Houtman, *Der Pentateuch: Die Geschichte seiner Erforschung neben einer Auswertung* (Kampen: Kok Pharos, 1994).

this opinion, were it not for the remarkable fact, which remained unrecognized until very recently, that most of the major historical works (in the sense of books describing events in the past) in the Hebrew Bible appear to have derived both their structure and the main course of the action from other works, in most cases inside the Hebrew Bible itself, but in the most striking case from a work outside it. Thus the book of Daniel derives its division into chapters or episodes from Ezra, as well as the switch from the Hebrew to the Aramaic language and back again; the series of dreams and visions has been copied rather precisely from those in the Life of Joseph in Genesis 37–50, and the shift of focus away from the protagonist in Daniel 3 evidently derives from the comparable phenomenon in Genesis 38. Ezra in turn is based in a similar manner on the book of Nehemiah, also a book that describes a return from the captivity in the East to Jerusalem. Finally, the Primary History, the historical books Genesis–2 Kings at the beginning of the Bible which present one continuous historical account from creation to the fall of Jerusalem to the Babylonians in 587 BCE, to our great surprise appears to derive its structure, with nine books divided into three parts, namely book 1, books 2–6 and books 7–9, from the Greek-language *Histories* of Herodotus of Halicarnassus (written between about 445 and 425 BCE). This ultimate proof of closure and of authorial intention suddenly and completely reverses our view of the discontinuities and discrepancies in these works: from indications of the historical development of the text, thinly veiled by editorial work, they become literary phenomena, to be studied and explained on the purely literary level. Each of these works can be subjected to an analysis that separates it into several different layers, because the authors deliberately created this option by choosing the literary form of what I would like to call the *linear literary dossier*: a series of supposedly more or less independent documents in roughly chronological order, with limited disagreements and discontinuities. Conversely, the constituent parts, and sometimes the entire work as well, lend themselves to a literary analysis because a number of coherent episodes have been created within them, and because the authors took care to insert indications of continuity throughout the work.[4]

4. See especially my 'Discontinuity, Congruence and the Making of the Hebrew Bible', *SJOT* 13 (1999), pp. 24-77, and 'Towards a New History of Israel', *Journal of Hebrew Scriptures* [www.arts.ualberta.ca/JHS or www.purl.org/jhs] 3 (2000–2001), article 2; PDF version pp. 1-21, and the earlier literature quoted there.

The rest of this book deals with the consequences of these observations for our view of Primary History as a literary and historical document. First I shall compare the flow of the narrative of the *Histories* and of Primary History. In the second chapter the literary methods of the author will be described in some detail, and a formal description of the relationship between the two texts will be given. Then in the third chapter some of the consequences for the study of Primary History in general will be given, and finally, in the fourth chapter, the consequences for the literary study of Primary History will be discussed by means of four case-studies.

I am grateful to the Netherlands Institute for Advanced Study in the Humanities and Social Sciences (NIAS) in Wassenaar and the Department of Semitic Languages of the *Vrije Universiteit* in Amsterdam for their hospitality in the academic years 1997–98 and 1998–99, respectively. This book proved rather difficult to write and to complete for several reasons, among others because of the hesitation to engage in an enterprise that could potentially change completely an entire established academic discipline, because of the necessity to refine and complete its unusual thesis as much as possible before its final presentation, and because it touches and tests my own and others' religious susceptibilities in a rather unexpected manner. I could not have done it without the continuing loving support of my wife, Françoise, and our children Nanja, Joram, Carel and Rolf.

ABBREVIATIONS

AB	Anchor Bible
AJP	*American Journal of Philology*
CBQ	*Catholic Biblical Quarterly*
ETL	*Ephemerides theologicae lovanienses*
GRBS	*Greek, Roman, and Byzantine Studies*
HALAT	Ludwig Koehler *et al.* (eds.), *Hebräisches und aramäisches Lexikon zum Alten Testament* (5 vols.; Leiden: E.J. Brill, 1967–1995)
HUCA	*Hebrew Union College Annual*
JBL	*Journal of Biblical Literature*
JEOL	*Jaarbericht…Ex Oriente Lux*
JSOT	*Journal for the Study of the Old Testament*
JSP	*Journal for the Study of the Pseudepigrapha*
OTS	*Oudtestamentische Studiën*
RSV	Revised Standard Version
SJOT	*Scandinavian Journal of the Old Testament*
VT	*Vetus Testamentum*
ZAW	*Zeitschrift für die alttestamentliche Wissenschaft*

Chapter 1

TWO GREAT HISTORICAL WORKS

The writing and telling of history appears to be an almost universal characteristic of human civilization, and there probably never was a period in
which people were not interested in ordering the events of the past and
telling about them. Yet it is generally accepted that historiography in its
modern sense—in contrast with earlier and more commonly known genres
such as annals, royal inscriptions and chronological lists—arose rather late
in antiquity, according to most more or less at the same time in Israel and
in Greece, in the seventh to fifth centuries BCE. Somewhat surprisingly, we
meet almost at once a sophisticated and lengthy work in both locations, in
which the definition of the identity of the author's group in contrast with
the others, the outsiders, plays an important role. Herodotus of Halicarnassus (c. 490–430 BCE) wrote a nine-volume work called *Historie* ('investigation'), usually called his *Histories*, about the wars between Greeks and
Persians during the reigns of the Persian kings Darius and Xerxes in the
period 492–479 BCE, in which he also exposed the roots of this conflict in
the history of Greece and the Near East in the two preceding centuries.[1]
The great historical work in Israel, the series of the nine biblical books
from Genesis to 2 Kings, has a much wider scope, starting with the

---

1. A new translation of large parts of the work, with short extracts from secondary
literature, is found in Walter Blanco and Jennifer Tolbert Roberts, *Herodotus. The
Histories: New Translation, Selections, Backgrounds, Commentaries* (New York:
Norton, 1992). Cf. also the translation by Aubrey de Selincourt (Harmondsworth:
Penguin, 1954), from which most of the quotations presented below were taken, and
the edition with translation in the Loeb series by A.D. Godley (4 vols.; LCL; London:
Heinemann, 1920–1924). On Herodotus's history of the Near East see R. Drews, *The
Greek Accounts of Eastern History* (Washington: Center for Hellenic Studies, 1973).
See also the comprehensive study by D. Lateiner, *The Historical Method of Herodotus*
(Toronto: University of Toronto Press, 1989), and the well-written and informative
essays in John Gould, *Herodotus* (London: Weidenfeld and Nicholson, 1989). Publi-
cations will be quoted according to the Revised Standard Version.

creation of the world, and continuing with stories about the patriarchs, explaining how the Israelites came to live in Egypt and how they were delivered from there through divine intervention and finally took possession of the land of Canaan. The work continues with Israel's history in the Promised Land until the taking of Jerusalem by the Babylonians and the beginning of the Babylonian exile in 587 BCE.[2]

It is hardly surprising that the work of Herodotus and these historical books of the Bible, which are nowadays usually designated 'Primary History',[3] have been compared numerous times in the past. These two works constitute elaborate histories of two nations that have exercised decisive influence on the development of the Western world, namely the Greeks and the Jews, and their identity is outlined very convincingly in these compositions. For these and other reasons there have been numerous scholars who put one beside the other, unfortunately with relatively limited results, as appears from some recent publications in this field.

The by now almost classic work by John Van Seters, *In Search of History*, engages in a general discussion of the position of Israelite historiography among historical texts from the ancient Near East and Greece, and has rightly been hailed as an impressive and innovative contribution to its study. Van Seters notes that, whereas we have numerous texts from the Near East with historical contents, only the Greek historians can be said to parallel the biblical historical texts in their distance from the past that is being described. Van Seters tends to keep the Pentateuch or Torah, the five so-called books of Moses, outside the comparison with other historical texts, presumably because many of the events described in them can hardly be interpreted as reflexes of historical events. He mentions a fair number of agreements in substance and style between the books Joshua–2 Kings, often taken to be the main part of the 'Deuteronomistic History' (together with the book of Deuteronomy itself), on the one hand, and a

2.   There is a host of recent literature dealing with various aspects of the history of Israel in the biblical period. Two important books: Thomas L. Thompson, *Early History of the Israelite People: From the Written and Archaeological Sources* (Leiden: E.J. Brill, 1992), especially the third chapter, 'Historicity and the Deconstruction of Biblical Historiography' (pp. 77-126), and Philip R. Davies, *In Search of 'Ancient Israel'* (Sheffield: Sheffield Academic Press, 1992).

3.   This designation, apparently coined by D.N. Freedman, here merely used as a neutral term for the books Genesis–2 Kings of the Hebrew Bible, because the alternatives 'Biblical History' and 'History of Israel', though both quite appropriate, have a number of extra connotations.

number of Greek historians, especially Herodotus, on the other, but refrains from attempting a precise definition of the nature of the relationship between these two traditions of history-writing, and merely states that mutual influencing cannot be excluded.[4]

By contrast, Sara Mandell and David Noel Freedman have written a book that deals exclusively with the comparison of Primary History and Herodotus' *Histories*. Their main interest is in the field of redaction, though style and contents receive attention as well. They note certain formal agreements between the two works, such as the division of both into nine volumes, and the intriguing phenomenon of both having the separation between the eighth and the ninth book in the middle of an episode: with Herodotus the story about the mission that the Persian general Mardonius sends to Athens, in the Bible the closely knitted 'Succession History', which extends from 2 Samuel 9 to 1 Kings 2. Their book is a veritable hoard of observations on parallels of various kinds between the two great works, and in those cases where they do not come to a final verdict, they have at least pointed out where others may continue their work. Even in their conclusion, however, the authors remain hesitant about the significance of these observations for the relation between the two works, cautiously suggesting that Herodotus may have been aware of the work of Ezra.[5]

An objection against the methodology of both books, in my view, is that for the purpose of the comparison with other historical texts they take as their point of departure the reconstruction of the prehistory of the biblical text as produced by the Graf–Wellhausen theory of different sources for the Pentateuch. Although in doing this they follow what is probably a majority among twentieth-century biblical scholars, especially for the line of research they propose this assumption should not in my view be made *a priori*. Occasionally, such an approach even leads to a remarkable disregard for information presented literally and explicitly in the text of the

---

4. John Van Seters, *In Search of History* (New Haven: Yale University Press, 1983), pp. 53-54. It is hardly possible to do justice to this learned work here, nor to the important book in the next note, as their approach is completely different from the one proposed here; see also the Preface. Cf. also Van Seters's *Prologue to History: The Yahwist as Historian in Genesis* (Louisville, KY: Westminster/John Knox Press, 1992).

5. Sara Mandell and David Noel Freedman, *The Relationship between Herodotus' History and Primary History* (Atlanta: Scholars Press, 1993), pp. 180-87.

Bible.[6] Whatever one may think about this sometimes hotly debated and always present issue, in my opinion for a comparison of Primary History with other works one should start with the text in its present shape, namely as a continuous historical work that runs from the creation of the world to the Babylonian exile. Only when it turns out to be unavoidable to have recourse to an earlier shape of these biblical books, for example in order to recognize certain parallels that are not visible in the present form of the work, should such reconstructions be taken into consideration, especially since there is considerable disagreement about boundaries and chronology, and even about the mere existence of these sources.[7]

Flemming Nielsen's valuable study in principle discusses only one aspect of the relationship between Primary History and the *Histories*, namely the tragic elements in both.[8] In a way, his is a less ripe work than the others mentioned so far, but as happens not infrequently, this has caused many interesting ideas to remain in it, rather than be pruned out by the experienced scholar's cautiousness. Thus Nielsen daringly tackles the problem of the discrepancies and contradictions within Primary History on the literary level, although he is also unable to shake loose from the idea of the 'Deuteronomistic History' supposedly running from Deuteronomy up to and including 2 Kings, and his final conclusion, that the tragic notions common to Herodotus and Primary History may derive from a common literary background, is somewhat meagre.[9]

In the work of many scholars, there is a remarkable explicit or implicit connection between taking the text of Primary History literally, as intended to mean more or less what it appears to say at first sight, and fundamentalist opinions about its origin and value, and conversely between critical study of this work and the assumption of a rather irregular process of growth of the text, whether or not one subscribes to historical criticism in the Wellhausen tradition. I shall attempt to show that the

---

6.   Note, for example, that the genealogy of Moses, which will play a significant role in our considerations here, though explicitly presented in Exod. 2.1 (without the names of his parents), in Exod. 6.13-26 (see also below) and in Num. 26.58, for this reason receives hardly any attention in these two books, and even in books exclusively dealing with him, e.g. John Van Seters, *The Life of Moses* (Kampen: Kok Pharos, 1994), which passes it over almost entirely.

7.   Cf. Houtman, *Der Pentateuch. Die Geschichte seiner Erforschung neben einer Auswertung* (Kampen: Kok Pharos, 1994).

8.   F.A.J. Nielsen, *The Tragedy in History: Herodotus and the Deuteronomistic History* (JSOTSup, 251; CIS, 4; Sheffield: Sheffield Academic Press, 1997).

9.   Nielsen, *The Tragedy in History*, esp. p. 164.

connection may well be the other way round, and that Primary History was most likely deliberately composed in the form in which we have it now, but that it probably is a text with a rather narrowly circumscribed time of origin and purpose. I shall refrain from taking sides in the recent debate about the relation between the picture drawn in the Bible of Ancient Israel and the realities of the history of Palestine and the neighbouring countries in the period described,[10] but try to point out the nature of Primary History as an ancient historical work, leaving the complex relationship with 'historical reality' entailed by its character as the view of a learned Jew of late Persian or early Hellenistic times on the history of his people to further research. We will see, however, that our literary study at least partly confirms the critical ideas recently evinced about Judaism as we know it having been the result of religious and political tendencies in the Persian period, and being based historically in forms of religion and society which certainly would not conform to its standards.

In this book it will be argued that the author of Primary History made extensive use of the work of Herodotus, especially for the part that deals with the period before 1000 BCE, i.e. before the beginning of the monarchy in Israel; and, perhaps more importantly, that Primary History can very well be read in contrast with Herodotus' *Histories*, indeed that it must be read in conjunction with that work in order to be properly understood. I shall in general only deal with questions and observations that are directly relevant for the evaluation of this thesis, and shall leave aside the many possible points of comparison between the two works that are of secondary significance only for this purpose, such as the use of poetry and other literary forms in the middle of narrative prose, the relationship with the divine, the lack of descriptions of emotions, or the technique of having two histories run side by side, shifting between the two every now and then; many of these are discussed in the books by Van Seters, Mandell and Freedman, and Nielsen mentioned above. The time has certainly not yet come for a full evaluation of these parallels, partly because the thesis set forth in this book may well lead to a new view on at least some of these also.

I shall first attempt to demonstrate that in both works in their present shape there is a common element, which, though well hidden and hitherto never noticed, is so characteristic that it is almost unthinkable that there would not be a direct connection between the two, namely the important

---

10. See the literature quoted in Chapter 3.

position of the key figures of Joseph, the son of the patriarch Jacob, who became viceroy of Egypt, on the one hand, and King Cyrus, the founder of the great Persian empire, on the other. I shall also try to show that there are a number of rather precise parallels between individual members of the families of Joseph and Cyrus, and that on this basis we can postulate a striking congruence between the genealogy of the patriarchs and that of the Persian–Median royal house, exposing a number of parallelisms between persons belonging to corresponding generations. The most surprising of these parallels is between the figures of Moses and King Xerxes, not in the description of their character, appearance or course of life, but in certain aspects of their careers as leaders of their people. It will be noted in this connection that the main subjects of Primary History and the work of Herodotus are surprisingly similar: a leader, summoned by the divinity, brings an enormous army into another continent across a body of water as on dry land in order to conquer a country there. In both cases, the conquest finally comes to naught when the last city remaining in the hands of the conquerors is reduced by means of a gruelling siege. We will also see that the theme of the deception of or by a family member, with each subsequent act of deception a reaction to the preceding one, runs on through several generations, and that some instances correspond very closely with those in the other work.

Joseph

The story of Joseph is one of the best known of the entire Bible. When he is seventeen years old, he arouses the anger and even the hatred of his half-brothers by denouncing them to his father Jacob and by telling them two similar dreams that he has had, which are understood without any hesitation by the members of his family as meaning that Joseph will finally rule over all of them. Joseph received from his father a beautiful garment ($k^e tonet\ pass\bar{\imath}m$, lit. 'garment of stripes', cf. the rendering in the Septuagint: *chiton poikilon*, 'many-coloured coat', RSV 'long robe with sleeves'), and he apparently wears it all the time, as it plays an important part in what follows.

> [Gen. 37.3] Now Israel loved Joseph more than any other of his children, because he was the son of his old age; and he made him a long robe with sleeves. [4] But when his brothers saw that their father loved him more than all his brothers, they hated him, and could not speak peaceably to him. [5] Now Joseph had a dream, and when he told it to his brothers they only hated him the more. [6] He said to them, 'Hear this dream which I have

dreamed: [7] behold, we were binding sheaves in the field, and lo, my sheaf arose and stood upright; and behold, your sheaves gathered round it, and bowed down to my sheaf'. [8] His brothers said to him, 'Are you indeed to reign over us? Or are you indeed to have dominion over us?' So they hated him yet more for his dreams and for his words. [9] Then he dreamed another dream, and told it to his brothers, and said, 'Behold, I have dreamed another dream; and behold, the sun, the moon, and eleven stars were bowing down to me.' [10] But when he told it to his father and to his brothers, his father rebuked him, and said to him, 'What is this dream that you have dreamed? Shall I and your mother and your brothers indeed come to bow ourselves to the ground before you?' [11] And his brothers were jealous of him, but his father kept the saying in mind.

One day Joseph is sent by his father, who apparently does not fathom the brothers' feelings of hatred towards him, to inquire after their well-being. At first Joseph cannot find them, but he is informed by a stranger that they have gone to Dothan. He travels on to that place and finds them there. While he is approaching his brothers they start to make plans against him:

[Gen. 37.18] They saw him afar off, and before he came near to them they conspired against him to kill him. [19] They said to one another, 'Here comes this dreamer. [20] Come now, let us kill him and throw him into one of the pits; then we shall say that a wild beast has devoured him, and we shall see what will become of his dreams.'

Reuben, the oldest of the brothers, intervenes and says that they should not kill their brother Joseph, and that they may as well throw him alive in a pit, with the implication that Joseph would die there of hunger and thirst. In reality Reuben has the intention, we are told, to liberate Joseph afterwards and to return him to their father. The brothers follow his suggestion, take off Joseph's many-coloured garment (later it becomes clear why they do so) and throw him into the pit. But while Reuben has apparently walked away, the other brothers see a caravan of merchants on their way from the other side of the river Jordan to Egypt. On the suggestion of Judah, another brother, they sell Joseph to the merchants and these take him along to Egypt.

The brothers then dip the many-coloured garment in the blood of a kid (s^e '*īr* '*izzīm*) and they send it to their father with the request to identify it. Jacob sees the stained coat, immediately assumes that Joseph has been killed by a wild animal (*ḥayyā rā* '*ā*) and mourns for his son. Joseph, meanwhile, is sold in Egypt to a certain Potiphar, the 'captain of the guard'.

The rest of the well-known story of Joseph is of less importance for our purpose here: how he lands in prison in Egypt, because the wife of his master Potiphar is impressed by his beauty (he is called y^e*pe to'ar wīpe mar'e*, 'beautiful of figure and beautiful of appearance'), tries to seduce him, and finally accuses him of assaulting her, how he gets out of prison through his capacity to elucidate dreams, and how the same ability enables him to attain the rank of viceroy of Egypt. Two points that need to be especially noted are the two instances of chapters that clearly interrupt the Joseph narrative. Genesis 38 contains the famous story of Judah and Tamar, the widow of two of his sons, who through a ruse succeeds in letting her father-in-law impregnate her, when he refuses to let his third son marry her: she sits with covered head by the roadside where Judah is to pass by, pretending to be a prostitute, and he has intercourse with her. One child of the twins born from this union has an especial significance, because this Perez is to become the ancestor of King David (according to Ruth 4.18-22). In any case the children are apparently (according to Gen. 46.12) two of the three direct male descendants of Judah, and consequently the ancestors of the large majority of the tribe of Judah. Genesis 49 contains a long address by the aged Jacob to his sons, in which he characterizes them and pronounces certain predictions about each of them, which are only fulfilled after they have entered the Promised Land and taken possession of it. In the next chapter Jacob dies, and some time later also his son Joseph, at the end of the cycle of stories describing his life.

Cyrus

The only person whose life Herodotus describes from birth to death is the Persian king Cyrus, who has made the Persians from a nation subservient to the Medians into the rulers of the entire Middle East, and thus created the conditions for the great conflict between Greeks and Persians that he describes. Cyrus's way to kingship was not easy, though he stemmed from a royal family. The story that Herodotus tells about this, and which according to him was only one of the versions known to him of Cyrus's birth and youth, runs as follows. The king of the Medes, Astyages, has a daughter of marriageable age, called Mandane. One night he has a dream, in which Mandane urinates so profusely, that his city and all Asia are flooded as a result. His dream-interpreters tell him that this means that Mandane's son—she has not yet borne any children—will take his place, and Astyages decides, somewhat unexpectedly for the reader, to forestall this outcome by letting her marry a Persian called Cambyses, because the Persians were esteemed far lower than the Medians and a son of such a humble marriage would not be able to pose a serious threat. In the first year of her marriage to Cambyses, however, Astyages has a second dream. Now he sees an enormous vine emerging from his daughter's vagina. He again seeks the advice of his dream-interpreters, who explain the dream more or less in the same way as the first time. Astyages decides to let Mandane have her baby at his court and to have it killed immediately afterwards (Her. I, 107-108).

When Mandane has indeed given birth to a son, Astyages orders a certain Harpagus, a courtier and distant relative, to see to it that the boy disappears. Harpagus understandably hesitates to do this, firstly because the child is also related to himself, and secondly because he fears that he will have to face Mandane's vengeance after Astyages' death. He consequently entrusts the child to a shepherd, enjoining him to lay the child in a desolate spot in mountains full of wild animals. The shepherd's wife, however, upon seeing how beautiful the child is, begs him to spare the boy. When he refuses, she proposes to dress their own still-born child in his golden and many-coloured clothes (*chrusoi te kai estheti poikilei*) and to expose it in his place. Thus it happens and the ruse succeeds: a member of Harpagus's guard sees that the child dressed in these garments has indeed died and buries it (Her. I, 108-13).

The little boy is raised in the shepherd's family, receiving a name from them; according to Herodotus the name Cyrus was given to him only later. When he is ten years old, he plays a game with his coevals that involves him being the king, and giving orders to the other children. One of these is the son of a high official of the king, who refuses to obey Cyrus, who then orders him beaten up. The boy complains to his father, who has Cyrus and his foster-father dragged in front of Astyages with the request to punish them severely. King Astyages, however, recognizes his grandson Cyrus by his appearance and his royal behaviour, lets himself be reassured by his dream-interpreters that through the game that Cyrus and his friends played his dreams have already been fulfilled, and consequently spares Cyrus and admits him to his court. He punishes Harpagus, however, with extreme cruelty for disobeying his orders, by feeding him the flesh of his own son at a banquet; Harpagus does not realize this until he is shown the head, hands and feet of his son on a separate tray. From that time onwards, Harpagus secretly seeks revenge and he manages to incite Cyrus against his grandfather. Cyrus then brings the Persians to revolt against their Median overlords, defeats Astyages in battle and becomes king of the Medians and Persians in his place (Her. I, 113-30).

King Croesus of Lydia in the western part of Asia Minor was connected to Astyages through bonds of marriage (his sister was married off to

Astyages to confirm the treaty that ended a war between Lydians and Medians) and goes to war with Cyrus to put matters in order again or to punish him for deposing his grandfather. Cyrus, however, defeats him also, besieges him in his capital Sardis, captures him and takes possession of his kingdom. In one of the best-known stories from the work of Herodotus, Cyrus puts Croesus on a pyre. While the flames are already raging, Croesus calls out the name of the Athenian Solon, whom he had previously discharged contemptuously because, even after being shown Croesus's fabulous treasures, he refused to call him the happiest person in existence before seeing how it all ended, since human fortune is variable. Cyrus hears what Croesus says, asks him about it, hears about the incident with Solon, and decides to spare Croesus. The fire, however, cannot be put out, and it seems as if Croesus is still going to die. He then cries out to Apollo, the Greek god upon whom he bestowed many sumptuous presents, and suddenly a heavy rain comes down and quenches the fire. King Croesus is then indeed taken down from the pyre and even appointed as one of Cyrus's counsellors (Her. I, 75-91).

After that, Cyrus goes to the eastern part of his empire, and leaves it to his generals, foremost among whom is the Harpagus mentioned before, to subjugate the Greek cities in Asia Minor, which had previously been subordinate to Croesus (Her. I, 141-77). After this, Cyrus campaigns against the kingdom of Babylon, which he also conquers (Her. I, 178-91). His last campaign, however, against the Massagetae in Central Asia, ends in disaster: Cyrus is killed and the Persians are routed, and his son Cambyses becomes king in his place. In the night after Cyrus entered the country of the Massagetae he has a dream in which he sees another distant relative, Darius son of Hystaspes, with wings spreading over both Asia and Europe. Cyrus takes this dream to mean that young Darius is plotting against him, and sends back his father Hystaspes in order to keep a check on him. The readers of Herodotus's work, by contrast, see that Cyrus's dream is fulfilled later, when Darius ascends the throne of Persia after Cambyses' death, and is the first to go to war against the Greeks in Europe, so that his dream has a completely different meaning from the one he gave it (Her. I, 201-14).[11]

11. On Herodotus's image of Cyrus see Harry C. Avery, 'Herodotus' Picture of Cyrus', *AJP* 93.4 (1972), pp. 529-46. On the accounts of his early years see Elisabeth Vandiver, *Heroes in Herodotus: The Interaction of Myth and History* (Frankfurt: Lang, 1991), pp. 249-53 ('Appendix C: Cyrus' Birth and Childhood').

Comparison of the Stories

Once we place the first parts of the biographies of Joseph and Cyrus beside each other, we are struck by a large number of agreements. The cause of all problems is in both cases two highly similar dreams which the jealous members of their family interpret, with or without the help of professional dream-interpreters, to mean that the key figure is going to rule over his family (Gen. 37.5-11; Her. I, 107-108). In both cases the members of the family attempt to prevent this prediction coming true by killing the key figure, a measure which to the reader appears rather radical in view of the absence of danger threatening the families (Gen. 37.18-20; Her. I, 108). By their actions to accomplish this, ironically, they are instrumental in establishing the situation they wanted to avoid, though it would not at first appear to be so. The key figure is saved in both cases by the intervention of two persons, mostly members of his family (Joseph's half-brothers Reuben and Judah in Gen. 37.21-22 and 26-27, and Harpagus and the shepherd in Her. I, 109 and 112-13), who apparently do not act this way out of love for him, but because they do not want his death on their conscience; in both cases the family relationship is expressly referred to. The first person causes a temporary reprieve by proposing or ordering the keyfigure to die from exposure instead of through violence, and the second one saves him by causing him to disappear from the view of his enemies. The result is that the key figures come to live in very modest circumstances (Cyrus in the house of the shepherd, posing as his son, Joseph as a servant in the house of Potiphar) and remain hidden from their families for many years (Cyrus for 10 years according to Her. I, 114, Joseph for 22 years according to a combination of Gen. 41.46, 42.53-54 and 45.5). Both key figures are said to be beautiful at the time of their disappearance (Gen. 39.6; Her. I, 112), both are dressed in a many-coloured garment, which is later used to convince their father or grandfather that they have been killed by wild animals (Gen. 37.3, 31-32; Her. I, 110, 111 and 113). Both receive another name when they finally come to power: the king whom we know as Cyrus bore another name at first according to Herodotus, and was only later called Cyrus (Her. I, 113, 114), Joseph receives an Egyptian name, *ṣopnat pa ᵃneaḥ*, from Pharaoh (Gen. 41.45). Both are said to be informed by the divinity about the future in dreams (Pharaoh against Joseph in Gen. 41.38-39, Cyrus about himself in Her. I, 209). Finally and perhaps most importantly, both key figures are the first to come to power in Egypt and the Lydian capital Sardis respectively, the places that were to be the starting point for the great campaigns of two generations later. At that time the great leaders of these campaigns, their family members Moses and Xerxes, clash with persons who are probably the grandsons of the rulers of these places during the days of Joseph and Cyrus, namely the Pharaoh of the Exodus, probably the grandson of the Pharaoh of Joseph, and Pythios, most likely the grandson of Croesus (see also below), with the death of their first-born sons as one of the consequences.

As noted above, in Herodotus's life of Cyrus we find two parallel dreams at the beginning of the story (and one dream at its end), whereas we find no less than three pairs of dreams in the story of Joseph: his own two dreams in Genesis 37, the similar dreams of the chief steward and the chief baker in the prison in Genesis 40, and finally the two dreams of Pharaoh in Genesis 41. Whereas the dreams of Genesis 37 agree with the two dreams of Astyages in their general contents, namely the prediction of power for the key figure, the central elements of Astyages' two dreams, the vine and the stream of urine, are not found there, though the vine returns in the chief steward's dream. Dream-interpreters such as those who explain Astyages' two dreams do not occur in Genesis 37, but are found with Pharaoh's dreams in Gen. 41.8. The parallel elements listed here are without exception relatively common and can be found in various stories from many times and places, but one will not soon find a comparable accumulation of them.

Other Agreements
Bearing in mind the parallels between the stories about mortal danger, salvation and ascension to power of Cyrus and Joseph, we easily notice a number of additional parallels between the first book of Herodotus, especially the part about Cyrus's campaign against Babylon, which also contains an elaborate description of the habits of the people of Babylon and Mesopotamia, and the history of Joseph in Genesis 37–50.

In Genesis 38 Tamar's behaviour is described, at least from the point of view of the inhabitants of the place where she offers herself to her father-in-law Judah, as a case of cultic prostitution: she is among other things described as a $q^e de\check{s}\bar{a}$, a 'woman who is sanctified [to prostitution]'. She sits with veiled face in a certain place called in Hebrew *petah 'enayim*, which is often translated as 'opening/gate of [the town] Enayim', but the first part of which is explained in rabbinical literature as a word for 'crossroads'.[12] The phenomenon of cultic prostitution is by itself well known in the Bible

12. For example in *Targum Onqelos ad loc.*, *pārāšut 'enayim*.

(though its laconic mention here is surprising), but still a look at Herodotus may be useful. His is one of the most famous descriptions of cultic prostitution in antiquity. In Babylon, he tells, every woman must once in her life go to the temple of the goddess Mylitta (nowadays known to Assyriologists as Ninlil), and prostitute herself for a small amount of money to one stranger, after which she will never do this again. The women are sitting, according to him, with covered head (*stefanon peri teisi kefaleisi echousai thominggos*, lit. 'with a wreath of rope on their heads') and arranged in a certain way (*schoinotenees de diexodoi panta tropon hodon echousi dia ton gunaikon*, lit. 'between the women they have straight crossroads in every way of roads'), and waiting until a man will come for them (I, 199). The element of a security given when buying a woman we find in Herodotus's description of the Babylonian 'marriage market' (I, 196), where a buyer has to give a security to ensure that he will indeed marry the woman he chose. There is also an interesting agreement between the fact that Judah appears to have taken his staff and signet (as well as the enigmatic $p^e t\bar{\imath}l\bar{\imath}m$, perhaps 'cords') with him, though he does not even carry the wherewithal to pay Tamar for her services, and Herodotus's remark that the Babylonians always have a staff and signet-ring (*sfregida de hekastos echei kai skeptron cheiropoieton*, 'everybody has a signet-ring and a hand-made staff': I, 195).

The habit of embalming the dead, as performed on Jacob and Joseph (in Gen. 50.2-3 and 26, respectively), seemingly such a typically Egyptian custom, is also mentioned in Herodotus's description of Babylon (I, 198), as are the laments of the Babylonians for their deceased ones, which he says to be much like those of the Egyptians; cf. Gen. 50.11, *wayyom^{e}ru 'evel kāved ze l^{e}mişrayim*, 'They said: This is a grievous mourning to the Egyptians'.

Of course these parallels are not significant when considered in isolation, and may then easily be considered coincidental, but their accumulation in these two books with all their other agreements is certainly striking. They are, however, not essential for the thesis of the connection between the two cycles of stories.

Place within the Work
Such an agreement in biography as we noted to exist between Cyrus and Joseph is interesting by itself, as well as in view of the other common elements of the two stories, and we would anyway have to consider seriously whether there may not have been a certain influence of one on the other, or a common source for the two. But the significance of this parallel

between biblical stories and Herodotus is greater. Both of these short biographies occupy a similar position within the larger works of which they are part. To start with their physical place: both occur in the second half of the first book of a series of nine. The division of Herodotus's *Histories* into nine books is often dated to Hellenistic times, but it may be earlier, and Primary History originally also had nine books, namely the five 'books of Moses', Joshua, Judges, Samuel and Kings (the division of Samuel and Kings into two parts is late, and Ruth, which comes after Judges in the Septuagint and in most Christian translations, is placed further on in the Hebrew canon, with the Writings).

In both works the key figure (Joseph and Cyrus, respectively) is the one who is at the beginning of the great developments described in the works, and the first origin of these developments lies in the parallel events just discussed. Because Joseph was sold to Egypt his family goes there from Canaan, which makes the Exodus and the conquest of the Promised Land necessary. Through Astyages' reaction to his two dreams Cyrus is born as the son of a Median princess and a Persian, and the course of his life is steered towards the dethroning of his grandfather and, as a direct consequence, the making of large conquests for his empire. Finally, as noted above, both Joseph and Cyrus provide the point of departure of the great campaign of two generations later by coming to power in Egypt and the Lydian capital Sardis, respectively.

Another remarkable agreement is that a family member who has unwittingly saved the key figure, Judah in the Bible and Harpagus with Herodotus, is the main person in an episode that interrupts the description of the life of the key figure; in both cases this episode is of great significance in the light of later events. The key figure himself is said to have left for another country: at the end of Genesis 37 we are told that Joseph is brought to Egypt and is sold to Potiphar, a sentence that is taken up again at the beginning of Genesis 39. In between we find the well-known story of Judah and Tamar, in which the origins of the ancestors of the later tribe of Judah and more specifically of King David (via a combination of Gen. 38.29-30 with information from Ruth 4.18-22) are expounded. With Herodotus, something comparable happens. While Cyrus has left for the eastern part of his empire, Harpagus subdues the Greek cities of Asia Minor (Her. I, 157-77), an event that will finally turn out to be the cause of the great conflict between Persians and Greeks. The same persons also play a role in recognizing the hidden key person: Harpagus in Her. I, 117, and Judah in Gen. 44.18-34 (the first one before and the second one after the episode in which he is the main character).

The chronologically preceding episode in the work of Herodotus, the intended burning of King Croesus, has a curious parallel in the same story about Judah and Tamar near the beginning of the cycle of stories about Joseph, where Tamar is accused of adultery (it is not yet clear that Judah himself is the father of her children). Judah condemns her to be burned, but when she is at the point of undergoing this fate together with her unborn children, she informs him that she has the three objects which he gave to her as a security. He consequently spares her and leaves her alone. Here we also see the theme of impending burning (Tamar apparently keeps the three objects back until the very last moment) and the revoking of the verdict by the person who had pronounced it, after the prospective victim utters a saying that makes him change his mind. In both cases this mercy has important consequences. As noted before, Tamar is the ancestor of a large part of the tribe of Judah (cf. Gen. 46.12), and in particular of King David; Croesus has a decisive influence on the course of Cyrus's last campaign, because his counsel apparently leads to the preservation of the Persian empire after Cyrus's death (Her. I, 207). A final agreement may be hidden in the connection that Herodotus apparently sees between the fourteen years of Croesus's reign and the fourteen days he had been besieged in his capital Sardis on the one hand, and the fourteen young men who are to be burned with him on the other (Her. I, 86); in later Jewish exegesis it is often pointed out that the number of the persons who are threatened with burning in Genesis 38, namely three, is equal to the number of Judah's securities, which Tamar produces as pieces of evidence for the identity of her children's father.[13] Of course coincidence is a likely possibility here, and we should not attach too much value to the agreement of the numbers.

It should be noted, by the way, that various themes of the complex and momentous episode of the relationship between Cyrus and Croesus are reflected in at least three different ways in Primary History, in different episodes. Firstly, the spoiling of the in-law has its parallel in Jacob's tricking most of Laban's possessions out of his hands (Gen. 30–31; see below). Secondly, the intended burning of the in-law is reflected in the treatment meted out by Judah to Tamar. Thirdly, we see the assumption of power over the starting point for the great campaign (Lydia and Egypt, respectively) in Joseph's becoming viceroy of Egypt and taking his family there.

---

13. See, e.g., R. le Déaut and J. Robert, *Targum du Pentateuque*. I. *Genèse* (Paris: Cerf, 1978), pp. 350-51. Note also that Tamar's pregnancy is said to have drawn attention after three months.

Finally, both Harpagus and Judah are represented as deceived deceivers: in Herodotus's story King Astyages takes his revenge on Harpagus for not executing his order with regard to Cyrus by feeding him his son's flesh at a banquet; in Genesis the request to Jacob to identify Joseph's garment bears a striking likeness to Tamar's asking Judah to identify the possessions that he gave her as security (both begin with the imperative *hakker-na*, 'do recognize…': Gen. 37.32 and 38.25, which are resumed by narratives of the same verb *nkr* (hiph.) in 37.33 and 38.26), thus establishing a close connection between Judah's taking the initiative in cheating Jacob in Genesis 37 and being deceived himself in Genesis 38.[14]

Just before the last episode of the life of the key figure, in which his death is described, we have in both cases a passage that looks far ahead to important events described further on in the historical work. In Genesis 49 the life of the twelve tribes of Israel after their arrival in and conquest of the Promised Land is described by the aged Jacob. In Her. I, 209 Cyrus has the dream which he interprets as exposing a supposed plot of Darius, the son of Hystaspes, against himself, but which the reader recognizes as a prediction of Darius's (and as a consequence, Xerxes') war against Greece.

Abraham and Cyaxares

There is also a noteworthy correspondence between the great-grandfathers of both key figures, Abraham and Cyaxares (cf. Fig. 1.1), who are described as great warriors, whose main accomplishment was the defeat of a group of foreign invaders (the kings of the east in Gen. 14 and the Scythians in Her. I, 103-106), who kept their lands subjected for a long period (12 years in Genesis, 28 years in Herodotus). In both cases the invaders make strikingly comparable forays across large part of the Near East, through Palestine to the border of Egypt and back to the north again. The Scythians are bought off by Pharaoh when they arrive at his border, and on their return commit sacrilege in a temple in Ashkelon (Her. I, 105); the kings of the east continue their punitive expedition against the kings of Sodom and Gomorrah and their allies along a more easterly route to El Paran and some other locations between Palestine and Egypt, overcome the local kings in battle and are finally overtaken and beaten by Abraham

14. This has been noted by many exegetes from early times onwards. See, for example, Robert Alter, *The Art of Biblical Narrative* (New York: Basic Books, 1981), pp. 9-12. See also below for the chain of deceptions running on through several generations in both works.

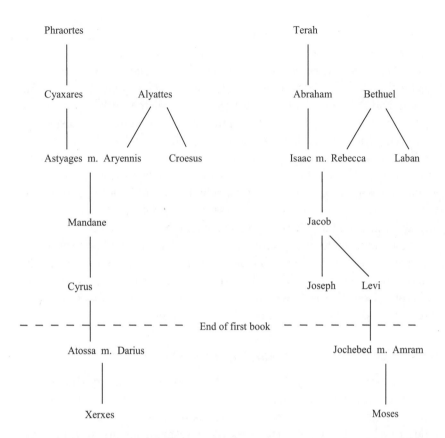

Fig. 1.1   *The genealogy of the Persian–Median royal family compared with the*
family of the patriarchs.

near Damascus (Gen. 14.5-15).[15] Both Cyaxares and Abraham complete a
great project of their fathers, both of whom die in northern Mesopotamia
without having accomplished it themselves (the journey to Canaan, begun
by Abraham's father Terah, who dies in Haran according to Gen. 11.31-
32,[16] and the taking of Nineveh, planned by Cyaxares' father Phraortes,
who dies in battle against the Assyrians in Her. I, 102). Both Cyaxares and

15. For a discussion of the Scythians in this episode of the work of Herodotus see
R.P. Vaggione, 'Over All Asia? The Extent of the Scythian Domination in Herodotus',
JBL 92 (1973), pp. 523-30.
16. Though Terah actually dies much later (11.32), he is said to have set out for
Canaan together with Abraham (11.31), but apparently stays behind in Haran when
Abraham continues the journey in 12.4.

Abraham fight a nightly battle against their enemies, Abraham in the story of Genesis 14 in the real night (Gen. 14.15), Cyaxares against the Lydians during an eclipse that had been predicted by Thales of Miletus (Her. I, 74, *en de kai nuktomachien tina epoiesanto...ten hemeren exapines nukta genesthai*, 'they fought a kind of night battle...the day suddenly became night' and 103, *hote nux he hemere egeneto*, 'when the day became night'). They are the only members of the families to be described as hospitably receiving foreigners (Gen. 18.1-8; Her. I, 106), though their treatment of them is rather different: Cyaxares uses this as a ruse to defeat and kill the Scythians, Abraham freely gives from his possessions to his divine guests, and ends with begging for mercy on behalf of sinful Sodom (Gen. 18.23-32). Of course some or most of these agreements may be mere coincidence, but cumulatively they gain considerable significance.

More importantly, both Cyaxares and Abraham are the first to establish contact with the starting point of the great campaign, Cyaxares in the above-mentioned war with the Lydians, Abraham in his famous journey to Egypt in Gen. 12.10-20, which, as is well known, in a number of respects resembles the Exodus of the Israelites from there.

Moses and Xerxes

Another striking family relation may be observed in Primary History and the *Histories*, namely between these key figures of Cyrus and Joseph and their family members of two generations later, who can doubtlessly be described as the main personages of these great historical works: the Persian king Xerxes in Herodotus and Israel's great law-giver Moses in Primary History. Xerxes has none to compete for this title but his father Darius, whose exploits are described in far less detail, and Moses only King David, who lived much later. Certain interesting analogies between the lives of these two can be observed. The greatest dramatic moment in the career of both is a journey from one continent to another one across a body of water as on dry land: in the case of Xerxes the crossing of the Hellespont by his tremendous army of (according to Herodotus) no less than 1.7 million men over two immense bridges of boats with packed earth on the bottom and fences on the outside (Herodotus VII, 33-56, this number in VII, 184; in VII, 186 he arrives at the even more staggering number of 5,283,220 for the size of the entire army through the addition of some other groups); with Moses the miraculous crossing of the people of Israel through the Red Sea (*yam suf*), which supposedly formed two walls of water on both sides of the passing Israelites (*weʰhammayim lāhem ḥomā*

mīmīnām umiṣᵉmolām, 'and the water was a wall for them on their right
and on their left', Exod. 14.22),[17] of whom the fighting men numbered
603,550 according to Num. 1.46, 2.32 (Exod. 14-15). Of these two tremendous groups, many or most were to die prematurely. The Persian
armies perish in the battles of Thermopylae, Salamis and Plataeae, so that
only a small number are able to return to their land.[18] The Israelites who
were above twenty years old during the Exodus incur the divine wrath in
Numbers 14 (cf. Num. 32.8-13), so that none of these except for Joshua
and Caleb enter the Promised Land: they die in the forty years that the
Israelites spend in the desert before entering the land of Canaan. In both
cases the crossing is preceded or accompanied by a number of portents,
though of a rather different nature (see Table 1.1). In Exodus, the so-called
'ten plagues' are mainly of an agricultural nature and serve the purpose of
punishing the Egyptians before the Exodus takes place (the first eight are:
water changing into blood, frogs, lice, flies, murrain, boils, hail and thunderstorm, locusts), whereas in Herodotus we find a number of more or less
conventional portents boding evil for the great campaign (a thunderstorm
in VII, 42, a panic at night in the army in VII, 43, and unusual miscar-
riages of cattle in VII, 57). Two other events are especially noteworthy, as
they agree closely in both works. The crossing is directly preceded by a
darkening of the light of the sun (Her. VII, 37, in Exod. 10.21-23 for three
days, as the ninth of the ten plagues)[19] and the death of one or more first-

17. Note that the rare word *ned* in Exod. 15.8 is also translated as *teichos*, 'wall', in
the Septuagint; see also below.
18. The famous scene of King Xerxes weeping at the crossing of the Hellespont, and
speaking with Artabanus about the vicissitudes and briefness of human life, though very
moving in itself, also carries a streak of sublime irony: note Herodotus's graphic
description of Xerxes leading the pitiable remains of his army, plagued by hunger and
disease, scrambling back towards the Hellespont, where they have to be ferried across, as
the bridges had been destroyed by a storm (Her. VIII, 115-20). The passing away of the
entire army in due time is also mentioned on this occasion by Xerxes as the reason for
his weeping: 'for of all these thousands of men not one will be alive in a hundred years'
time', which in a way strengthens the parallel with the biblical story. It may not be
superfluous to point out that Herodotus's account is hardly in agreement with the actual
state of affairs during and after Xerxes' Greek campaign, as Persian military supremacy
in fact continued right to the end of the war, and according to many authors only gross
incompetence allowed them to snatch their ultimate defeat from the jaws of victory. See,
for example, A.T. Olmstead, 'Persia and the Greek Frontier Problem', in Blanco and
Roberts, *Herodotus. The Histories*, pp. 377-89 [reprinted, with omission of the footnotes,
from *Classical Philology* 34 (1939), pp. 305-22].
19. Additionally, it may be noted that both the Persian army and the Israelites start

The Origin of the History of Israel

Table 1.1 *The plagues of Egypt compared with the events connected with Xerxes'*
army, in the order of the plagues. Between brackets: events in Herodotus's work not
connected with the crossing of Xerxes' army.

Exodus		Herodotus	
1. water to blood, no drinking from river	7.14-25	too many people, no drinking from river	VII, 43
2. frogs	8.1-11 [8.5-15]	–	
3. dust becomes lice	8.12-15 [8.16-19]	(cloud of dust)	(VIII, 65)
4. flies	8.16-28 [8.20-32]	–	
5. murrain	9.1-7	(pest of man and animal on Crete)	(VII, 171)
6. boils	9.8-12	(pest and dysentery)	(VIII, 115)
7. hail, thunderstorm	9.13-35	thunderstorm	VII, 42 (VIII,12; 37)
8. locusts	10.12-20	–	
9. darkness	10.21-26	darkness	VII, 37
10. death of first-born	11.4-7; 12.29-30	death of Pythios's eldest son	VII, 38
–		miscarriages of cattle	VII, 57

sons (the tenth of the plagues and the episode of Pythios, see below) and
accompanied by a mustering and elaborate description of the army (see
below). Both leaders, finally, had to look at the destination of their journey
helplessly from behind a second water-barrier, without being able to arrive
at their intended goal by crossing it: Moses from Mt Nebo to the Promised
Land on the other side of the river Jordan, which God had forbidden him
to cross (Deut. 32.49-52 and 34.1-4), Xerxes from his throne to the island
of Salamis, where part of the Athenians had fled, and where he would
never come because of the defeat of his fleet at Salamis (note his feeble
attempts to build a bridge of boats to the island in VIII, 97).

These are not, however, the only possible parallels between the books
Exodus–Joshua and Xerxes' campaign against Greece. It would seem, in
fact, that the events from the Exodus to the battle with Amalek in Exodus
17 and the arrival at Mt Sinai in Exodus 19 run more or less parallel to those
between the departure of Xerxes' army from Sardis and the battle of Thermopylae, and that there is an additional parallel between Balaam, the seer

their journey in the dark, the first because of this eclipse, the second because they leave
Egypt during the night.

who is hired by King Balak to curse the Israelites but blesses them instead and pronounces a detailed prediction about their future (Num. 22–24), and the Greek in Persian service, Dikaios, who predicts the defeat of his own overlord (Her. VIII, 65). It should also be noted, though this is hardly unexpected for either account, that the armies are mustered and counted in long descriptions of the groups they are composed of, either before or after the crossing of the sea (Her. VII, 60-100 just before the crossing of the Hellespont, Num. 1–4 one year after the crossing of the Red Sea). I shall briefly discuss these parallels below. Though one can, of course, hesitate in individual cases, it seems extremely unlikely that all the analogies would be mere coincidence. (See the survey in Table 1.2, which can only be of a tentative nature, as there are bound to be accidental agreements between such stretches of narrative text dealing with comparable subjects.)

Table 1.2 *Main events of Exodus–Deuteronomy compared with Xerxes' campaign. The episodes in Primary History that do not conform to a linear correspondence with Herodotus's work are in italics.*

Bible		Herodotus	
Moses is ordered to bring Israel to the Land of Canaan and conquer it; he is reluctant, but is forced to do so through divine intervention	Exodus 3	Xerxes is advised to conquer Greece; he is reluctant, but is forced to do so through divine intervention	VII, 5ff.
genealogy of Moses and Aaron	Exod. 6.14-26	genealogy of Xerxes	VII, 11
darkness	Exod. 10.21-23	darkness	VII, 37
presents of Egyptians	Exod. 11.2, 12.35-36	presents of Pythios	VII, 28; 38
first-born dead	Exod. 12.29	Pythios' eldest son dead	VII, 39
leaving Egypt	Exod. 12.37	leaving Sardis	VII, 40
(plagues of Egypt)	*Exod. 8–13*	thunder and lightning	VII, 42
Baal Zephon	Exod. 14.2	Pergamon of Priamus	VII, 43
panic among Egyptians (night)	*Exod. 14.24-25*	panic in army (night)	VII, 43
murmuring of Israel at the sea	Exod. 14.10-12	advice of Artabanus	VII, 47-52

Table1.2 (cont.)

crossing of sea between continents through miracle	Exod. 14.21-31	crossing of sea between continents over bridges of boats	VII, 54-56
songs of praise	Exod. 15	words of praise	VII, 56
(plagues of Egypt)	*Exod. 8–13*	strange miscarriages	VII, 57
murmuring of Israel in Marah	Exod. 15.24	advice of Demaratus	VII, 101-105
no water in desert of Shur	*Ex. 15.22*	river Lissos dries up through drinking of army	VII, 108
bitter water at Marah	*Exod. 15.23*	salt water at Pistyros	VII, 109
people encamped at Elim	Exod. 15.27	army encamped at Therme	VII, 127
murmuring of Israel in desert of Sin	Exod. 16.3	–	–
feeding the people	Exod. 16	feeding the army	VII, 119; 187
murmuring of Israel in Rephidim	Exod. 17.2-3	advice of Demaratus	VII, 209
war with Amalek, Moses sits and stands, brother Aaron and Hur support him; written record, monument	Exod. 17.8-16	battle of Thermopylae, Xerxes sits and stands, brother Achaemenes and Demaratus give advice; written record, monument	VII, 201-38
Mt Sinai, thunderstorm	Exod. 19	Mt Parnassus, thunderstorm	VIII, 35-39
mustering and counting of the people	*Num. 1–4*	mustering and counting of the army	VII, 60-100
prediction of Balaam	Num. 22–24	prediction of Dikaios	VIII, 65
Moses not to enter Promised Land, looks at it from behind river Jordan	Deut. 32.52	Xerxes not to go to Salamis, looks at it from behind the sea	VIII, 97
Joshua crosses river Jordan through miracle	*Joshua 3–4*	Xerxes attempts to build bridge of boats for crossing sea to Salamis	VIII, 97
Moses dies	Deut. 33.5	Xerxes leaves Greece	VIII, 115-20

The attitudes of Moses and Xerxes at the beginning of their great adventures are remarkably similar also. At the beginning of his seventh book, Herodotus tells his readers that Xerxes is at first not really enthusiastic about the prospect of waging war against Greece, and convenes a council for discussing the options only after his nephew Mardonius presses him to go to war with Greece and especially the Athenians, firstly in order to exact revenge for the Persians' defeat at Marathon under the reign of his father, and secondly because the spoils would be worth while:

> And to the arguments for revenge he would add that Europe was a very beautiful place; it produced every kind of garden tree; the land there was everything that land should be—it was, in short, too good for anyone in the world except the Persian king (Her. VII, 5).

During the conference Mardonius argues strongly in favour of war, whereas Xerxes' uncle Artabanus opposes it. Xerxes first accepts Mardonius's view and reproaches Artabanus, then changes his mind shortly before retiring to bed that day, and decides to shelve the plan. He then falls asleep and dreams that a man tells him not to change his mind and orders him to go to war with Greece. At first he does not attach any value to the dream, and the next day tells his councillors that he has decided against the undertaking. The following night the same man appears in his dream and threatens him with losing his royal power if he does not comply and refrains from starting the campaign. He then persuades Artabanus to take his place for the day and sleep in his bed at night, wearing the king's royal garments all the time, in order to see whether the man will appear to him also. Artabanus indeed dreams and sees the same man, but the man is not taken in by the change of attire and threatens Artabanus with having his eyes gouged out with red-hot irons if he continues to advise against the campaign. Artabanus worriedly wakes up and henceforth advocates waging war against Greece, which clinches the matter. Preparations for the great campaign are started.

The calling of Moses is one of the best-known episodes of his life. After killing an Egyptian who was beating an Israelite, he had to flee to Midian, where he married the daughter of a local priest and herded his cattle. One day he sees a thorn-bush burning without being consumed. Approaching the bush in amazement, he is addressed by God, who orders him to take off his shoes, as this is a holy spot (it later turns out to be Mt Sinai, the place of the divine revelation to Moses and his people). After identifying himself to Moses as the God of the Patriarchs, God explains his plans to him and assigns Moses his own role in them:

[Exod. 3.7] Then the Lord said, 'I have seen the affliction of my people who are in Egypt, and have heard their cry because of their taskmasters; I know their sufferings, [8] and I have come down to deliver them out of the hand of the Egyptians, and to bring them up out of that land to a good and broad land, a land flowing with milk and honey, to the place of the Canaanites, the Hittites, the Amorites, the Perizzites, the Hivites, and the Jebusites. [9] And now, behold, the cry of the people of Israel has come to me, and I have seen the oppression with which the Egyptians oppress them. [10] Come, I will send you to Pharaoh that you may bring forth my people, the sons of Israel, out of Egypt.'

Like Xerxes, Moses has severe misgivings about the campaign he is enjoined to carry out. Only after a heated interchange does God make it clear to him that there is no way to escape from this assignment:

[Exod. 4.10-15] But Moses said to the Lord, 'Oh, my Lord, I am not eloquent, either heretofore or since thou hast spoken to thy servant; but I am slow of speech and of tongue.' [11] Then the Lord said to him, 'Who has made man's mouth? Who makes him dumb, or deaf, or seeing, or blind? Is it not I, the Lord? [12] Now therefore go, and I will be with your mouth and teach you what you shall speak.' [13] But he said, 'Oh, my Lord, send, I pray, some other person.' [14] Then the anger of the Lord was kindled against Moses and he said, 'Is there not Aaron, your brother, the Levite? I know that he can speak well; and behold, he is coming out to meet you, and when he sees you he will be glad in his heart. [15] And you shall speak to him and put the words in his mouth; and I will be with your mouth and with his mouth, and will teach you what you shall do.'

Thus we see as common elements in these accounts, which are otherwise very different, the proposal or command to the leader to go to a foreign country that is now in the hands of its own people, who have lived there for a very long time, and to take it away from them; and the representation of this country as very beautiful and fruitful, which is somewhat exaggerated both in the case of Canaan and of Greece when they are compared with countries such as Egypt and Mesopotamia. Furthermore, both leaders want to avoid this campaign, but are finally forced to go through divine intervention.

When Xerxes arrives in Lydia with his army, he is greeted there by an extremely rich old man called Pythios, son of Atys, of whom Herodotus seems to suggest (surprisingly refraining from discussing the possibility) that he is the grandson of King Croesus of Lydia, who indeed had a son called Atys (I, 34-45), possessed legendary riches (I, 30) and entertained close relations with the Delphi oracle of Apollo Pythios (I, 46 and *passim* until I, 92). Pythios offers Xerxes all the money that he possesses as a present, but Xerxes, instead of accepting this offer, supplements Pythios's capital to the next round amount of four million darics. Just before the army leaves Sardis in Lydia, an eclipse of the sun takes place. Immediately afterwards Pythios comes to meet Xerxes again, and humbly requests that the oldest of his five sons be exempted from service on the campaign to Greece. Herodotus tells his readers that the eclipse (which is not historical, at least not for this time and place) was regarded as an evil portent, which he suggests made Pythios desire to have at least one of his sons survive in order to succeed him. Unfortunately for him, Xerxes appears to see his request as a sign of distrust in the outcome of the Greek campaign (his suspicion may have been reinforced by Pythios being the grandson of Croesus, perhaps entertaining ambitions of returning to his grandfather's throne), and orders the hapless oldest son to be cut in half, and the army to pass between the two pieces of his body on their departure from Sardis.

The Pharaoh of the Exodus, probably the grandson of the Pharaoh who elevated Joseph to a high position (at least, it is stated that he was his successor's successor, see Exod. 1.8 and 2.23), after he and his people have been struck by a number of increasingly severe plagues, is finally convinced to let the Israelites leave when his country is shrouded in utter darkness for three days (Exod. 10.22-23). This is not the end of his tribulations, however: on the night of the departure of the Israelites, all the firstborn sons of the Egyptians, including his own, are slain by the Lord (Exod. 12.29). Within the framework of the cycle of stories dealing with the Exodus, this is clearly a punishment for the Egyptians' attempt to kill all male offspring of the Israelites (Exod. 1.16, 22).

Although these elements of the enigmatic darkness, the death of one or more first-born sons and the departure of the army clearly have a natural place within the respective works, their occurring together in the same order in both is very remarkable. The relation of Pythios to Croesus and of the Pharaoh of the Exodus to the Pharaoh of Joseph as offspring of the second generation—in both cases suggested, though not stated explicitly—strengthens this congruence, as does the element of the Egyptians surprisingly giving presents to the Israelites (Exod. 11.2; 12.35-36), more or less paralleling Pythios's presents for Xerxes and his campaign (Her. VII, 27-29).

From Sardis, the Persian army goes to the Hellespont via the location of ancient Troy, where Xerxes offers on the Pergamon of King Priam enormous sacrifices to an evidently non-Persian goddess, who is identified as Athena Ilias by Herodotus (VII, 43); directly before this we have the story of many soldiers of the army being killed through lightning at the foot of Mt Ida. This element of the story may or may not correspond to an episode found in the same location in the Exodus account, namely the Israelites encamping 'in front of Pihahiroth, between Migdol and the sea, in front of Baalzephon' (Exod. 14.2). This Baal Zephon (*ba'al ṣāpon*), of course, is to be identified with the Egyptian Mt Casius of the classical authors, and is (like its North Syrian counterpart, which is especially well known from the Ugaritic texts) a holy mountain of the god Ba'al, well known as the main non-Israelite god to be mentioned in the Hebrew Bible, and probably to be identified with the weather-god Hadad.

In both cases the divinity is addressed directly after the crossing of the sea. In Herodotus, after the crossing an anonymous man cries out: 'Why, O God, have you assumed the shape of a man of Persia, and changed your name to Xerxes, in order to lead everyone in the world to the conquest and devastation of Greece? You could have destroyed Greece without going to that trouble' (VII, 56). In the Bible, Moses and the Israelites sing the Song of the Sea in Exodus 15, to which the women of Israel react in Exod. 15.20-21. The Song describes God as a valiant warrior, and specifically mentions his own Name: 'The Lord is a man of war; the Lord is his name' (Exod. 15.3). While Herodotus's man hyperbolically identifies Xerxes with Zeus, or with the divinity in general, the Song assigns God a role that is compared to that of a human warrior, and makes it clear that he acts under his own Name. In both, the divinity is directly addressed (in the Song from v. 6 onwards).

While everything goes smoothly during the march of the army into central Greece, Xerxes receives several warnings about the hazards connected with the campaign, both from Persians and from Greek allies. Directly after the crossing of the Hellespont, his uncle Artabanus, whom we have already met in the episode of Xerxes' dream, warns him of the logistical problems caused by the enormous size of his fleet and army (VII, 47-52). Later on, the Greek Demaratus, a Spartan of royal family, who had got into trouble in his homeland and had therefore taken his refuge at the Persian king's court, twice warns the king against the Greeks, and especially against the Spartans and other Peloponnesians among them (VII, 101-105 and 209).[20]

---

20. See about this remarkable figure D. Boedecker, 'The Two Faces of Demaratus', *Arethusa* 20 (1987), pp. 185-201.

In the book of Exodus, there are also several episodes in which doubt about the outcome of the campaign is expressed, this time not in the form of sage counsel (which would, after all, hardly be possible against a divine assignment), but as complaints and protests of the people of Israel. The first time this happens in the Exodus account is when the pursuing Egyptians are approaching the fugitives, near the Red Sea (Exod. 14.10-12), then after they fail to obtain drinkable water in the desert of Shur and in Marah (Exod. 15.24), when they are hungry in the desert of Sin (Exod. 16.3), and finally in Rephidim, when they are again thirsty (Exod. 17.2-3).

It would seem, though the agreement is not as complete as one would like, that the places of the warnings that Xerxes receives about his campaign largely correspond with the location of the complaints of the people of Israel about Moses having taken them from Egypt to the desert. Thus Artabanus's advice before the crossing of the sea seems to correspond with the Israelites' complaints at the sea, and Demaratus's advices are paralleled by the complaints about lack of water in Marah and Rephidim. Only the occasion just before the giving of the manna in Exod. 16.3 seems to lack a corresponding advice in Herodotus. It can however be maintained that the difference could be the result of the different ways in which Herodotus and Primary History view the problem of keeping the people in supply: a tremendous logistical problem solved by conventional human means versus an occasion for divine providence.

Still, both works deal at some length with the problem of obtaining sufficient food and water for the multitudes. Herodotus describes the way in which the Persians requisition food for their army, whereas Primary History mentions the miraculous gift of the manna in corresponding places in the narrative (Her. VII, 119 [cf. also 187], and Exod. 16 [cf. also Num. 11], respectively); and another point of agreement between Primary History and Herodotus's account is formed by the problems with finding enough drinking water for all the people (Exod. 15.22-23; 17.1 versus the recurrent theme of the Persian army drinking dry the rivers they pass: e.g. VII, 108, perhaps 109, 127 and 187). These are apparently not to be found in exactly corresponding places in the text.

A striking parallel can be observed between the two typical battles recounted after this: the desperate stand of the Greeks, especially the Spartans under King Leonidas, at the pass of Thermopylae, where they hold back the enormous Persian army for some days (VII, 201-38), and the battle with Amalek, the archetypal enemy of Israel who is said to fight against it throughout history, in Exodus 17. In both cases the leader looks on at the battle from a convenient vantage point. Xerxes is said to have jumped up and sat down again several times during the battle (VII, 212); Moses has to keep his arms up in order for the Israelites to win, and, when he tires of standing, he is given a stone to sit on for that purpose (Exod. 17.11-12). After the battle, Xerxes confers with his brother Achaemenes and again with Demaratus (Her. VII, 234-37), whereas Moses is supported during the battle by his brother Aaron and by a certain Hur, from the tribe of Judah (Exod. 17.12). While the Greeks later commemorated the battle through a number of monuments and inscriptions there (VII, 228), Moses is said to have written down (the first reference to writing in the Bible) the account of the divine wrath against Amalek, and to have built an altar on the spot (Exod. 17.14-16).

The episode of the arrival of Moses' father-in-law Jethro in Exodus 18, and the advice he gives to Moses with regard to the appointment of judges in order to alleviate his administrative duties, may also be connected in some way with the advice Achaemenes gives to his brother Xerxes after Thermopylae, but this is far from certain.

A final parallelism between the account in the book of Exodus and Xerxes' campaign in Greece may perhaps be visible in the episode of the Persians attempting to enter Apollo's sanctuary in Delphi and plunder its treasures, and being barred from this by lightning and rocks falling down from nearby Mt Parnassus, Apollo's sacred mountain, in agreement with the god's promise that he would himself protect his sanctuary (Her. VIII, 35-39), in comparison with the story of the Israelites arriving at the foot of Mt Sinai, which they are forbidden to approach and from where thunder, lightning and smoke emerge (Exod. 19, *passim*).

When we make an inventory of those passages in Herodotus's books VII–VIII and in the narrative portions of the Pentateuch (mainly Gen. 12–50, Exod. 1–19, Num. 10–25) that do not lend themselves to the linear parallelism described above, we see that usually these would be inappropriate in the other work, such as the naval affairs in Herodotus, for which there is definitely no room in the land-bound narrative of the Pentateuch, or local Greek affairs that do not pertain directly to the great conflict, or specifically Israelite affairs in the Bible, but that otherwise the mutual coverage is surprisingly high; it seems possible that there are further analogies between the military acts connecting the parallel events in both works, but these are certainly not very striking and may in fact be absent altogether.

A Common Main Subject

The consideration of the course of the two campaigns brings us to a surprising and very important observation. In spite of the considerable attention that has been given to the comparison of Herodotus's work with Primary History, no scholar seems to have commented on the most striking point of agreement between the two, perhaps because it is so obvious that no one deemed it necessary to dwell on it: namely that the main action in both works is highly similar, if not identical for all practical purposes. In these works a leader sets out at the head of an enormous army to conquer a foreign country on another continent, which does not belong to him or his people except by natural or divine right, and is firmly in the hand of other nations: in the Bible Moses, after protesting at first, receives a divine command to do so, in the work of Herodotus Xerxes is also forced by divine intervention to go on with his expedition after he has all but cancelled it. Both lead their people across the sea separating the two continents as if on dry land. A striking difference is, of course, that in Exodus there are two groups, with the Egyptians chasing the Israelites but drowning when the sea suddenly overwhelms them, whereas Xerxes crosses the Hellespont unchallenged by anyone; but it can be maintained that this is a more or less logical consequence of the difference in the situation of departure, the Israelites having served as slaves in Egypt, whereas the all-powerful Persian king embarks upon the campaign from his own land.

It may be significant that there is a parallel in Herodotus for some of the key elements of the fate striking the Egyptian army. The sea receding, an attacking army taking the opportunity to march on the sea-bed and a sudden flood drowning all or most of them, are also found in Her. VIII, 129, where the Persians investing the city of Poteidaia, situated at the entrance of the peninsula of Pallene in northern Greece, make use of an uncommonly low ebb to attempt to wade to Pallene. They are, however, surprised by an enormous flood, the like of which there had never been before; Herodotus reports that this is supposed to have been a divine punishment for committing sacrilege against a sanctuary of Poseidon, the god of the sea, near the city. Note that both in the Red Sea story and in this episode drowning is a punishment closely connected with the crime for which it is meant, as the Egyptians clearly suffer this fate because they ordered the Hebrew boys to be drowned in the Nile. The biblical account contains elements of both Xerxes' crossing of the Hellespont and the Pallene affair (see Fig. 1.2).

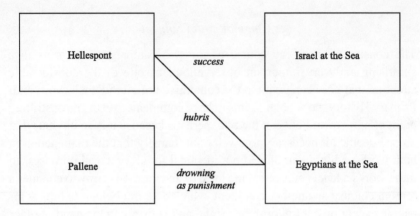

Fig. 1.2   *The two crossings of the sea in the* Histories *compared with the crossing of
the Sea of Israel and the Egyptians in Exodus.*

Both in Herodotus and in Primary History the main crossing of the sea is
used as a chronological pivot. In the *Histories*, the date given for Xerxes'
invasion when his army enters Attica, the sixth year after Darius's death
(Her. VII, 7, 20), being identified with the magistracy of Calliades (Her.
VIII, 51), is the only point of attachment between his ancient Near Eastern
and classical Greek chronology.[21] In the Bible the Exodus from Egypt is
situated between the patriarchal early history of the world, in which chronology depends on the information provided about the long lives of early
men, and the history of the Israelite kingdoms with its counting of regnal
years, related to the date of the Exodus through the indication that Solomon
started to build his temple 480 years after the event (1 Kgs 6.1); otherwise
there is no way to close the gap between them, as there are considerable
chronological lacunas in the account of events between the two.

   In neither case does the leader succeed in his plans. Moses and Xerxes
can only look at their final destinations from a distance, and disappear
from the centre of the stage shortly afterwards: a short time after the defeat
of his fleet in the battle of Salamis, Xerxes returns directly to Persia and no
longer plays any role in the campaign in Greece, while Moses dies at the
end of the book of Deuteronomy. The big difference is, of course, that
Moses' successor Joshua succeeds in conquering the land of Canaan, or at
least part of it, whereas the Persians never conquered Greece, but we can

   21.   H. Strasburger, 'Herodots Zeitrechnung', in W. Schmitthenner and R. Zoepffel
(eds.), *Studien zur Alten Geschichte* (Hildesheim: Olins, 1982 [1956]), pp. 627-75.

hardly be surprised about this—had things been otherwise there need not have been a Primary History at all. Still, even allowing for this aspect there are parallels with Herodotus. Xerxes' abortive crossing of the sea-arm between the mainland and Salamis by means of yet another bridge of boats (Her. VIII, 97) is mirrored in the Bible by the success of Joshua's miraculous crossing of the river Jordan (Josh. 3–4), which has a number of traits in common with the crossing of the Red Sea.[22] Note also that as Xerxes, after his departure from Greece, is succeeded by Mardonius as leader of the great campaign, so Joshua becomes Moses' successor after his death at the end of the book of Deuteronomy. Both successors had already led the armies during the first great battles of the campaign, in Thermopylae and against Amalek, respectively,[23] and both finally attain a partial conquest of Greece and Canaan, respectively; the big difference is again that Mardonius's conquest is annulled straight away through his defeat and death, whereas Joshua's results form the basis for Israel's finally taking possession of the entire land of Canaan.

The final outcome of the military campaign of conquest, however, is highly similar again, though the position with regard to the episodes that have hitherto been discussed is very different. Both conquests finally come to naught: the Persian expedition to Greece ends in disaster within one year of Salamis, the Israelite conquest of Canaan is effectively annulled more than seven hundred years (of narrated time) after Moses, when the last vestiges of Israelite political power are wiped out by the Babylonians. The account of this final phase mainly consists of an episode of siege and capture at the end of each work: that of the prolonged siege of the town of Sestos on the European side of the Hellespont and that of the Judean capital Jerusalem. The outcome of Xerxes' campaign is thus effectively reflected three times in Primary History: once with a more or less identical interim result, with Moses like Xerxes staring at the land he can no longer reach (at the end of Deuteronomy), once with a contrary result, in the success of Joshua in conquering the Holy Land (in the book of Joshua), and once more with a comparable outcome, when the Babylonians take

22. Cf. Van Seters, *Life of Moses*, pp. 139-49, who supposes that the crossing of the sea was secondarily developed out of the crossing of the river Jordan (he is not the only one to do so; see C. Houtman, *Exodus*, I [Kampen: Kok, 1986], p. 194).

23. Though Mardonius is not mentioned even once in the actual account of the battle of Thermopylae, he can safely be presumed to have commanded the Persian army there, because later on in the *Histories* he is said to have ordered the mutilation of the dead body of the Spartan king Leonidas there, together with King Xerxes (IX, 78).

Jerusalem and carry its populace into exile, thus in a way undoing the conquest of the land by the Israelites (at the end of 2 Kings).

This is not to say, of course, that the subject matter of both works is not very different: Primary History is mainly concerned with the very special relationship between God and his chosen people Israel, and his promise to give them the land of Canaan as an eternal heritage, while it is not so easy to formulate one general subject for Herodotus, unless one is satisfied with the conventional description of the work as the history of the wars between Greeks and Persians. One could, in fact, maintain that one of Herodotus's main points of interest is also of a religious nature: time and again he is concerned with the influence of the divine on very earthly matters, including the beginning and the course of Xerxes' great campaign, but there is no equivalent of the religious atmosphere pervading Primary History. In Fig. 1.3 the main themes in both works have been represented showing both correspondences and differences.

Of course, the great campaign, and with it the life of the main person, are not told in corresponding parts of the works involved. After telling about Cyrus's career in his first book, Herodotus describes the reigns of his successors Cambyses and Darius at length in his books II–VI, before starting his elaborate account of Xerxes' campaign in books VII–IX. In Primary History, by contrast, the life of Moses and the Exodus directly follow the first book with its description of Joseph's life and career in Genesis 37–50, namely in books 2–5, Exodus through Deuteronomy; the partial conquest of Canaan follows in the book of Joshua. As noted above, in the succeeding books Judges, 1 and 2 Samuel and 1 and 2 Kings (originally the book of Samuel and the book of Kings, respectively) the history of the people of Israel in its land during a much longer period is told, and only with the similar ending (see below) does the story run once more parallel to Herodotus's work. See also Fig. 1.4.

The phenomenon of a literary description of a campaign of one group against another is very common, but the express purpose to take possession of the other's land certainly is not; this becomes especially clear if one examines a number of famed examples of such wars in the literatures of the Mediterranean and the Near East in antiquity. The Trojan war, for example, whether it was waged to get Helen, who had been abducted by the Trojan king's son Paris, back to her husband Menelaus in Greece, or was fought for ulterior motives, certainly did not have as its stated objective to conquer the area of Troy for the Greeks. In the Ugaritic epic of King Keret, the king goes to war against his colleague King Pabil of Udum in order to secure his daughter for marriage, not in order to conquer his territory.[24] This is not to say, of course, that wars of conquest or their description were unusual in antiquity: as is well known, the reverse is the case (we need only think of the Neo-Assyrian royal inscriptions and the like), but as a pattern in a literary work it is very rare.[25]

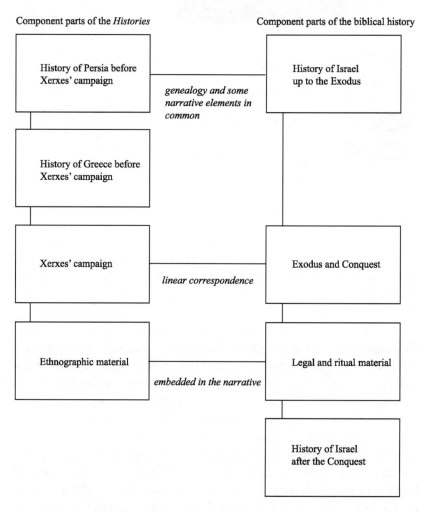

Fig. 1.3   *Dominant themes in the* Histories *and in Primary History with and without equivalent in the other work.*

24. J.C.L. Gibson, *Canaanite Myths and Legends* (Edinburgh: T. & T. Clark, 1978), pp. 19-23 and 82-102.
25. Cf. also K.L. Younger, *Ancient Conquest Accounts: A Study in Ancient Near Eastern and Biblical History Writing* (Sheffield: JSOT Press, 1990).

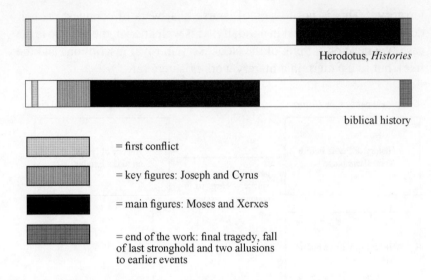

= first conflict

= key figures: Joseph and Cyrus

= main figures: Moses and Xerxes

= end of the work: final tragedy, fall
of last stronghold and two allusions
to earlier events

Fig. 1.4   *Relative position of similar parts in Herodotus and in Primary History.*

In both instances the direct link to the generation of the key figure is via
the mother, while the father is a comparatively distant relative. This
mother is also said to have influenced her son's career decisively. Xerxes
was the son of Darius, son of Hystaspes, who ascended the throne of Persia
after the death of Cyrus's son Cambyses and the defeat of the person
passing for his brother Smerdis, and also the grandson of Cyrus through
his mother Atossa; Darius, though, was also related to Cyrus, stemming
from the same family of the Achaemenids. Via his mother Jochebed Moses
was the grandson of Joseph's brother Levi; his father Amram was also a
grandson of Levi via his father Kohath. In both cases these genealogies are
not given when the main person is first introduced, but at the beginning of
the great adventure. Xerxes mentions his genealogy during the delibera-
tions about the merits of undertaking the Greek campaign (Her. VII, 11:
'[if that would happen,] let me be [from my father's side] no child of
Darius, the son of Hystaspes, the son of Arsames, the son of Ariaramnes,
the son of Teispes, [and from my mother's side] the son of Cyrus, the son
of Cambyses, the son of Teispes, the son of Achaemenes!'); the family
members of Moses are enumerated in a genealogical interlude, which
contains the descendants of Reuben, Simeon and Levi, in the story about
his first contacts with Pharaoh (Exod. 6.14-26). Neither in Herodotus nor
in the Bible is the direct descent via the female line commented on, though
it is alluded to in both cases: Xerxes simply leaves out his mother Atossa

from his genealogy (he calls himself 'the son of Cyrus'); in Exod. 6.9 we find, somewhat more explicitly, 'Amram took to wife Jochebed his father's sister [not: 'the daughter of Levi', as she is called, but then without her name, in Exod. 2.1] and she bore him Aaron and Moses…'. In both the biblical account and Herodotus, however, the mother's intervention on behalf of her son is mentioned. Atossa, assisted by the Spartan exile Demaratus, sees to it that Xerxes takes precedence over his half-brothers, who had been born before Darius ascended the throne (Her. VII, 2-3). Jochebed saves the little Moses from Pharaoh's decree, that all little Hebrew boys were to be killed by throwing them into the Nile, by her ruse of putting him in a basket in this river, whether or not she foresaw or hoped that Pharaoh's daughter would find him and take care of him (Exod. 2.3-6); this finally leads to his becoming the leader of the Israelites, in effect taking precedence over his older brother Aaron. It should be noted, by the way, that the significance of the Exodus genealogy within Primary History far surpasses that of Xerxes in Herodotus's work. The latter exhibits his especial interest in the figure of Xerxes by providing the family tree of the Achaemenid royal family only here; in the much longer genealogy of Exodus 6 we can perceive intertextual links to many and varied texts, such as the list of Jacob's sons in Gen. 46.8-27 or the death of Aaron's sons in Lev. 10.1-2.[26]

Two Families

In this way a remarkable congruence becomes visible between the family tree of the Persian–Median royal family, which plays an important role throughout Herodotus's work, beginning with military adventures under the Median king Phraortes and continuing with the war waged on Greece under the great kings Darius and Xerxes, and the genealogy of the ancestors of the people of Israel as found in the biblical books Genesis and Exodus, which runs from Terah to Moses. In both cases we are dealing with seven generations, which are listed in Fig. 1.1; in Table 1.3 we see some striking agreements between the corresponding generations. It is notable that in both cases the brother-in-law of the third generation plays an important part, namely Croesus with Herodotus and Laban in the Bible (Gen. 24 and 29–31).

26. See the survey of the interpretations of the Exodus genealogy in A. Marx, 'La généalogie d'Exode vi 14-25: sa forme, sa fonction', *VT* 45 (1995), pp. 318-36.

Table 1.3 *Summary of the parallels between the corresponding generations of the two families. 'A deception' = deceives someone else; 'P deception' = is deceived by someone else (see Table 1.4).*

Herodotus	Characterization	Characterization	Biblical history
Phraortes	begins attack on Nineveh; dies there	begins with journey to Canaan, reaches Haran; dies there	Terah
Cyaxares [P+A deception]	fights a nightly battle; fights against robbers advancing across the Middle East to the border of Egypt; is the first to establish contact with the ruler of Lydia; (no) hospitality	fights a nightly battle; fights against robbers advancing across the Middle East to the border of Egypt;is the first to establish contact with the ruler of Egypt; hospitality	Abraham
Astyages [P+A+P deception]	brokered marriage with woman from another country (Aryennis); rich brother-in-law (Croesus), whose possessions are appropriated by grandson (Cyrus)	brokered marriage with woman from another country (Rebecca); rich brother-in-law (Laban), whose possessions are appropriated by son (Jacob)	Isaac [P deception]
Mandane	brokered marriage with man from another country (Cambyses); thinks that her son is dead	brokered (?) marriage with women from another country (Rachel, Leah etc.); thinks that his son is dead	Jacob [P+A+P deception]
Cyrus (Harpagus [A+P+A deception])	two dreams (of his grandfather) about his future power; jealousy of grandfather; life is threatened; lives hidden from his family for many years; attains power as result of attempts to kill him; brings his people to the starting point of the great campaign (Lydia)	two dreams (of himself) about his future power; jealousy of brothers; life is threatened; lives hidden from his family for many years; attains power as result of attempts to kill him; brings his people to the starting point of the great campaign (Egypt)	Joseph (Judah [P deception], Levi)

Atossa	married to man from the same family (Darius); through a ruse causes her son to be leader of his people instead of his older brothers	married to man from the same family (Amram); through a ruse saves her son, and consequently causes him to be leader of his people instead of his older brother	Jochebed
Xerxes	summoned by the divinity to conquer Greece; takes his multitudes from Lydia across the Hellespont in order to conquer it; finally looks at his destination helplessly beyond the water	summoned by the divinity to conquer Canaan; takes his multitudes from Egypt across the Red Sea in order to conquer it; finally looks at his destination helplessly beyond the water	Moses

In both cases an earlier state of hostility with the brother-in-law is ended through a treaty, in which the marriage or marriages constituting the family link play a certain part: the treaty between Medians and Lydians is confirmed by the marriage of Aryennis to Astyages; the treaty between Jacob and Laban explicitly deals with the relationship of Laban's daughters Rachel and Leah to their husband Jacob (Her. I, 74; Gen. 31.43-55). It should, moreover, be noted that the marriages that form the origin of the relationships with Laban and Croesus, respectively, are among the very few that are explicitly said to have been brokered in both family histories: Abraham's servant sets out for Mesopotamia in order to find a wife for his son Isaac in Genesis 24; Astyages' marriage with Aryennis, as noted before, seals the treaty between Lydians and Medians in Her. I, 74. The corresponding marriages in the next generation, of Mandane with Cambyses and of Jacob with Rachel and Leah (the only other marriages whose conclusions are mentioned explicitly), both also involve a partner from another country, though their arrangement is rather different: Astyages marries off his daughter to the Persian Cambyses, whereas Jacob goes to Mesopotamia and himself apparently desires to marry Rachel, with Leah deviously thrown into the bargain by Laban. Still, it should be noted that, beside the danger threatening Jacob from his brother Esau, the wish to find a wife from the daughters of Laban had also been given as the motivation for his journey to Mesopotamia by his parents (Gen. 27.46 and especially 29.1-2). Both marriages can thus also be described as having been brokered. The very rich brothers-in-law lose at least part of their possessions to a scion of the main family: Jacob cheats Laban out of large flocks of small cattle (Gen. 30–31), whereas Cyrus gains the riches of Lydia when he conquers its capital Sardis and captures Croesus (Her. I, 88). Finally, in both works the first five generations are treated in the first book of a series of nine.[27]

There is an additional agreement between various members of these families, albeit not always in exactly corresponding generations. In Herodotus's work a number of Scythians, who as revenge for an insult put before Cyaxares the flesh of a young Median man, telling him that it was the game that they had brought him, flee to Alyattes, the father of Croesus (Her. I, 73). In Genesis it is Jacob who has to flee 'to the house of Bethuel', Laban's father (Gen. 28.2), after cheating his father Isaac by disguising himself and pretending to be his brother Esau in order to get his blessing, and giving him the meat of two kids ($g^e d\bar{a}ye$ '$izz\bar{\imath}m$) which he said to be Esau's game (Gen. 27.6-29). In the work of Herodotus, an apparently causally connected train of instances of deception appears in his first book. As mentioned above, Cyaxares takes his revenge on the Scythians by treacherously killing them during a banquet, thus confirming the power endangered by them. His son Astyages loses the royal power bequeathed by his father through being deceived by Harpagus twice: first when he spirits away the little Cyrus (I, 108-13), then when he incites Cyrus to revolt through sending him a message hidden in a hare (Her. I, 123-24); the second instance of deception is caused by the first one through Astyages' cruel deception of Harpagus when he feeds him the flesh of his son as revenge for disobeying his command with regard to the little Cyrus. Just as the theme of eating human flesh, always popular in Greek mythology,[28] returns with Herodotus in Astyages' revenge on Harpagus, and, more generally, all these instances of deception in Herodotus are characterized by the connection of eating and death, so the theme of the deception with small cattle runs on throughout the stories around Jacob: he is deceived about the identity of the woman he marries (he expected Laban's daughter Rachel, but at first gets her sister Leah), in order that he will herd Laban's small cattle even longer (Gen. 29.21-27), he then cheats Laban with it (Gen. 30.25-43) and is deceived himself when Joseph's brothers, after selling him to Egypt, dip his coat in the blood of a kid (s^e '$\bar{\imath}r$

27. If we indeed assume this to have been the original number. In any case, however, the death of the key figures Cyrus and Joseph would be a very natural place for the end of the first book in both works.

28. The most famous example, of course, being the story of Atreus, who fed Thyestes the flesh of his son.

'izzīm; Gen. 37.31), thus making it appear that he was devoured by a wild animal. Judah, who in his function as saviour of the key figure can be compared to Harpagus in Herodotus's work, and who took the initiative for deceiving Jacob about Joseph, is then deceived in the episode of Tamar, where the kid (*g^edī 'izzīm*) is mentioned again as the fee she is to receive for her services (Gen. 38.17, 20, 23).

Table 1.4 *Deception and reaction in the first books of Herodotus and Primary History. Similar elements are in bold characters.*

Herodotus	Other common elements	Genesis
(1) Scythians deceive Cyaxares about **game**	**deceivers have to flee**	(1) Jacob deceives Isaac about **game**
(2) Cyaxares deceives Scythians with hospitality	**feast**	(2) Laban deceives Jacob about Rachel and Leah
		(3) Jacob deceives Laban about small cattle
(3) Harpagus deceives Astyages about fate of his **grandson** Cyrus	**disappearance of descendant, soiled and torn coat, wild animals**	(4) Judah and his brothers deceive Jacob about fate of his **son** Joseph
(4) Astyages deceives Harpagus about son	**unknowingly doing something shameful with a relative**	(5) Tamar deceives Judah about her identity
(5) Harpagus deceives Astyages with hare		

The theme of deception thus runs on through a number of generations of the family in both cases, and the various instances of deception and their order within the story are also strikingly similar in a number of instances (see Table 1.4): Cyaxares and Isaac with the supposed game that they eat, Astyages and Jacob with the supposed death of their progeny and the object that is used to deceive them, Harpagus and Judah with unknowingly doing something shameful within their families through not recognizing their own relatives—in both cases because their *heads* are not visible. The first two correspondences seem to have shifted one generation down in the genealogy of Genesis (one would have expected Cyaxares-Abraham and Astyages-Isaac).[29] It should of course be noted—it has already become

---

29. The reason may have been that in Genesis there was no place for a female figure corresponding to Mandane; see below.

partly clear from the above—that family relations in Genesis are far more extensive and involved than they have been represented as being in the table; this does not, however, invalidate my conclusions about the congruence of the family trees and a number of the persons in them.[30]

It will be clear that in the preceding paragraphs we have mainly dealt with the agreements between the structure of the two families and the acts of persons in corresponding generations, and we should now also give some attention to what makes them different, in order to avoid the bias of noting only the congruences and not the variations. Still, this does not change the general picture very much. Many, if not most, of the obvious differences between the patriarchal genealogy and the family of the Persian kings can be supposed to represent characteristically Jewish religious and historical preoccupations and tendencies. The patriarchs appear to marry almost exclusively among their own families: Abraham's wife is also his half-sister (Gen. 20.12), Isaac marries his remote relative Rebecca, the great-granddaughter of his grandfather Terah, and Jacob's wives Rachel and Leah are Rebecca's cousins; especially marrying a woman from among the Canaanites is looked upon askance in Gen. 24.3 and 27.46–28.1. Only in the next generation do these habits seem to change somewhat: Joseph marries Asenath, the daughter of the Egyptian priest Potiphera (Gen. 41.50), and Judah the daughter of the Canaanite Shua (Gen. 38.2).

In contrast with the story of the birth of Cyrus, where the shepherd and Harpagus have the main roles together with his grandfather Astyages, the persons involved in Joseph's disappearance are all his brothers. The roles of Judah and Joseph in the cycle of stories around Joseph have probably been inspired at least in part by later history, Judah being the supposed ancestor of the population of the southern kingdom, which in Primary History is said to carry on the Israelite traditions alone, and Joseph, in his son Ephraim, representing its northern counterpart, which was pre-eminent for centuries, but fell before the Assyrians in 720 BCE and subsequently disappeared from the stage completely. This distinction is paralleled by Judah and Joseph having different mothers, Leah and Rachel, respectively. Comparable reasons may be behind the fact that Moses and Aaron are said

30. The main extras are the branching off of a number of other families (and subsequently, nations) through Abraham's son Ishmael, Isaac's son Esau and Abraham's nephew Lot (son of his brother Haran), and Jacob's marriages with Laban's daughters Rachel and Leah. Of course the Median–Persian royal family is also much larger than the persons represented here.

to descend from Levi, the ancestor of the groups of Levites and priests. Note also that the system of twelve tribes itself, many of which (especially those said to have issued from Jacob's concubines Bilhah and Zilpah) play only a perfunctory role in Primary History, has numerous parallels in ancient history. In the work of Herodotus we may note especially the Ionian league, composed of twelve cities, which plays an important part in the dealings between Greeks and Lydians at first, and then between Greeks and Persians (I, 142-43).

Beginning, Final Episodes and General Character of Both Works

Having noted the agreement between the subjects of the two works, it is appropriate to scrutinize their beginnings, in order to see whether the way in which they introduce this subject may have elements in common. Herodotus starts his work with a half-mythological story about the first strife between Greeks and Asians. He tells about the beautiful Io from Argos, who was abducted by a group of Phoenicians, and continues with the tit-for-tat abduction of Princess Europa from Tyre, Medea from Colchis and finally of Helen, which was the cause of the Trojan war, the first armed conflict between Europe and Asia, generally regarded as analogous to the wars between Persians and Greeks, both by the Greeks and by the Persians and their allies, and to later conflicts.[31] Herodotus concludes this introduction with a small but significant variant of the story which, he says, the Phoenicians tell: Io would really have fallen in love with a Phoenician captain and become pregnant by him, sufficient reason for her to join the Phoenicians and to decline a return to her land of origin. Directly afterwards, Herodotus starts his account of the real history with the figure of Croesus, who 'was the first foreigner so far as we know to come into direct contact with the Greeks, both in the way of conquest and alliance, forcing tribute from Ionians, Aeolians, and Asiatic Dorians, and forming a pact of friendship with the Lacedaemonians' (Her. I, 6); in this account he treats the string of historical events which finally led to the great conflicts that form the main subject of his work.

Primary History sets out with the creation of the world, which is said to have taken the six working days of the first week, after which God himself

---

31. See, for example, P. Georges, *Barbarian Asia and the Greek Experience: From the Archaic Period to the Age of Xenophon* (Baltimore: The Johns Hopkins University Press, 1994), pp. 58-71.

rested on the Sabbath-day. Humankind is said to have been created after everything else on the sixth day.

> [Gen. 1.26] Then God said, 'Let us make man in our image, after our likeness; and let them have dominion over the fish of the sea, and over the birds of the air, and over the cattle, and over all the earth, and over every creeping thing that creeps upon the earth.' [27] So God created man in his own image, in the image of God he created him; male and female he created them.

In Genesis 2, however, a slightly different version of the creation, especially of man, is given.

> [Gen. 2.4] These are the generations of the heavens and the earth when they were created. In the day that the Lord God made the earth and the heavens, [5] when no plant of the field was yet in the earth and no herb of the field had yet sprung up—for the Lord God had not caused it to rain upon the earth, and there was no man to till the ground; [6] but a mist went up from the earth and watered the whole face of the ground—[7] then the Lord God formed man of dust from the ground, and breathed into his nostrils the breath of life; and man became a living being.

Thus, man is created before all other living beings in this version. This dual account of creation is very remarkable, and historically served as one of the first reasons for assuming various sources in the Pentateuch.[32] Of course one could argue that the two accounts can be harmonized or that they go back to different sources, but the basic fact remains that they have been left one beside the other in more or less the most conspicuous place of the entire work, which virtually precludes anything but intentional juxtaposition as an explanation of the way in which they are found now, irrespective of the question what their origins may have been.[33]

Both the work of Herodotus and Primary History thus start with a story, one detail of which is given in a somewhat different version also. With this beginning, however, Primary History has not even started with giving a background for its great theme, the conquest of the so-called land of Canaan by the Israelites, in contrast with Herodotus, who straight away presents what he considers to be the first instance of a conflict between Europe and Asia. A few chapters later, however, the readers are indeed for the first time given a reason why this 'land of Canaan' was to be taken

---

32. Houtman, *Der Pentateuch*, pp. 62-67.
33. See Chapter 4 for a general discussion of the function of such contradictory stories in Primary History.

away from its original inhabitants and given to the Israelites. After his salvation from the Great Flood, together with his wife and his three sons Ham, Japheth and Shem, Noah had settled down to become a husband-man, planted vines, harvested grapes and made wine. He subsequently indulges in drinking wine and in his drunkenness lies down naked. Ham enters the tent where his father lies, leaves again and tells his two brothers what he has seen. They enter the tent backwards, in order to avoid seeing their father's sorry state, and cover his nakedness. After Noah has come to his senses again, he somewhat surprisingly curses not Ham himself but his offspring, and more specifically his youngest son Canaan:

> [Gen. 9.20] Noah was the first tiller of the soil. He planted a vineyard; [21] and he drank of the wine, and became drunk, and lay uncovered in his tent. [22] And Ham, the father of Canaan, saw the nakedness of his father, and told his two brothers outside. [23] Then Shem and Japheth took a garment, laid it upon both their shoulders, and walked backward and covered the nakedness of their father; their faces were turned away, and they did not see their father's nakedness. [24] When Noah awoke from his wine and knew what his youngest son had done to him, [25] he said, 'Cursed be Canaan; a slave of slaves shall he be to his brothers.' He also said, [26] 'Blessed by the Lord my God be Shem; and let Canaan be his slave. [27] God enlarge Japheth, and let him dwell in the tents of Shem; and let Canaan be his slave.'

As in Herodotus's work, the first roots of the great conflict over the land are traced to a seemingly unrelated episode of quarrel between the two parties, which is not said to be causally connected with the later history of the conflict. The 'real' cause of the taking possession of the land of Canaan by the Israelites is given a number of chapters later. Together with his father Terah and the rest of his family, the patriarch Abram sets out from Ur of the Chaldees in southern Mesopotamia, but at first they do not go any further than Haran in northern Mesopotamia, where Terah dies (Gen. 11.31-32). Either in Haran or perhaps when he is still living in Ur, Abram receives a divine promise that God is to give a certain country, which he will show to Abram, to his descendants, and he is ordered to go there. It soon turns out that this is the land of Canaan. Whether or not he knows this already, Abram travels there from Haran, arrives in the Prom-ised Land and is told by God in the location of Shechem: 'To your descendants I will give this land' (Gen. 12.7). These promises are reit-erated many times to Abraham and to the other patriarchs and are later taken to be the legal title to the land of Abram's descendants: 'And I will bring you into the land which I swore to give to Abraham, to Isaac, and to

Jacob; I will give it to you for a possession. I am the Lord' (Exod. 6.8); 'Remember Abraham, Isaac, and Israel, thy servants, to whom thou didst swear by thine own self, and didst say to them, "I will multiply your descendants as the stars of heaven, and all this land that I have promised I will give to your descendants, and they shall inherit it for ever"' (Exod. 32.13); 'The Lord said to Moses, "Depart, go up hence, you and the people whom you have brought up out of the land of Egypt, to the land of which I swore to Abraham, Isaac, and Jacob, saying, 'To your descendants I will give it'"' (Exod. 33.1); 'Surely none of the men who came up out of Egypt, from twenty years old and upward, shall see the land which I swore to give to Abraham, to Isaac, and to Jacob, because they have not wholly followed me' (Num. 32.11); 'Behold, I have set the land before you; go in and take possession of the land which the Lord swore to your fathers, to Abraham, to Isaac, and to Jacob, to give to them and to their descendants after them' (Deut. 1.8); 'Not because of your righteousness or the upright-ness of your heart are you going in to possess their land; but because of the wickedness of these nations the Lord your God is driving them out from before you, and that he may confirm the word which the Lord swore to your fathers, to Abraham, to Isaac, and to Jacob' (Deut. 9.5); 'And the Lord said to [Moses], "This is the land of which I swore to Abraham, to Isaac, and to Jacob, 'I will give it to your descendants'. I have let you see it with your eyes, but you shall not go over there"' (Deut. 34.4).

Thus we see that the work of Herodotus and Primary History both begin with a story for one aspect of which a variant tradition is given. Herodotus combines this story with his account of the first origins of the great conflict that he describes; Primary History reserves this for a later passage. In both cases a first origin for the great conflict is given in the form of a story placed in the remote past (Io *et al.* and Noah), while a more or less his-torical explanation (Croesus and Abraham) is presented further on in the work, in a period which falls within the main chronological and narrative framework.

An additional agreement is that at the end of both works, which have often been noticed to conclude very abruptly, without an epilogue or something like it, there appears to be a reference to the key figure and to the main person's crossing of the sea. With Herodotus, this reminiscence of the key figure is done explicitly through mentioning a dialogue between the ancestor of the Persian governor Artayctes, about whose death he has just told his readers, and King Cyrus as to whether the Persians should leave their infertile country to live in more pleasant lands (Her. IX, 122)—one of the important themes in Herodotus's view of the Persians. Primary

History is concluded with a reference to the liberation and restoration to a honourable position of Zedekiah's nephew, King Jehoiachin, who had been incarcerated for many years after having been taken away from Jerusalem by King Nebuchadnezzar in 597 BCE (2 Kgs 25.27-30). We have no difficulty recognizing one of the themes of the story of Joseph, who had also been in a prison in a foreign country, and was liberated from there in order to take an important position at court. Herodotus also tells that the Greeks kill Artayctes by crucifying him in the exact spot where Xerxes had built his great bridges across the Hellespont (Her. IX, 120), an event apparently so striking in his eyes that he has already mentioned it when describing the building of the bridges (Her. VII, 33). For this case we do not have a direct reference to the corresponding event in the Bible, but there is an allusion of sorts in the directly preceding story of the murder of the Babylonian governor Gedaliah and the flight of the people to Egypt out of fear of reprisals (2 Kgs 25.25-26)—exactly the other direction compared to Moses and Israel crossing the Red Sea.

Before these final episodes we find the last military action: in both works the investing and capture of the last stronghold in the possession of the conquerors. In the work of Herodotus this is the already mentioned town of Sestos, which is situated on the Hellespont more or less at the location of Xerxes' bridges; in the corresponding place in Primary History we find the capture of Jerusalem. Thus the taking of the town of Sestos, the last small Persian stronghold in Europe,[34] surprisingly corresponds with what is probably the most momentous event in ancient Jewish history, the fall of David's city Jerusalem to the Babylonians and the subsequent deportation of its inhabitants to Mesopotamia. This correspondence is hardly accidental: the fate of King Zedekiah, who escapes in the night from beleaguered and hungry Jerusalem, is pursued and captured, and has to watch his sons being killed before his eyes, after which he is blinded, bound in fetters (*n°huštayim*) and taken to Babylon (2 Kgs 25.4-7), is very similar to what is related of the Persian governor Artayctes in this concluding episode of Herodotus's work: he flees at night from the town of Sestos, which had long been invested by the Athenians, so that its inhabitants had been reduced to dire necessity, is pursued, overtaken and fettered, and after he has been crucified, his son is killed before his eyes (Her. IX, 118-20). Thus, the last thing that the commander of the last stronghold sees in both works is the death of his offspring.

---

34. At least (implicitly) according to Herodotus's account; in reality the Persians retained some footholds in Europe, notably Byzantium.

In this way, of course, Primary History finds a conclusion that is to some degree more convincing than the way Herodotus's work ends:[35] it has the Jews returning to Egypt and Babylon, the lands that they are said to have left at the beginning of their history (in Exod. 13–14 and Gen. 12, respectively)[36], and the city of Jerusalem with its central role in the earlier history being taken and burned by the Babylonians, and thus exhibits a fitting epilogue to the history it describes, especially in view of the following considerations.

There is also a more general similarity of literary character between the two works, which finds its clearest expression in and just before these final episodes. It should be realized that from the Persian point of view, which was undoubtedly at least partly shared by the Jews of Jerusalem, Herodotus's work is a thoroughly tragic one: each and every one of the Persian kings whose career he describes at length becomes the victim of his own ambitions, or rather of his *hubris*. Cyrus is killed in an unnecessary battle against the Massagetae (I, 214), Cambyses dies after having committed sacrilege in Egypt (II, 64-66), Darius suffers a humiliating defeat against the Scythians (IV, 121-43), and Xerxes not only is defeated by the Greeks, but is said to suffer terribly in his personal life near the end of the narrative, just before the episodes concluding Herodotus's work which allude to Cyrus and the crossing of the Hellespont: his wife tortures and mutilates the wife of his beloved and respected brother Masistes, whom Xerxes had at first fallen in love with. Masistes himself then revolts against Xerxes and is killed (IX, 108-13). In a comparable way the tragic event *par excellence*, the fall of Jerusalem to the Babylonians and the destruction of Solomon's temple, is related before the two episodes at the end of Primary History; it effectively combines the fall of Sestos, with its symbolical value

35. Though there are, in fact, good reasons why the *Histories* end the way they do. See especially D. Boedecker, 'Protesilaus and the End of Herodotus' Histories', *Classical Antiquity* 7 (1988), pp. 30-48. She points out that it is hardly accidental that it ends with the death of Artayctes, who desecrated the sanctuary of Protesilaus, the first Greek to be killed in the Trojan war, at more or less the location of Xerxes' great bridges. Lateiner (*The Historical Method of Herodotus*, p. 134) adds the insight that by inflicting this wicked punishment the Athenians (in the person of Pericles' father Xanthippus) in turn cross the boundaries set by nature in more or less the same way Xerxes did when crossing the Hellespont, which bodes evil for their future.

36. As already noted by Mandell and Freedman, *Herodotus' History and Primary History*, pp. 166-69. This grand *inclusio*, by the way, appears to mirror Herodotus's implicit references to Homer's work at the beginning and end of his *Histories*.

of indicating the demise of the conquest, with the tragical aspects of the story about Masistes' wife. Like the work of Herodotus, the great historical work stretching from Genesis to 2 Kings is indeed a tragic history, and was probably meant to be just that.

Chapter 2

A REMARKABLE PROCEDURE

To our modern sense of composition it is a rather remarkable and unusual procedure to copy structural elements from an existing literary or literary-religious work into a new one without the intention of a parody or paraphrase that would be evident to every educated reader. It would seem, however, that it was sometimes done in antiquity. It has even been observed that the notion is not foreign to Jewish literature. Thus Devorah Dimant has demonstrated that the apocryphal book of Tobit derived many elements from the book of Job, and that even their order is often the same in both books, though the plot is entirely different:

> These affinities with the story of Job are notable because they are present without any explicit reference to Job or the Book of Job. Moreover, the materials of the plot are not taken from Job or a similar biblical figure, but are independent of them. The use made by Tobit of biblical motifs differs, then, in purpose and form from that of narratives of the rewritten Bible or pseudepigraphic biography type. The referential value lies in the coincidence of motifs and some of the terms, but it leads to a comparison between the new and old texts, and not to an integration of the old in the new, as was the case in the pseudepigraphic or 'rewritten Bible' narratives.[1]

I attempted myself to demonstrate that the structure of the book of Daniel is largely based on a combination of structural elements in the history of Joseph and in the book of Ezra, supplemented with information derived from Herodotus's description of the life of Cyrus, which is, of course, somewhat ironic in the light of what has been set forth above,[2] while the

---

1. Devorah Dimant, 'Use and Interpretation of Mikra in the Apocrypha and Pseudepigrapha', in M.J. Mulder and H. Sysling (eds.), *Mikra: Text, Translation, Reading and Interpretation of the Hebrew Bible in Ancient Judaism and Early Christianity* (Assen: Van Gorcum, 1988), pp. 379-419 (417-19).

2. See my *De eenheid van het boek Daniel: Openingscollege van de Faculteit der Godgeleerdheid UvA, 3 September 1993* (Amsterdam: [privately published], 1993) and *Language, Style and Structure in the Book of Daniel* (forthcoming).

book of Ezra, though officially joined with Nehemiah in one book of the Hebrew Bible, seems to be secondary to Nehemiah in more or less the same manner.[3] Although the likeness to the sources is much more evident for Daniel than with Tobit and Job, Ezra and Nehemiah, or Primary History and Herodotus's *Histories*, the general pattern is clear: in certain Israelite groups there was an accepted literary habit of reusing characteristic structural elements of certain highly valued and more or less classical books when writing a new work. In those cases where certain established themes and other clearly recognizable patterns have also been copied, the relationship between these works has been noted in the past already, but if such elements have been transformed in some way it is far more difficult to discern the relation, as the works may have very little likeness on the surface.

For this reason the possibility should be considered very seriously that this method of copying the structure of existing works for a new one was far more common than we have hitherto realized. By the very nature of this procedure the agreement will usually not be very striking: our usual classifications according to literary genre and contents will often obscure the parallel rather than reveal it. The story of Cyrus's birth has been compared with other stories about children being exposed, such as Oedipus with the Greeks and Moses in the Bible,[4] but rarely, if ever, with the beginning of the Joseph narrative, for which other stories about dream-interpretation are adduced as parallels.[5] The approach proposed here may in the long run prove fruitful for the study of certain other types of ancient literature; see below for the illuminating parallel of the origin of Virgil's *Aeneid*.

A direct application of the theory of literary transformation proposed here may be found in the well-known phenomenon of biblical stories that exhibit significant similarity of the use of certain expressions, personal names or structure of the narrative. More or less well-known examples are the story of Judah and Tamar (Gen. 38) in comparison with that of Amnon and the other Tamar (2 Sam. 14), the elimination of the first three sons of

3.   Wesselius, 'Discontinuity', *passim*.

4.   Cf. D.B. Redford, 'The Literary Motif of the Exposed Child (cf. Ex. ii 1-10)', *Numen* 14 (1967), pp. 209-28. There may, in fact, be a secondary relation between the birth stories of Moses and Cyrus, in view of shared elements such as the danger for the child from the king, the exposure and the foster-mother who saves its life.

5.   R. Gnuse, 'The Jewish Dream Interpreter in a Foreign Court: The Recurrent Use of a Theme in Jewish Literature', *JSP* 7 (1990), pp. 29-53.

Jacob and David from the succession, making way for the desired successors Judah and Solomon,[6] and the story about the inhospitality of the inhabitants of Sodom (Gen. 19) compared with the episode of the Levite and his concubine in Gibeah (Judg. 19). It has been remarked that in many such cases we are dealing with parallels between stories in the Pentateuch on one side and in Judges, Joshua and the books of Samuel and Kings, the Former Prophets of the Jewish canon, on the other, which are in this way apparently deliberately connected.[7] On another level, it is well known that the story of the patriarch saying of his wife that she is his sister, with all the complications that result from it, is told three times in the book of Genesis, twice of Abraham and once of Isaac, and although these instances can hardly be completely independent from one another, each has its own distinct function within its context.[8] It would seem that in all these cases structural elements of one story have been incorporated into another in more or less the same way that we meet elements of the work of Herodotus in the biblical historical work. We may be justified in concluding that in this way we have identified one of the leading principles of the literary composition of Primary History, which has largely remained unrecognized through its unexpectedness and location outside of current literary models. Maybe it should be pointed out once more that all this does not imply 'primary' or 'secondary' usage of words and themes, at least as far as literary value is considered: each occurrence has its own value and its own distinct place within the literary work as a whole.

All this does not mean, of course, that there is a really significant similarity between the figures of Cyrus and Joseph in character, appearance or way of life, and this is even more true for the other parallel figures and the events of their lives in Herodotus and Primary History. There is very little likeness, of course, between Xerxes, the tyrannical king *par excellence*, whimsical, cruel, magnanimous at times, but cowardly at heart, and Moses,

---

6.   The eldest sons Reuben and Amnon commit incest (Gen. 35.22 and 2 Sam. 13), Simeon and Levi disobey their father by violently avenging the rape of their sister Dinah (Gen. 36), and Absalom and Adonijah by making a bid for royal power without David's consent, the former after taking violent revenge for the rape of his sister Tamar (2 Sam. 15–19 and 1 Kgs 1). See the brief note about the parallel in B. Halpern, *The Emergence of Israel in Canaan* (Chico, CA: Scholars Press, 1983), p. 124 n. 49.

7.   Cf., for example, E.L. Greenstein, 'The Formation of the Biblical Narrative Corpus', *AJS Review* 15 (1990), pp. 151-78, who gives a thorough description of the phenomenon, but deliberately refrains from attempting an explanation.

8.   See the illuminating comments by Robert Alter, *The World of Biblical Literature* (New York: BasicBooks, 1992), pp. 145-48.

the God-sent law-giver and leader of the people of Israel, who is said to tower above all who have come since (Deut. 34.10); or between the noble and hospitable Abraham, who wins his victory over the kings of the east through sheer valour, and the treacherous king Cyaxares, who gains his great victory over the Scythians through inviting them to a banquet, making them drunk and then attacking them suddenly. These pairs of persons are not similar, i.e. they do not really look like each other, but they are congruent: they undergo or commit similar acts, or there are other agreements that do not seem essential for their description. The parallels do not, therefore, link these persons only, but more especially the texts in which they figure, and in this case they connect Primary History very closely with the work of Herodotus. This purpose of the parallelism is stressed by making the family trees congruent also.

The Significance of the Agreement between Herodotus and Primary History

The first question that should now be asked is whether the similarities discussed above may be treated as a whole, or should be divided into, for example, the agreements in the stories about Cyrus and Joseph, and likewise between Abraham and Cyaxares, and Moses and Xerxes. In that case the agreement between Herodotus and the Bible would be reduced to some very remarkable observations, all of which could, however, if necessary be explained from parallel development or from a common origin in one literary model. One could imagine that the stories of the provenance of Joseph and Cyrus have a common background in birth-stories of a type that was quite common in the Near East, that the similarities between Abraham and Cyaxares concern more or less general characteristics of many historical persons, and that the stories of Moses and Xerxes elaborate well-known themes of a leader bringing an enormous army to attain aims in a distant country, and that the comparable position of these stories and their main persons within the cycle of stories would be grounded in a normal and accepted method of setting up historical works. This approach, however, does not provide a convincing explanation. Firstly, it must be said that the story of Joseph is not a birth-story at all, that the agreements with the story of Cyrus are hardly characteristic of any particular genre, and that more or less the same goes for Abraham/Cyaxares and Moses/Xerxes. Secondly, the position of these stories within their respective works seems to be too specific to be explained from a common model—apart from the problem that we know of no other work with this structural framework. The series of cases of deception in the first book of both works, both starting from making a member of the family concerned believe that a certain piece of meat is the venison brought to him, whereas it is, in fact, something completely different (two kids in the case of Isaac, and the flesh of a young Median man with Cyaxares), and resulting in certain important changes in the lives of the key figures Joseph and Cyrus, are very much alike, in spite of the evident differences of details, and would by themselves constitute a highly significant similarity. A coincidental occurrence of all these similarities at the same time seems very unlikely. When the congruence between the family trees and the persons figuring in them is added, coincidence can effectively be excluded as a cause.

It may be added that, by contrast, some old problems with the text of Primary History as we now have it may be solved by having recourse to the parallel with Herodotus. Thus we can now explain why Abraham's father Terah already set out for Canaan, why Moses is so closely related to Levi in spite of the chronological and practical problems involved (the number of Israelites is said to have grown from 70 to several millions between the lifetime of grandfather and grandson), and why we have two instances of the people of Israel crossing waters as if on dry land.

If there is indeed a direct connection between the work of Herodotus and the History of Israel in Genesis–2 Kings, especially with regard to the history and position of Abraham, Joseph and Moses versus Cyaxares, Cyrus and Xerxes, the next question is what direction the influence has taken. On the one hand one could suppose that Herodotus, either during his travels or on some other occasion, would have made the acquaintance of the national history of Israel, which would then already have received more or less the form which we know, and would have used part of its structure for his own work. On the other hand one could think that the author or redactor of Primary History knew the *Histories* of Herodotus, whether in the present form or in an earlier one, and used their framework for ordering the material that was doubtlessly already at his disposal. It would seem that the second theory about the connection between Herodotus and Primary History is much more likely than the first one for the following reasons.

A comparison of the position of the common elements within the two works would be very useful in principle, but at first appears not to provide an unambiguous result. Of course both Herodotus and the author and redactor of Primary History must have felt bound to certain historical and literary information that they were unable or unwilling to contradict, and in theory this should make it rather easy to determine which account is the original one. The problem is that we have very little information about earlier stages of the traditions that they employed. Thus it seems very likely that the author of Primary History already had part of the genealogy of the patriarchs at his disposal, but proof is hard to come by. On the other side, there were certainly variant traditions about the defeat, intended burning and salvation of King Croesus, of which Herodotus apparently chose the one that suited him best,[9] and he explicitly tells his readers that he found a number of stories dealing with the background and birth of Cyrus, of which he chose the one he considered most likely (Her. I, 95).

There also seem to be certain inconsistencies of substance and chronology in the Joseph story in Genesis in connection with those elements that it shares with Herodotus. I shall mention only a few. We are not told where Reuben, the first one to save Joseph, was when his brother was sold to the merchants, nor is it clear why Joseph, who apparently longed to see his father and his brother Benjamin again, did not attempt to get in touch with them during his first nine years as viceroy of Egypt. Finally, it has often been noted that the story of Judah and Tamar does not fit in the chronological framework of the cycle of Joseph, as there simply is not enough time to generate the grandchildren of Judah who are mentioned in Gen. 46.12, even if we assume with several ancient and modern authors that the events of Genesis 38 took place before those of Genesis 37.[10] Experience has taught, however, that one should be very cautious with such considerations, as the laconic style and terse mode of composition of biblical Hebrew prose texts often engender apparent contradictions which later turn out not to be contradictions at all.[11]

There is one very famous episode, however, where the priority of Herodotus's account is very likely, namely the stories of the crossing of the sea by the people of Israel and by Xerxes' army. In the latter case we are dealing with a reasonably well-documented historical event, in which a very real barrier for the Persian king's army was crossed by means of two bridges of boats, to the amazement of the contemporaries.[12] The case of the crossing of the Red Sea, by contrast, is regarded as highly problematic

9. Gould, *Herodotus*, pp. 34-35 n. 1.

10. See, for example, B. Jacob, *Das erste Buch der Tora: Genesis* (Berlin: Schocken Verlag, 1934), p. 710.

11. See below (in Chapter 4) on the literary aspects of these supposed contradictions or discontinuities.

12. See, for example, Aeschylus's *Persians*, 65-72; 125-32; 721-24; 744-50.

by many scholars who have commented on it. The indications for its location, for example, are so ambiguous that numerous identifications have been proposed for the place where it all happened, and nearly every body of water between the Mediterranean and the Red Sea (in the modern sense) has at some time been regarded as the correct location.[13] If there is indeed a relationship between the two episodes, the Exodus account must be dependent on the Herodotus story, not the other way round. This does not automatically mean that such a thing as the Exodus never took place or that there were no prior traditions about it when Primary History was written, only that its present position in the biblical account must be the result of the parallel with Herodotus. What should be noted, moreover, for this event as for several others in Primary History, is that the parallel with the *Histories* is by itself sufficient to explain the course of events in Primary History, and that historically speaking the latter text provides empty information only: when the link with the *Histories* is observed, no independent claim to historical correctness results. Again this cannot be used to prove that there is no historical reality underlying the description in the text, as such a reality may, in fact, have triggered the use of the parallel in the first place. True, the application of the narrative framework of the *Histories* to the question of how Israel came into the possession of the country where it used to live can well lead independently to something much like the narrative in Primary History. The hypothesis of a similar Great Campaign from another continent across a body of water to conquer the land of Canaan automatically leads to an Egyptian episode, and this episode, combined with the characteristic features of the Life of Cyrus in Book I of the Histories, in turn may well bring into being something like the Life of Joseph in Genesis. It must be observed, however, that a real earlier tradition about an Egyptian provenance of the nation or part of it would considerably strengthen the tendency to use the framework of the *Histories* in this way.

The case of another parallel is even more convincing. The congruence of the genealogy of the well-known royal house of Persia with that of the patriarchs can only be explained as a borrowing of the latter from the former. It can also be observed that in some places the biblical account encounters certain logical problems. As noted above, Moses' position as a third-generation descendant of Jacob is especially difficult to explain, unless one assumes a dependence of the biblical genealogy on Herodotus.

Another consideration is also very important. The polemicists in favour

13. C. Houtman, *Exodus*, I, pp. 115-16.

of and against Judaism around the beginning of our era noted, either with pleasure or with dismay, that neither Herodotus nor any of the other early Greek historians and other authors gives any attention to the Jews, a fact that is even more striking in the case of Herodotus because he mentions the 'Syrians' or 'Palestinian Syrians', as well as the country they live in, rather frequently.[14] It is hardly likely that Herodotus would not have mentioned the Jews by name at some length if he had such a thorough knowledge of a substantial part of the Jewish sacred literature that he could derive part of the structure of his work from it. By contrast, there must have been several aspects of Herodotus's *Histories* that were bound to be very interesting to Jewish readers. In particular, the portrait of King Cyrus must have appealed to them, because he was the king who allowed the Jews, around 539 BCE, to return from the exile into which King Nebuchadnezzar of Babylon had led them after the fall of Jerusalem in 587 BCE, and to rebuild Jerusalem and its Temple. Cyrus liked to have himself represented as the monarch who, in marked contrast with his Babylonian predecessors, respected and even supported the religious traditions of the nations subject to him. This official view has understandably found its way into the Bible, especially into the second part of the book of the prophet Isaiah (from ch. 40 onward, the so-called Deutero-Isaiah), in which Cyrus is mentioned with great respect (cf., for example, Isa. 45.1-3, 'Thus says the Lord to his anointed, to Cyrus, whose right hand I have grasped, to subdue nations before him and ungird the loins of kings, to open doors before him that gates may not be closed: [2] "I will go before you and level the mountains, I will break in pieces the doors of bronze and cut asunder the bars of iron, [3] I will give you the treasures of darkness and the hoards in secret places, that you may know that it is I, the Lord, the God of Israel, who call you by your name..." '), which led to the situation that Cyrus is the only king from the ancient Near East whose official

14. See, for example, E. Gabba, 'The Growth of Anti-Judaism or the Greek Attitude towards Jews', in W.D. Davies and L. Finkelstein (eds.), *The Cambridge History of Judaism* (Cambridge: Cambridge University Press, 1989), II, pp. 614-56; M. Stern, *Greek and Latin Authors on Jews and Judaism*, II (Jerusalem: Israel Academy of Sciences and Humanities, 1980). Cf. also A. Momigliano, 'Die Juden und die griechische Kultur', in *Die Juden in der alten Welt* (Berlin: Klaus Wagenbach, 1988), pp. 28-48, and L.H. Feldman, *Jew and Gentile in the Ancient World* (Princeton: Princeton University Press, 1993). Several passages in Herodotus's work have been taken by some authors as referring to the Jews without naming them, but by itself this does not change the argument that he does not refer to them explicitly.

reputation, propagated by himself, has managed to exercise its influence until the present day.

An interesting result of these observations would be that for the first time we have a real *terminus post quem* for the redaction of Primary History in the form in which we now have it: it must have been done after Herodotus's work received its final form, which happened almost certainly in the third quarter of the fifth century BCE. Primary History must therefore have received its present form after 425 BCE—if we assume that it must have taken some time for Herodotus's work to become widely known in the world. The accessibility of an originally Greek work to a Jewish author in the late fifth or the fourth century BCE may seem unlikely at first,[15] but we should keep in mind that the Greeks of Asia Minor were a not inconsiderable group of the population of the Persian empire, that many Greeks attained high office among the Persians, and that we should therefore not be surprised about a non-Greek knowing the Greek language, nor (perhaps) about a translation of Herodotus's work into one of the languages of the Near East. Such contacts are therefore by no means impossible, though still very remarkable.[16] A possible solution to this problem would be to push the date of the final composition of Primary History forward into the Hellenistic age (after c. 330 BCE), when the work of Herodotus would be readily available to educated Jews in Egypt or Palestine. Though this would agree with the ideas of some modern scholars, especially N.P. Lemche,[17] it is difficult to believe that only a few decades would separate the final redaction of Primary History from its translation into Greek, unless one would put the date of origin of the Septuagint considerably

15. Even if we reject the rather extreme view of S. Flory, 'Who Read Herodotus?', *AJP* 101 (1980), pp. 12-28, that Herodotus's work was simply too unwieldy to attract a sizeable readership.

16. Though Clearchus of Soloi's story about his teacher Aristotle making the acquaintance of a learned Jew is certainly not very reliable, the story proves that to the contemporaries such a person was by no means unimaginable, and there is no real argument against small groups of Jews or individuals perhaps living in Greece itself and acquiring Greek learning in this period. Cf. Momigliano, 'Die Juden und die griechische Kultur', p. 35. Finally, there is the possibility of Primary History having been composed by a literate Greek who had converted to Judaism, probably in collaboration with someone who knew Hebrew very well.

17. N.P. Lemche, 'The Old Testament: A Hellenistic Book?', *SJOT* 7 (1993), pp. 163-93.

later than the conventional third century BCE.[18] Still, the possibility cannot be excluded that the Hebrew text and the Septuagint of Primary History, or at least part of it, belong more closely together than one is inclined to think. Lemche rightly points out that it is hardly possible to prove that the Hebrew text predates the Septuagint by any prolonged period of time.[19] It should be noted, furthermore, that in some cases the Septuagint appears to facilitate the comparison with Herodotus, for instance in its rendering of the nature of Joseph's coat (Hebrew *k*e*tonet passīm*, Septuagint *chiton poikilon*, as in Cyrus's story) and of the way in which the waters of the Red Sea are said in the Song of the Sea to have stood when the Israelites passed by (Exod. 15.8, in the Hebrew the rare word *ned*, in the Septuagint *teichos*, 'wall'[20]). Further investigation is needed here.

It can be added to these considerations that a considerable linguistic and literary development can be observed between Primary History and late biblical books such as Chronicles or Ezra; this would be difficult to account for if only one century separated Primary History from these books, which can hardly be dated much later than 200 BCE, even if one takes into account the possibility that they originated in a different group in another location. Besides, the natural place of Primary History would seem to be in the movement of religious revival in the second half of the fifth century BCE, rather than much later.[21] For the time being, however, such a late date should not be excluded. The upper and lower limits for the composition of Primary History can in any case safely be taken to be 425 and 300 BCE, respectively.

A Possible Course of Events

It seems rather likely that Primary History derives from a situation in which the history of the Israelite kingdoms was known until some time after the reigns of David and Solomon, but the earlier history of the people of Israel had been lost in the fog of the past and probably only some disparate traditions about it were known. Apparently a need was felt, on

18. On the Septuagint and its date see E. Tov, *Textual Criticism of the Hebrew Bible* (Assen: Van Gorcum, 1992), pp. 134-48 and the literature quoted there.

19. 'The Old Testament: a Hellenistic Book?', p. 189.

20. Note, however, that this translation may have been influenced by the use of *ḥomā*, the ordinary word for 'wall', in Exod. 14.22.

21. See Chapter 3 for the possible connection with the Passover Letter from Elephantine.

the one hand to fill out the blanks in this history by pressing the description of the nation's history as far back in time as possible, and on the other hand to give an explanation of how the Israelites entered into the possession of their land; the simple and possibly quite correct explanation that they, or at least part of them, had always lived there, among many other population groups, was probably as unattractive then as it is to many modern scholars and laypersons. A likely course of events in this case would be that the author of the Primary History, either because he was impressed by Herodotus's work and wanted to emulate it for the history of his own people, or because he was looking for a suitable model for this history, while probably making use of materials that were already available to him (maybe large parts of the Pentateuch and a history of the kings of Judah and Israel, as found in the books of Samuel and Kings), decided to use certain structural elements of this work, which may have appealed to him in the first place because of the important role played in it by King Cyrus. One can well imagine that an extra impulse for this derivation was given by Herodotus's elaborate description of the crossing of the Hellespont by Xerxes, a human endeavour that our author may have associated and contrasted with an event that he believed to have a divine background, namely the crossing of the Red Sea by the people of Israel under the guidance of Moses. Of course, as noted above, it can also be observed that the dynamics of Herodotus's narrative, when applied to the history of the people of Israel, make an Egyptian episode almost unavoidable: the only simple direction from which the campaign to conquer Canaan could have come, as well as the only place from where it would be necessary or possible to go from one continent to another, would be the land of Egypt. In the latter case the traditions about Egypt and the Exodus might well be a radical innovation by our author, something that simply did not exist before his work. A full reconsideration of all the evidence for the Egyptian episodes would be necessary to determine which of the two is the right explanation.

Additionally, the episode at the end of the *Histories* of the lone town of Sestos holding out for a long time against the Greeks before finally being taken may have suggested an association with the sad fate of Jerusalem at the hands of the Babylonians. But above all, the phenomenon of the divinely sanctioned campaign of conquest against another country must have inspired the author of Primary History, and must have given him the idea of using Herodotus's work for the construction of his own, in which his sympathies and interest, in marked contrast with Herodotus, lay entirely with the conquerors instead of with the conquered.

For this reason, our hypothetical author decided to copy certain structural elements from this work, and in order to achieve this he made at least certain changes in and additions to the stories of Abraham, Joseph and Moses, which does not exclude, of course, the possibility that he intervened more heavily in certain places; thus, for example, the theme of the 'double dream' is elaborated much more in the history of Joseph than in Herodotus's work (Gen. 37.5-11; 40.5-23; 41.1-36), and its purpose is stated explicitly, in contrast with Herodotus: 'And the doubling of Pharaoh's dream means that the thing is fixed by God, and God will shortly bring it to pass' (Gen. 41.32). It is also not entirely clear to what degree the author modified the information he had about the ancestors of the people of Israel in the generations between Terah and Moses, though it is hardly likely that the agreement between the genealogy of this family and the family tree of the Persian and Median kings is entirely the result of coincidence. It may not be superfluous to point out that, although Herodotus's main interest is in the Greek side of the great conflict, the narrative and historical continuity of his work is provided by his description of the lives and times of the kings of Persia and Media, so it is hardly surprising that the author of Primary History took this to be highly characteristic of his work. Still, we must be wary of drawing precipitate conclusions about the historical and literary reliability of our author and his work. The fact that he ordered his information in a certain way does not by itself imply that his rendering of it would be completely or largely unreliable, or that he would have largely invented it himself. In this light we may have to look at the other agreements described here: from the supposed wealth of traditions about the patriarchs and about the Exodus he may have chosen those that would accentuate the similarities to certain aspects of Herodotus's work, but we cannot exclude the possibility that his own influence was far more fundamental. In other words, it is impossible to ascertain what traditions he had or did not have about, for example, the patriarchs Abraham, Isaac and Jacob, let alone to conclude anything about their historicity.

We can only guess at the motives to provide Primary History with this structure. It is certainly possible that our Jewish author and redactor of the late fifth or fourth century BCE, acquainted with the work of Herodotus, wanted to show that the history of his own people was of far greater significance for the world than the episode of the war between Greeks and Persians, which he probably considered in the last resort of very limited importance, and that many of the major events related by Herodotus could also be found in a morally superior form in the history of the people of

Israel, the forefathers of whom were also superior in this respect to the Persian monarchs. In general it can be observed, as I noted at the beginning of this book, that there are several cases where such intertextual links are at the basis of the structure and contents of books in the Hebrew Bible, and that they provide closure and completeness to works whose nature as more or less linear literary dossiers precludes most other ways to achieve this sense of completeness and unity.

Our author apparently derived certain crucial structural elements from Herodotus precisely to make this connection, and strengthened it by making some interesting collocations of events, noted above, such as the invasions of Palestine as far as the border of Egypt by the kings of the east in Genesis 14 and by the Scythians in Her. I, 103-106, or the deaths of Phraortes and Terah in northern Mesopotamia before they are able to accomplish their projects (Her. I, 102 and Gen. 11.31-32). The cleverest part of his work, however, was the radical geographical shift from an invasion of Greece, setting out from Sardis in Lydia, and crossing the sea between Asia and Europe, to an invasion of the land of Canaan which took its departure from Egypt, and involved a crossing of the Red Sea, on whatever location on the border between Africa and Asia one supposes it to be located. The persons who are involved in the affairs of the jumping-off points, Egypt and Lydia, constitute three corresponding pairs: Abraham and Cyaxares, who are the first to establish contact with the country and with the dynasty ruling there (in Gen. 12.10-20 and Her. I, 73-74),[22] Joseph and Cyrus, who attain power over this location, and finally Moses and Xerxes, who start their great campaigns from there. The basic differences, of course, are, first, that the Exodus represents a return to the land where the patriarchs used to live, whereas the Persian kings, hailing from Persia and Media in the East, previously had no direct involvement in mainland Greece before the invasions of Darius and Xerxes, with the result that Media/Persia and Greece are in a way merged into the 'land of Canaan' of Primary History; and, secondly, that the Israelites had lost the power wielded by Joseph after his death, so that their campaign started

22. In both cases, the subject of a marriage between the main family and someone from this country seems to play a role: Croesus's sister Aryennis is married off to Astyages to seal the treaty between the two countries (Her. I, 74), and Sarai, Abraham's wife, is taken away to Pharaoh's palace and returned after a series of plagues which seem to foreshadow those of the Exodus (Gen. 12.14-20). Note also the case of Abraham's servant and mother of his son Ishmael, the Egyptian maidservant Hagar (Gen. 16, 21.8-21); we are not told, however, when or where she was acquired by Abraham or Sarai.

under completely different and far less favourable circumstances, developing the characteristics of a flight in addition to those of a campaign of conquest. This enhanced focus on the land is probably the reason why, instead of only one prediction of the great conflict or its consequences at the end of the life of the key figures Joseph and Cyrus (Gen. 49 and Her. I, 209), Primary History also has an entire series of additional promises to the patriarchs. See Fig. 2.1 for the way in which the land of Canaan in Primary History corresponds with either Media/Persia or Greece, and Egypt with Lydia, in the work of Herodotus, and Fig. 2.2 for the same observation about the parallel use of Egypt and Lydia in combination with their distribution over the nine books of both works; in both figures these phenomena are also linked to the generations of the main families.

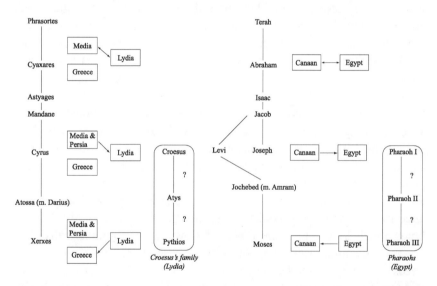

Fig. 2.1   *Routes of the members of the main families to and from Lydia and Egypt.*

The attractiveness of the work of Herodotus to a Jewish reader, provided he or she would not be overly offended by the religious differences, must have been considerable. Precisely those elements that tainted his reputation in the eyes of later historians are those that we find paralleled in Primary History, especially his tendency to discern certain religious patterns in history and to accept a lot of less likely accounts for that purpose, and his 'moral' view of history, in which the ever-present *hubris* of rulers takes more or less the same place that is allotted to the theme of religious loyalty and defection as the driving principle of history in Primary History.

Whatever the exact reason for this procedure of deriving the structure of

Primary History from the work of Herodotus, it was certainly not unique in antiquity, and we may have to look for its background in the way readers and authors looked upon matters of originality, imitation and emulation in antiquity; the parallel with Virgil's *Aeneid* discussed below is very illuminating in this respect.

A difficult practical problem must have been created by the fact that the episodes that Primary History was to describe occupied a far longer period than Herodotus's, even if we leave the primeval age of Genesis 1–11 out of consideration: some 800 years just from the Exodus to the fall of Jerusalem, against about two centuries for Herodotus's entire work, and less than two years between Xerxes' crossing of the Hellespont and the final failure of his campaign. Our author apparently solved this problem by inserting the account of this long period into the story of the attempted conquest of the land, between the episode of the first leader staring across the water towards his unattainable goal and the concluding episodes of the work describing the utter failure of the conquest; the stories told in the books of Joshua, Judges, 1 and 2 Samuel and 1 and 2 Kings thus take the place of the parts of the Greek campaign after Salamis in Herodotus's work (though strictly speaking only the events described in the book of Joshua belong to the Great Campaign itself). If our author wanted to imitate the *Histories* also by keeping the number of nine books with the caesura between the Great Campaign and the rest of the work between the sixth book and the seventh, and the separation between the last book and the one before that in the middle of an episode,[23] the present-day imbalance in size, with these books, especially those of Samuel and Kings, being much longer than the others, follows almost automatically. By contrast, our author saw no opportunity or reason to parallel the lives and deeds of Cambyses and Darius (books II–VI of the *Histories*) in his work, and consequently spent little space on the generations between Joseph and Moses (only Exod. 1 and the beginning of Exod. 2). In literary terms, the result is that the themes of the Great Campaign and of ordinary history have changed places in the two works; see Fig. 2.2 for a visualization of this shift and Table 2.1 for a formal description of this structural derivation (see also below).

It may be that our author continued the pattern of the preceding episodes by assuming a multiple of the size of the series of generations from Terah to Moses, but then probably counted along the masculine line (Moses being a

---

23. See the statement to this effect in Mandell and Freedman, *Herodotus' History and Primary History*, p. 179.

great-grandson of Levi through his father), as the backbone for the construction of the latter part of his work (see Fig. 2.3).[24] From Terah to the generation of the great-grandsons of Jacob (the generation of Moses' father) we count seven generations, the same number as from Moses to David's father. From David onwards we have three times seven kings both in the northern and in the southern kingdom; during the reign of the fourteenth king of Judah (Hezekiah), the northern kingdom came to an end. This agreement in numbers can hardly be accidental, and the author of Primary History has probably somewhat manipulated the king-lists as known to him in order to attain this result. Whereas the chronological scheme probably goes back to the parallel with Herodotus, the contents of this part of Primary History seem to have relatively little in common with his work. Our author and redactor, however, concluded his work, as we have seen, with passages continuing, in marked similarity to Herodotus, the fall of the last stronghold of the conquerors. These passages exhibit certain other resemblances to Herodotus by indirectly resuming the two great themes of the first part of the work, the Exodus from Egypt and the life of Joseph, while also agreeing in stressing the tragic end of the history described.

An Unexpected Parallel: Virgil's Aeneid

There is also a parallel situated well outside the Jewish world, within the mainstream of Graeco-Roman culture. Although it is several centuries later than the latest possible date of origin for Primary History, it is especially significant for two reasons. First, certain parallel developments are discernible in the reworking of the text lying at its base, but this time in a reasonably well-known historical and literary context, so that we see at least one possible scenario for the origins of a work such as Primary History and its relation to an earlier work. Secondly, and perhaps even more importantly, the work concerned is also a story of the origin of a nation, whose structure has been derived from one of the classical works of ancient Greek literature, though the attitude of this nation towards the Greeks was by no means exclusively positive.

---

24. It should be noted that we need the genealogical information from the book of Ruth (see above) for these calculations, otherwise there would be a gap between Judah's grandson Hezron and David's father Jesse. Note that the information provided in the book of Ruth is also necessary for evaluating other passages in Primary History: without it, for example, we would not know that the prince of the tribe of Judah, Nahshon son of Amminadab, who is mentioned in Num. 1.7 and elsewhere in that book, is a direct ancestor of King David.

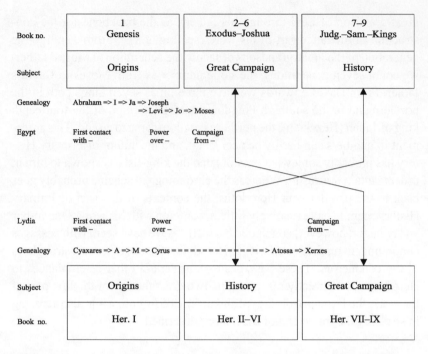

Abbreviated names: I = Isaac; Ja = Jacob; Jo = Jochebed; A = Astyages; M = Mandane.

Fig. 2.2   *Relation between genealogy, contact with the starting point of the Great Campaign, the parts of the* Histories *and Primary History, and their subjects.*

Ever since Virgil wrote his *Aeneid*, and even during the actual writing, it was well known that this work about the Trojan Aeneas, who escapes from conquered and destroyed Troy and after many peregrinations and combats becomes the forefather of the Romans and the originator of their state, is based upon the *Iliad* and *Odyssey* by Homer, works likewise dealing with events during and after the war of the Greeks against Troy. Only in modern times, however, have the techniques that Virgil applied to transform Homer's poems in Greek into his own work in Latin been systematically scrutinized, especially by G.N. Knauer.[25] Some of his conclusions are worth quoting here:

25.   G.N. Knauer, 'Vergil's *Aeneid* and Homer', reprinted in S.J. Harrison (ed.), *Oxford Readings in Vergil's* Aeneid (Oxford and New York: Oxford University Press, 1990), pp. 390-412 [originally appeared in *GRBS* 5 (1964), pp. 61-84], and at length in G.N. Knauer, *Die Aeneis und Homer: Studien zur poetischen Technik Vergils mit Listen der Homerzitate in der Aeneis* (Göttingen: Vandenhoeck & Ruprecht, 1964). See also K.W. Gransden, *Virgil's Iliad: An Essay on Epic Narrative* (Cambridge: Cambridge University Press, 1984).

Generation	Fam. Joseph	Fam. Moses	Fam. David	N. Kingdom
A/1	Terah	<=	<=	
A/2	Abraham	<=	<=	
A/3	Isaac	<=	<=	
A/4	Jacob	<=	<=	
A/5	Joseph	Levi	Judah	
A/6	Manasseh	Kohath	Perez	
A/7	Machir	Amram	Hezron	
B/1		Moses	Ram	
B/2			Amminadab	
B/3			Nahshon	
B/4			Salmon	
B/5			Boaz	
B/6			Obed	
B/7			Jesse	
C/1			David	<=
C/2			Solomon	<=
C/3			Rehoboam	Jeroboam
C/4			Abijam	Nadab
C/5			Asa	Baasha
C/6			Jehoshaphat	Elah
C/7			Joram	Zimri
D/1			Ahaziah	Omri
D/2			Jehoash	Ahab
D/3			Amaziah	Ahaziah
D/4			Uzzia	Joram
D/5			Jotham	Jehu
D/6			Ahaz	Jehoahaz
D/7			Hezekiah	Joash
E/1			Manasseh	Jeroboam II
E/2			Ammon	Zechariah
E/3			Josiah	Sallum
E/4			Jehoahaz	Menahem
E/5			Jehoiakim	Pekahia
E/6			Jehoiachin	Pekah
E/7			Zedekiah	Hosheah

Fig. 2.3   *Survey of the five sets of seven 'generations' of Primary History.*

In these [books] Aeneas is represented throughout as a hero surpassing his Greek counterpart, Odysseus, who had passed through the same or similar situations shortly before him (in epic time). Odysseus, the victor, destroys Ismaros in Thrace; Aeneas, the exile (3. 11), founds Ainos in the same region. On his way home to the patris, Ithaca, west of the Peloponnesus, Odysseus is shipwrecked by a storm at Cape Maleia; Aeneas, in spite of a storm, successfully passes this cape (cf. 5. 193) on his way to the west, where in the end he will find the promised patria, Hesperia. Here for the first time one begins to sense Vergil's purpose in following Homer.

Furthermore we can assume that Vergil clearly realized how Homer conceived the structure of the *Odyssey* and that Vergil therefore did not simply imitate sporadic Homeric verses or scenes. On the contrary he first analysed the plan of the *Odyssey*, then transformed it and made it the base of his own poem.

The complete structure of the Homeric epics, not simply occasional quotations, was no doubt the basis for Vergil's poem. I cannot explain these findings otherwise than by the suggestion that Vergil must have intensively studied the structure of the Homeric epics before he drafted in prose his famous first plan for the whole *Aeneid*.

It seems clear that Aeneas, who excelled Odysseus in the first part of the *Aeneid*, now surpasses the Greeks who had been victorious in Troy. [...] The way in which he completes the divine mission to found a new Troy, that is Rome, elevates him morally far above the Greek heroes.[26]

Most of these surprising observations also apply to Primary History in comparison with Herodotus's work. It would appear that the author of Primary History likewise performed a penetrating literary analysis of the *Histories*, transformed the enemies of the Greeks from rightly beaten adversaries into the (at least temporarily) successful heroes of his own work, and made them not only emulate but outdo the heroes of the other work: just as Moses is superior to Xerxes, and Abraham to Cyaxares, so Aeneas outdoes Odysseus, for example when he keeps his ship afloat during a storm at exactly the same spot where Odysseus was shipwrecked under similar circumstances. Even this element of such a collocation of comparable events is found in Primary History also, where the biblical heroes appear superior to the Persian and Median kings (see above).

Knauer finally states as Vergil's probable intention in following Homer's blueprint the desire to make clear that his account of the early history of the Romans emulates Greek history as described in the *Iliad* and the

26. Knauer, 'Vergil's *Aeneid* and Homer', pp. 398, 401-402, 409-10.

Odyssey, in the last resort (via a prediction derived from the seer Tiresias's prediction for Odysseus's safe return home and tranquil life after that) pointing to the period of Augustean peace after the battle of Actium in 27 BCE.[27] This thesis, in combination with the idea that Herodotus's *Histories* foreshadow the events of Greek history during the later part of the fifth century BCE,[28] makes one wonder whether the implicit purpose of Primary History may not have been to prepare the stage for the end of the captivity, the rebuilding of city and Temple and the religious reforms effected in Jerusalem during the fifth century (see below). This brings us to the problem, which I shall leave for later discussion, of whether Primary History was intended to be read or interpreted together with certain other books of the Hebrew Bible, such as Nehemiah or some of the prophetical books.

A Question of Proof

Of course there is not much room for doubt that there is a considerable amount of literary dependence between *Histories* and Primary History if one studies the figures in this chapter. Still, one may desire a higher degree of certainty in such a case as this one, where the basic tenets of Hebrew Bible scholarship are at stake. In order to provide this proof for Primary History as well as for the other supposed instances of this structural derivation in the Hebrew Bible I posited elsewhere the necessity of the existence of a limited set of simple, clear and unambiguous rules governing the transformation of generally recognized main events and divisions of one work into an other.[29] There are basically three types of rule. Analytical statements describe the main contents and literary structure of the original work or source text, rules of transformation serve to indicate whether the results of these observations are transferred in their original form (copying) or are mirrored (with two phenomena changing places), and rules of adaptation indicate the unavoidable adaptation of the result to the requirements of the target text. In Table 2.1 these rules are given for the relationship between *Histories* and Primary History. As long as such rules cannot be given, literary dependence cannot be excluded and may sometimes even be rather likely, but can certainly not be considered proven. If, by

27. Knauer, 'Vergil's *Aeneid* and Homer', pp. 411-12.
28. Cf., for example, Georges, *Barbarian Asia and the Greek Experience*, pp. 157-63, and Lateiner, *The Historical Method of Herodotus*, p. 134.
29. Wesselius, 'Discontinuity', *passim*.

contrast, such simple rules can be discovered, their very existence becomes a literary problem that can only be resolved through the assumption of such dependence. Once this has been established, the rules form a literary link between the two texts, which explains both the creative process taking place in the author's mind when writing the target text and the way in which it was undoubtedly meant to be read by the perceptive reader.

Table 2.1 *Rules for the structural derivation from* Histories *to Primary History.*

Analytical statements

The work is in three parts: *Origins* (of the Persian empire) in book 1; *History* (of the empire until Xerxes) in books 2-6; *Great Campaign* (of Xerxes, from Lydia against Greece) in books 7-9.

The grandfather of the leader of the Great Campaign (on his mother's side: Cyrus) gains power over its starting point (Lydia); his ancestor in the fifth generation (Cyaxares) is the first to establish contact with it.

The death of the person who gains power over the starting point of the Great Campaign (Cyrus) concludes the first book.

Rules of transformation

Copy the division in three parts over nine books.

Mirror the position of History and Great Campaign.

Copy relationship between persons in the genealogy of the leader of the Great Campaign and contacts with its starting point.

Copy position of person who gains power over the starting point at the end of the first book.

Rules of adaptation

Divide the generation of the grandfather of the leader of the Great Campaign over the eponyms of the tribes of Israel.

Chapter 3

CONSEQUENCES FOR THE STUDY OF PRIMARY HISTORY

The assumption of a single author or final redactor of Primary History, as advocated above, makes one curious after his or her identity. The philosopher Benedictus de Spinoza (1632–1674), who also assumed one author for the biblical books Genesis–2 Kings and thus in a way pre-empted my conclusions, proposed to assume until further notice that Ezra wrote these books, making use of earlier material, which he had no opportunity to harmonize completely.[1] Spinoza's argument is still largely valid today: it can be noted, among other things, that Ezra is the only person to whom scribal activities are attributed in the books Ezra and Nehemiah, and that an especially important event in the book of Nehemiah is the reading of the Law by Ezra (Neh. 8, dated to the twentieth year of Artaxerxes I, 445 BCE). It has been noticed by many ancient and modern exegetes that this Law was evidently to some degree new to the hearers, as they are said to react by obeying it, something that they apparently did not do before. This is probably the origin of well-known stories current in antiquity such as

1.   Benedictus de Spinoza, *Tractatus Theologico-Politicus* ([Amsterdam: J. Rieuwersz.], 1670), chapter 8. As is well known, Spinoza attributed this opinion to Abraham Ibn Ezra, whom he supposed to have noted this in a veiled, but nonetheless very clear form. There are reasons to assume that such opinions were not uncommon among medieval Jewish exegetes, but could for obvious reasons (especially the denial of the Mosaic authorship of the Torah) only be expressed in a very implicit form. In his commentary on the Former Prophets (books 6–9 of Primary History), the famous Isaac Abarbanel provided exactly those arguments for a late redaction of these books which in later works belong to the standard stock of arguments against Mosaic authorship of the Torah, which he strongly affirmed in the very same passage; see E. Lawee, 'From the Pages of Tradition. Don Isaac Abarbanel: Who Wrote the Books of the Bible?', *Tradition* 30.2 (1996), pp. 65-73 (only a suspicious reading of Abarbanel will reveal this, and the author did not notice it). Cf. also Houtman, *Der Pentateuch*, pp. 40-43. For Houtman's own well-balanced defence of the unity of the books Genesis–2 Kings see *Der Pentateuch*, pp. 421-55.

that Ezra wrote various books of the Bible again from memory or through
divine inspiration, after they had been lost during the Babylonian captivity.[2] Whether or not the story in Nehemiah 8 is a reliable description of
what actually happened in Jerusalem in the year 445 BCE, it seems rather
likely that religious innovation indeed issued from there in the second half
of the fifth century, as we seem to have a reflex of this movement in the
documents of the Jewish community of Elephantine in Egypt around that
time.

It is well known that in the fifth century BCE the Jews of Elephantine, an
island in the Nile in Southern Egypt, most of them mercenaries employed
by the Persian overlords of Egypt, at first professed a kind of Judaism very
far removed from the religion that we encounter only one or two centuries
later. Syncretism was rife and the standard religious holidays of later
Judaism were apparently not observed as prescribed in the Bible. During the
last decades of the existence of this community (it was apparently dis-
banded or disappeared in some other way around 400 BCE) a growing
influence of Jerusalem on the Elephantine affairs can be noticed. One of the
important events in these developments appears to have been the visit of a
certain Hananiah, who has been assumed by many scholars to be identical
with Nehemiah's brother Hanani (Neh. 1.1 and elsewhere), to Egypt in
order to supervise Jewish religious affairs there. One of the documents
reflecting this influence is the famous Passover Letter sent by Hananiah to
the Elephantine community in winter or early spring of the fifth year of
Darius II (419 BCE), in which the Jews of Egypt are enjoined to celebrate
the festival of Passover, which commemorates the Exodus from Egypt, as
far as can be seen from this fragmentary document according to the standard
biblical procedure.[3] Interestingly, the Jews living in Nippur in Mesopotamia
at the time seem to have undergone a comparable process of adaptation to
stricter 'biblical' standards.[4]

We need not assume, of course, that the writing and 'publication' (if one
may use the term) of Primary History was the origin of this movement, but
it certainly seems rather likely that it was closely connected with this religious revival. Reviewing the evidence, even if it is more limited than we

2.   Houtman, *Der Pentateuch*, pp. 11-13, 21-23 and 32-33.
3.   On the Passover Letter and the identity of Hananiah, see B. Porten, *Archives
from Elephantine* (Berkeley: University of California Press, 1968), pp. 128-33 and
279-82.
4.   See R. Zadok, *The Jews in Babylonia During the Chaldean and Achaemenian
Periods According to the Babylonian Sources* (Haifa: University of Haifa, 1979), pp.
84-85.

would like it to be, we may therefore be justified in assuming that Primary History was indeed published in Jerusalem after 425 BCE, perhaps only a limited number of years later, and was at once used (perhaps expressly written for the purpose) to assist in restructuring Jewish religious life in Jerusalem and also, probably at a somewhat slower pace, in diaspora communities such as those of Elephantine and Nippur.[5] Of course such a movement could hardly have gained any momentum without the active support of the Persian kings, and there is ample evidence that this was indeed forthcoming, probably because of the important position of Judaea on the border of the Persian empire with Egypt.[6]

An additional reason for the writing of Primary History—perhaps the most important one—must have been the desire to provide testimony of venerable antiquity for the history of Judaism. It is difficult to estimate how important this purpose was for the actual writing of the work, but in Hellenistic times and later this work served to lend an aura of antiquity, and consequently also respectability, to Judaism even in the eyes of its worst detractors.[7] This respectability extended also to Primary History itself and to the Hebrew Bible as a whole, so that among the many anti-Jewish writers denouncing Judaism, its tenets and its main figures, there were many who gave a negative twist to the account of Primary History, especially attacking the figure of Moses, but apparently none questioned the trustworthiness and antiquity of Primary History itself.[8]

One final question about the dates of origin and publication must be addressed. If Primary History was indeed written in the second half of the fifth century or even later, why did it end with the release of King Jehoiachin during the captivity, and did not describe the momentous events of Cyrus's edict and the return of the exiles, let alone the revival supposedly effected by Ezra and Nehemiah? Again, the reason may have to be sought partially in the parallel with Herodotus, though it is very difficult to go beyond educated speculation. A number of possible motivations can be

---

5. It should be noted that if we assume that the Elephantine Passover Letter presupposes the existence of Primary History, that is, if we assume that the stay in Egypt and the Exodus first made their appearance in this work, we can pinpoint the date of origin of Primary History to within one decade at most, namely 430–420 BCE! But for the moment this should be considered highly uncertain.

6. Compare, for example, Peter Frei and Klaus Koch, *Reichsidee und Reichsorganisation im Perserreich* (Freiburg: Universitätsverlag, 1996), *passim*.

7. See, e.g., Feldman, *Jew and Gentile*, pp. 177-200.

8. Feldman, *Jew and Gentile, passim.*

found, which may have been combined. First, the intention may have been to emulate the tragical character of Herodotus's work (see above), which would only be possible before Cyrus's edict heralded new possibilities and perspectives. Secondly, it may not be entirely accidental that Primary History ends more or less where Herodotus's history of the Near East begins, the middle of the sixth century BCE and the beginning of the seventh, respectively. This may have served the purpose of establishing that Israel's history went much further back than that of the nations around it. The end of Herodotus' *Histories*, furthermore, with the taking of the town of Sestos, would make the capture of Jerusalem one of the final events of Primary History, once the siege and capture of the two would be taken to be parallel (see above). Finally, the reason may also lie partly in the desire to project a likely author for the work. It seems rather likely that Primary History, probably written in the last half of the fifth century BCE, was originally meant to pass as a work written more than a century before, during the Babylonian captivity, by an anonymous author. The question whether it was originally intended to be ascribed to one of the persons living during the captivity whose names have been preserved in the Hebrew Bible—and of course the names of Jeremiah and his pupil Baruch come to mind immediately[9]—must probably remain undecided. In any case, it appears quite possible that Primary History really is a work by an anonymous author that was to represent the work of a fictional, but likewise unnamed predecessor. Because we are so thoroughly accustomed to the idea of this anonymous historical work, in which the author only refers indirectly to himself and his circumstances, we are inclined to think that this was a common genre when Primary History was written. The possibility cannot be excluded, however, that this anonymity was a deliberate choice and to some degree a radical innovation, meant to ensure acceptance as an authoritative source of historical and legal material. It is certainly possible that its present form was intended to suggest an author (alternatively, a number of authors) living during the captivity, while not attaching a name to him that might become a focus of criticism concerning his reliability. In any case, the concept of the anonymous and even personally absent author has had some very important consequences for the final form of the work, which I shall discuss very briefly here.

9.   The idea of Jeremiah being the author of the 'Deuteronomic History' is in fact to be found in the work of R.E. Friedman, *Who Wrote the Bible?* (New York: Summit Books, 1987), p. 146. On the figure of Baruch, see Walter Brueggemann, 'The Baruch Connection', *JBL* 113 (1994), pp. 405-20, and the literature quoted there.

Derivation and Originality

It should be pointed out that this derived character of plot and structure of vital parts of Primary History did not prevent its author composing a work that is startlingly original and well formed. Even in those instances where he apparently derived certain elements straight from the work of Herodotus, he imbued them with a meaning and intertextual significance that firmly anchor them within his own work. A good example is the episode told in Genesis 38, the story of Judah and Tamar, which I noted to correspond in some respects with the story of Croesus and Cyrus in the *Histories*. It has often been argued that this story has only secondarily been inserted in the place where we find it now, directly after the first chapter of the cycle of stories dealing with Joseph, but this pre-occupation with the history of the text is not relevant for our purpose, as we intend to study the text of Primary History in its final form (see above). There are, in fact, weighty arguments in favour of its present place being a very natural one, in spite of the fact that it clearly interrupts the story of Joseph in the strict sense. Judah plays a key role in the deception of Jacob in Genesis 37, and his own deception by Tamar in the next chapter bears all the signs of retribution for it (see above). Chastened by this experience, Judah is indeed the right person to show the virtuous behaviour at Joseph's court and back home in Canaan that is related in Gen. 43.1-9 and 44.14-34. Without the interlude of Genesis 38, his change of character would be difficult to account for. Apart from these and similar considerations, only Genesis 38, in combination with Gen. 49.8-12 (the oracle about Judah pronounced by Jacob), places the story of Joseph within the chain of history where it belongs, which ends in the tribe of Judah being the only carrier of the traditions of ancient Israel at the end of 2 Kings.

It may well be that the very natural association of the somewhat unexpected verdict of burning for Tamar with the death foreseen for a priest's daughter who plays the harlot (Lev. 21.9) was intended from the beginning, especially in view of the priestly functions performed by the patriarchs (though the idea of an arbitrary heavy punishment of pre-Sinai times seems slightly more likely), but this mode of execution itself, as well as the element of the sudden rescue at the point of being burned, have probably been derived from the story of Croesus, as discussed above. The uncertainty about the reason for this punishment may in fact also derive from Herodotus, who expresses his hesitation about it in the following way.

> The Persians brought their prisoner into the presence of the king, and Cyrus
> chained Croesus and placed him with fourteen Lydian boys on a great pyre
> that he had built; perhaps he intended them as a choice offering to some god
> of his, or perhaps he had made a vow and wished to fulfil it; or it may be
> that he had heard that Croesus was a god-fearing man, and set him on the
> pyre to see if any divine power would save him from being burned alive
> (Her. I, 86).

As in Herodotus's story about Croesus, we are left in the dark about
Judah's motives for ordering burning as a punishment, but in contrast with
that episode this uncertainty is left unexpressed in the blunt description of
Judah's command with regard to Tamar:

> About three months later Judah was told, 'Tamar your daughter-in-law has
> played the harlot; and moreover she is with child by harlotry.' And Judah
> said, 'Bring her out, and let her be burned' (Genesis 38.24).

Thus we see that uncertainty about one and the same matter, the unexpected verdict of burning for one of the main persons, is apparently
expressed in completely different ways in the two works: Herodotus
explicitly voices his doubt and hesitation, and presents various options to
his readers, whereas in the Bible the unexpected event is presented without any commentary, and the uncertainty is in a way imposed directly on
the readers by the briefness of Judah's utterance. It also becomes clear
that the origin of various elements in this story should be carefully
distinguished from their function in the story and within the rest of
Primary History: the theme of burning leads to completely different
associations.

A second example is the case of the death of the first-born of Egypt, a
theme that is resumed or alluded to several times in Primary History
(only in the books of Exodus and Numbers: Exod. 34.19-20; Num. 3.11-
13; 8.16-19; 33.4), and also in the book of Psalms (Pss. 78.51; 105.36;
135.8; 136.10). In the work of Herodotus, the corresponding episode of
the death of Pythios's eldest son appears to have a firm place within the
narrative of Xerxes' campaign as a whole: at its beginning Pythios is thus
punished for implicitly expressing the fear that none of his five sons
would return from the Greek expedition (VII, 38-39); immediately after
the account of Xerxes' return to the Hellespont Herodotus tells his
readers the story of the king of the Bisaltians, who had refused to give
his six sons permission to join Xerxes' army, and on their unexpected
safe return orders them all blinded as a punishment for disobeying their

father's command (VIII, 116). Besides, the story of Pythios fits perfectly in Herodotus's genre of stories dealing with fathers losing their sons.[10]

In Primary History, the story of the death of the first-born also has firm attachments, though they are very different from those in Herodotus's work. First, the episode itself is followed by the description of the ritual of *pidyon habben*, 'redemption of the son', which is explicitly derived from this event (Exod. 13.1-16). More importantly, the death of the Egyptian first-born is evidently a punishment meted out to the Egyptians for attempting to kill all the Israelite male children by throwing them into the river Nile (Exod. 1.22); together with the first of the ten plagues (the water of the Nile transformed into blood) this last one mirrors the crime of the Egyptians in their punishment. The death of Pharaoh's own first-born son is furthermore explicitly connected with his refusal to let Israel, God's 'first-born son', leave Egypt, in Moses' initial assignment (Exod. 4.22-23). In this example also, the origin of part of a story can be demonstrated to be of limited relevance for its present function within Primary History: it has been reworked and integrated in a masterly fashion.

A particularly nice instance of the intertextual significance of an element with a close parallel in the work of Herodotus is the case of Joseph's coat. We have already seen that the function of this particular coat in the life of Joseph largely agrees with that of the golden and many-coloured clothes of the little Cyrus. Within Primary History, however, this piece of clothing is echoed in the story of the rape of Tamar, the daughter of King David, by her half-brother Amnon in 2 Samuel 13. It thus belongs with the fairly large number of parallels between the stories of the patriarchs, especially Jacob, and the description of the life and career of David. It would seem, therefore, that we see the creative mechanism of the composition of Primary History operating before our eyes: it seems rather likely that the author or authors, having derived the element of Joseph's coat from the story of Cyrus, looked for a good link within the stories about David, and came up with the nice invention of making Joseph wear a typically feminine coat (as explained in 2 Sam. 13.18), which he could make good use of in one of the fateful episodes of the Succession History. This case also allows us once more to see the function of such intertextual links: not a quotation from another authoritative text, as supposed by

10. D.L. Gera, 'Bereaved Fathers in Herodotus', *Scripta Classica Israelica* 12 (1993), pp. 36-50.

many, but a deliberate connection between key episodes in the history of Israel (see below).[11]

The journey of Abram to Egypt in Gen. 12.10-20 corresponds with the earliest contact of the Medians with the Lydians to be related by Herodotus, the war between Cyaxares and the Lydian king Alyattes. In the Bible, however, this story has been transformed from an independent event to a literary parallel of the stay of the Israelites in Egypt and the Exodus, as is evident from details such as the famine causing the journey to Egypt, the divinely ordained plagues and the presents that are given.[12]

A last example is the genealogy of Moses and Aaron in Exodus 6 in comparison with Xerxes' genealogy in Her. VII, 11. The significance as well as the limitations of the parallels with Herodotus for the study of biblical literature also become very clear here. The parallel passage in Herodotus furnishes the reason why this genealogy is present in this place at all, but as noted above, the masterly art of the narrator has given it a significance far surpassing that of Herodotus's genealogy of Xerxes: Herodotus clearly marks King Xerxes as the main person of his narrative by pointing out his descent very clearly, even putting it into his own mouth, whereas the Exodus genealogy, while doubtlessly also serving the same purpose, has numerous connections with other texts in Primary History.[13]

Finally, it should also be kept in mind that the corresponding of events or persons with those in the work of Herodotus does not by itself prove the information provided by Primary History untrustworthy. The fall of Jerusalem at the end of the work, for example, though it closely corresponds with the taking of Sestos at the end of the *Histories*, both with regard to its position within the work and with regard to a number of details of the story, and though it is not attested in extra-biblical sources, need not be an invention by the author of Primary History: we simply do not have sources that would be expected to mention it. Still, the text of 2 Kings itself seems to indicate that the fall of Jerusalem under Jehoiachin in 597 BCE (attested in the so-called Babylonian Chronicle), the exile of the king and part of the population, and the pillaging of most of the Temple

11. Against, for example, Alter's note about this in his otherwise very good discussion of these parallels in *The World of Biblical Literature*, p. 165.

12. But note that here, as elsewhere the author of Primary History may have been led also by parallels between the events already to be found in Herodotus, such as the sudden eclipse of the sun related of both episodes (I, 74 and VII, 37).

13. See Chapter 1. Note also that the Exodus genealogy is characteristically put in the form of a list; on the function of such lists in Primary History, see also below.

treasures was in fact of far greater historical moment than the revolt of the Babylonian puppet-king Zedekiah, reigning over a depopulated and despoiled Jerusalem, against his overlord Nebuchadnezzar.[14] This correspondence between the sieges of Sestos and Jerusalem may, however, indicate an additional reason why Primary History ends as it does, and why its account does not continue for long after the taking of Jerusalem.

Consequences of the Anonymity of the Author of Primary History

The choice of method and literary form made by the author or redactor of Primary History entailed certain practical problems that are not encountered in writing a historical work such as Herodotus's *Histories*. A comparison with certain aspects of that work is again very illuminating. The almost complete absence of the personal aspect of the narrator makes it impossible to express his personal thoughts and feelings, as is done so cleverly in the *Histories*, to such a degree in fact that many scholars want to separate Herodotus the author who wrote the *Histories* from the Herodotus who is said to tell them to his readers, because they rightly identify this as a sophisticated literary device, rather than as a real intrusion of the author into his work (if such a thing could really exist).[15]

This apparently made it necessary to invent or apply various literary techniques that enable an anonymous narrator to express doubt about motives for this or that act, such as the multi-level motivation that is to be found frequently in the stories around King David,[16] or to introduce the programme of a book through purely literary means, for example at the beginning of 1 Samuel.[17] I shall discuss below the possibility that the well-

14. A survey of the literature dealing with the last years of the Judaean monarchy can be found in M. Cogan and H. Tadmor, *II Kings* (AB; Garden City, NY: Doubleday; 1988), especially pp. 310-24.

15. On this aspect of Herodotus's work see especially C. Dewald, 'Narrative Surface and Authorial Voice in Herodotus' Histories', *Arethusa* 20 (1987), pp. 147-70.

16. J.-W. Wesselius, 'Openbare en verborgen motieven voor handelingen in de verhalen rondom koning David', *Amsterdamse Cahiers voor Exegese en Bijbelse Theologie* 11 (1992), pp. 42-64 [in Dutch] and Chapter 4, Section 2 below.

17. J.-W. Wesselius, 'Samuël en de zonen van Eli: De betekenis van de structuur van 1 Samuël 2 en 3', in E.G.L. Schrijver, N.A. van Uchelen and I.E. Zwiep (eds.), *The Literary Analysis of Hebrew Texts. Papers read at a Symposium held at the Juda Palache Institute, University of Amsterdam (5 February 1990)* (Amsterdam: Juda Palache Instituut1992), pp. 35-44 [in Dutch] and Chapter 4, Section 1 below.

known phenomenon of conflicting information is also caused by the desire to juxtapose different versions of an event, without having the option of letting the author (or rather, the persona acting for him) say that they are variant versions. It is not clear whether there is also a connection with the often-discussed reticence of the biblical narrator to relate human emotions, except insofar as they are visible from the outside, whereas he is completely aware of things that have happened in deep secret and can hardly have become known in a natural way within the framework of the narrated world.[18]

It is well known that even with such highly restrictive limitations, an author can find ways to impart his or her personal opinion to the reader. He or she can, for example, attempt to draw on a supposedly common reservoir of personal reactions and ethical standards, and describe the action in such a way that the desired reaction is provoked in the reader. The main problem with this method is that the reader may have a completely different set of moral standards, which would make it very arduous for him or her to discern the author's subtleties; or a reader may fail to recognize the author's set of standards, even though in fact they are by and large shared by author and reader. Thus the cruel episode of the Levite's concubine in Judges 19 is for many readers evidently deliberately framed as a depiction of the moral disintegration and very base behaviour of most persons involved, whereas there have indeed been people who took it to be simply an amoral description of an event that was supposedly not very remarkable in ancient Israelite society.

Another method that is much more objective, though it is evident that it can also be overlooked or misinterpreted in many cases, appears to have been favourite with the author of Primary History. The basic procedure is almost universal. It is possible to lift words, sentences, stories and virtually any part of a text out of their unobtrusive place by letting them repeat a counterpart elsewhere, be it far away in the text or directly in the preceding sentence. In this way the identical elements are linked with each other, a connection that often extends to their contexts. The aim and the result of such a link can be very different. In some cases the word or sentence itself that is repeated in the story receives extra stress, and we can note it to be important in the context of the narrative. In other cases a sentence refers back to a completely different episode in order to connect

---

18. On literary aspects of the biblical narrator see for example Alter, *The Art of Biblical Narrative*, pp. 155-77; S. Bar-Efrat, *Narrative Art in the Bible* (Sheffield: Almond Press, 1989), pp. 13-45.

the two situations. Nice examples can be found below, in the chapters about the 'wise women' of 1 Samuel 14 and 20, where David's course of action seems to have been contrasted with the way Joseph's brothers act against him, and in the passage about David and the Amalekite in 2 Samuel 1, where the self-characterization of the Amalekite appears to refer back to the passage dealing with Amalek in Deuteronomy 25. There are, in fact, also many other links of various kinds between the stories about David's life and the patriarchal stories. Of course one could attempt a historical explanation, one series of stories supposedly having been available to the author of the others, but the basic fact remains that in the text as we now have it these cycles of stories are intimately connected in this way, and that whatever origin one supposes for them, someone must have had very clear ideas as to why these parallels were to be established. It seems at least possible that these parallels arose from a desire to show continuity in Israelite history, in other words to make it clear that this history had a more or less uniform character of its own, in which certain typical situations, locations and names kept recurring. In that case the priority in time of one episode of Primary History over the other, if it can be proved at all (see above for some cases where this seems indeed possible), is certainly not very important. The view proposed here of the authorship and nature of Primary History makes the assumption of a deliberate literary parallel between these episodes very likely.

Parallel situations are apparently also found several times within the patriarchal narratives, such as the main person describing his wife as his sister (twice of Abraham and once of Isaac), or of the prospective bride found near a well (of Rebecca in Gen. 24.13-21, of Rachel in Gen. 29.1-10, of Zipporah in Exod. 2.16-22). As for the first series of parallels, Robert Alter has already noted that each of the three cases fits very well in its own context (see Chapter 2), and we can now add that such usage fits with the general approach of the author to his work, and that there is no good reason left for supposing that in such cases we have anything but intended literary parallels, indicating continuity of the early history of Israel in completely different circumstances, as in the instances mentioned above; the question of whether they were ever transmitted independently recedes into almost complete insignificance.

Sometimes the repetition of words or sentences in a series of stories seems to serve to indicate overall structure, usually with the crucial episode of the series in the middle. Thus we can observe that in the so-called Succession History of David (2 Sam. 9–1 Kgs 2) we can distinguish pairs of stories linked through identical words, names and phrases, indicating as the most important point in this series and as nadir of David's life the battle of his soldiers against the army of his rebellious son Absalom. Additionally, such parallels may function in the same way as stated below for the comparison of stories, namely to invite the reader to compare and contrast the accounts in which the identical words and names are found; see the nice example 2 Samuel 14 and 20 in Chapter 4, Section 3.

A very striking option is to use identical, almost identical or parallel words for making two different accounts of the same event look like each other, so that the reader is invited to compare the two. Thus the two stories about the death of Saul, one told by the narrator in 1 Samuel 31 and the other by a young Amalekite man in the next chapter, 2 Samuel 1, are connected through the use of parallel phrases (see Chapter 4, Section 2), and the narrator's two different accounts about the way in which David first meets King Saul, in 1 Samuel 16 and 17, respectively, also have a number of striking phrases in common (see Chapter 4, Section 4).

Thus even in this very brief review we see how the author of Primary History applied this method very often and in very many different ways. It may be useful to note that this observation eliminates the need to assume errors, differences of sources or accidental agreements in very many cases where these have been supposed in the past, though this is hardly the place to weigh the arguments against and in favour of assuming this literary method in every suitable passage.

There is, however, one significant agreement in relation to the position of the author in both works, which sets them apart from many other ancient historical compositions. Herodotus probably wrote his *Histories* shortly before or during the Peloponnesian War between Sparta and Athens and their respective allies (431–404 BCE), but deliberately refrained from drawing even the most obvious parallels between his own time and the episode of half a century earlier that he describes.[19] Likewise, the author of Primary History does not say anything about the edict of King Cyrus and the permission to the exiles to return to their country. Although we cannot exclude the possibility that his work was meant to give the impression of having been written shortly after the last event recorded in it, the release and restoration to high position of King Jehoiachin of Judah, it seems

---

19. Except, of course, for the story of the birth of Pericles in VI, 131. Note that his father Xanthippus also plays a role in the Sestos episode at the end of the *Histories* (IX, 114-20).

rather likely that he emulated Herodotus in this respect of refraining from reflection on later events.

Unity and Variety

The concept of the basic unity of Primary History forces us to give attention once more to the variety that is clearly and undeniably present in the work. There are basically two phenomena that interrupt the unitary structure, and partly also the rigid linear time-line of the narrative. First, we have the division into books, which largely corresponds with certain divisions in style and content. Secondly, there are a fairly large number of instances where we seem to have various and often conflicting accounts of one and the same event, or where terminology and style seem to vary considerably within a single passage, series of passages or book. The historical-critical method, with its recognition of separate sources, largely rests on a cross-section of these two types of variety, and evaluating this variety is necessary for a preliminary determination of whether or not the historical-critical approach can survive, whether partly or completely, my observations about the unitary structure of Primary History.

Once we realize that there is probably the hand of one conscientious redactor behind all this, it becomes rather unlikely that this variety is the result of mere sloppiness or haste on the part of this person, who then supposedly would have used elaborate literary structures on the one hand, and have left glaring inconsistencies in his text on the other, and it becomes attractive to try to find a reason why such variety would have been introduced or left standing deliberately in the text as we now have it. This does not mean, of course, that there may not have been a process of growth behind the text: it seems entirely possible that certain books each have their peculiar character because they were originally at least partially separate entities, and that various versions of one story once circulated independently. Still, it seems rather far-fetched to assume that this capable redactor or author would not have removed certain very obvious contradictions, especially in cases where they are found at a short distance from each other, and could not have imposed one theological and literary pattern on all these books if he had wanted to. It would seem, instead, that he deliberately assigned each of the nine books (I leave aside the problem of the original place of the booklet of Ruth) a character of its own, whether or not he found it partly or completely available in his sources, perhaps in partial agreement with each book's place within the history of Israel. Thus we find the A-generations of Fig. 2.3 in Genesis, B in Exodus up to and including Judges, of which Exodus–Deuteronomy basically contain only Moses' generation, and C–E, apart from King David's generation, which is largely in Samuel and is in fact interrupted by the separation between Samuel and Kings,[20] in the book of Kings. As noted above (Chapter 2), an additional reason for this division may need to be sought in the fact that the break between the episode of the Great Campaign and the remainder of history is to be found between the sixth book, Joshua, and the seventh, Judges, in remarkable agreement with Herodotus' *Histories*, where we also find such a caesura between the sixth and seventh books—with the interesting difference that the Great Campaign is found before the break in Primary History, i.e. before 'ordinary' history and preparing the way for it, and after it in the *Histories*, serving as the main action of the entire work. Whether such considerations are indeed part of the background of the division into books or not, the result is a series of nine books, each of which has its own character, style and to some degree also a separate theological point of view, but which, when taken together, furnish one continuous narrative of the History of Israel, almost completely linear in time, as well as a reasonably consistent view of its religious and cultural background. In view of the parallel with Herodotus, both with regard to the number of books and the other agreements between the overall structure of the two works, it seems rather likely that this was the intended form of the work: unity expressed through the variety of nine separate books, each with a character of its own.

In such a literary context it will hardly have been felt as a problem, rather as an advantage, that some books also show a number of linguistic traits that set them apart; the best-known example, of course, is the book of Deuteronomy. Such diversity among the books may indicate a different origin and later insertion into Primary History, but this is by no means necessarily the case, as the possibility of various authors each working on their own part of Primary History. But a deliberate literary strategy of the author of Primary History seems the most natural explanation, whether or not in combination with these other possibilities, is also a viable option for explaining this state of affairs.

20. The overall structure of the Succession History, which describes the latter part of David's reign, in fact runs on across the separation between the two books. See for example J.-W. Wesselius, 'Joab's Death and the Central Theme of the Succession Narrative (2 Samuel ix–1 Kings ii)', *VT* 40 (1990), pp. 336-51 (340-43). Note that this running on of an episode across the separation between the penultimate book and the last one is also found in the work of Herodotus.

The matter of variety and internal contradictions within smaller units, such as the separate books, within Primary History is more complicated and deserves a separate treatment here.

Variant Traditions within One Historical Work

In the light of the well-known phenomenon of Herodotus giving various explanations for a fact (e.g. the annual rising and falling of the Nile, as well as several other aspects of this river in II, 19-34), presenting several versions of a story (as in the episode of the youth of Cyrus in I, 122) or discussing the sources that were available to him (as in the story of Io mentioned above), it seems at least possible that we may have to study the numerous and well-known instances of apparent contradiction and variety in Primary History again, with the link between the *Histories* and Primary History in mind. Instead of harmonizing conflicting versions or ascribing them to the clumsiness of a redactor (explanations that may still be valid in some instances), we may have to assume that their juxtaposition within one work was intentional, that they were deliberately left unharmonized, or may even have been intentionally written as contradictory accounts, to be assessed in each other's light. One could, for example, accept that the death of Saul is ascribed to the Philistines in 2 Sam. 21.12 by mistake, the accounts in 1 Samuel 31 and 2 Samuel 1 leaving only a choice between Saul himself and an anonymous Amalekite,[21] but the juxtaposed contradictory accounts of how David came to know King Saul (taken to the court because of his music-making in 1 Samuel 16 or come to the attention of Saul when slaying Goliath the Philistine in 1 Samuel 17),[22] or the two accounts of the creation of humankind in Genesis 1 and 2 (see above), cannot be explained in this way, unless one would assume a hopelessly incapable redactor. Likewise the text in its present state clearly mentions two persons who are said to have killed Goliath the Philistine, once David in the famous story in 1 Samuel 17, and once a certain Jaare-oregim, like David from Bethlehem, in a list that contains several important pieces of information concerning David's reign, in 2 Sam. 21.19. One therefore wonders whether the author may not have intended his work to look as if

21. Cf. J.P. Fokkelman, 'A Lie, Born of Truth, too Weak to Contain it', *OTS* 23 (1984), pp. 39-55.

22. See, for example, the collection of essays by various authors in D. Barthélemy *et al.*, *The Story of David and Goliath: Textual and Literary Criticism. Papers of a Joint Venture* (Freiburg: Editions Universitaires, 1986), who address this problem.

at various places different sources had been incorporated, and whether he may have consciously presented multiple versions of a story next to one another.[23] It may be noted in this connection that such contradictions were often noticed and recognized as such by the author of the books of Chronicles and by the makers of the Septuagint, who in various clever ways removed many of them. It seems at least possible that we are dealing in such cases with the phenomenon of deliberately putting certain conflicting accounts one beside the other, probably with the purpose of achieving more or less the same literary effect aimed at by Herodotus's method of presenting various versions of the same event or explanation.[24]

In a recent study, I proposed to see a conscious plan behind a number of these apparent contradictions, which together cover a large part of the text of the first eight books of Primary History. It would seem that in each of these instances two alternative courses of narrative history are offered to the reader, one of which (usually the second) carries on the narrative and is referred to several times in what follows, until the point where it is surprisingly denied explicitly, though usually in an unobtrusive place such as a list of persons, or the other alternative is strongly confirmed. In that light, to the cases discussed above one could add the account of Joseph's abduction in Genesis 37 and the curious case in the chapters at the end of the book of Judges, where the entire foundation story of the people of Israel as told in the books Exodus–Deuteronomy is placed in doubt because of the chronological contradiction and the strange light thrown on the families of Moses and Aaron.[25]

To a degree, the same explanation may be valid for those instances where a single person, location or God himself is called by different names, a phenomenon surprisingly common in Primary History and another cornerstone of the historical-critical approach. Of course, there are a number of instances where a change of name has a function within the narrative, such as the case of Abram becoming Abraham and Sarai becoming Sarah, by which names they are always referred to after the events related in Genesis 17, but in most cases the distinction between the two names is less than completely clear. Thus we see the mountain where God revealed himself to Israel designated as either Horeb or Sinai,

23. See Chapter 4, Section 4 below.

24. See also the illuminating parallel between the verdicts of burning passed on Tamar and Croesus which has been discussed in Chapter 1.

25. See my 'Towards a New History of Israel', *Journal of Hebrew Scripture* 3 (2000–2001), *passim*.

the Midianite father-in-law of Moses being called either Jethro or Reuel (besides other names), and the patriarch Jacob being called alternatively Israel and Jacob after he has received the first name in Gen. 32.28. The most fascinating of all these cases is, of course, the matter of the name of the God of Israel himself, who is designated by numerous different names, some of which seem to have belonged to the standard stock of divine designations in the western part of the Near East. In particular, the distinction between the four-letter name YHWH, traditionally not pronounced and replaced in reading the Bible text by *ᵃdonāy*, 'Adonay', lit. 'my lord', and therefore represented in many ancient and modern translations as 'the Lord', and the designation Elohim, 'God', has traditionally received much attention. In some biblical texts there seems to be a clear-cut distinction noted as such in rabbinical literature, between Elohim, suggesting God as judge or exercising comparable functions, and YHWH, suggesting his merciful aspect, but in others there is no evident reason why one name or the other has been used.[26] We cannot and should not try to solve this problem here and now, but we must seriously consider the possibility that this variety really served as a conscious programme, pointing out that the ancestral God was called by several different names throughout history (apart from their function of distinguishing the two accounts of Creation in Gen. 1–2), and that there were also variant traditions about the place of his revelation and the names of the patriarchs of the people of Israel and their families.

The considerations of this section and of the preceding one should make us wary of attempting to reconstruct the prehistory of the text of Primary History, as the text as we now have it was probably intended to be that way, with all its variations. Although such variation may originate in many cases from differences of provenience, it is probably not feasible to distinguish in individual instances whether variety is a result of different origins or of the design of the author.

Embedding of Non-Narrative Material

In recent years, attention has been given to the use of various literary genres such as laws, poetry and covenant as part of a single narrative line.

---

26. On the distribution of divine names in some very characteristic instances in narrative texts see H. Magonet, 'The Names of God in Biblical Narratives', in J. Davies *et al.* (eds.), *Words Remembered, Texts Renewed: Essays in Honour of John F.A. Sawyer* (Sheffield: Sheffield Academic Press, 1995), pp. 80-96.

This mixture has been shown to be highly characteristic of narrative texts in the Hebrew Bible.[27] Still, this device seems so sophisticated that one is tempted to look for external models for its use in Primary History.

Another literary device that our author may therefore have derived from Herodotus is the insertion of long digressions at appropriate places in a basically narrative text: whereas Herodotus has long ethnographic elaborations about the nations and lands that occur in his narrative, much of the ritual and legal material found in the Pentateuch is attached to certain aspects of the events described. Thus we find some of the rules regarding the redeeming of the first-born directly after the killing of the first-born of Egypt (Exod. 13.11-15), an outline of the Sabbath laws connected with the story of the manna miraculously coming down six days of the week, but not on the seventh (Exod. 16.23), and a description of the festival of Passover within the account of the Exodus (Exod. 12.43-49).

Larger units of ritual and legal material are, of course, presented at certain occasions in the narrative when they are said to have been enjoined upon Israel by God via Moses. Thus the prescriptions for the Tabernacle and the service to be performed in it are given when it is to be set up at the foot of Mt Sinai (Exod. 25–31), within the framework of Moses ascending the mountain and receiving these prescriptions together with the two Stone Tables (Exod. 24.18 and 31.18); the laws of Deuteronomy are said to have been part of an address of Moses to Israel in the land across the river Jordan before his death (Deut. 1.1-5 and 31.24-29), and likewise with other legal and ritual passages. Even without the observations made here with regard to the structural relationship between Herodotus and Primary History, it is clear that by and large the same procedure has been followed in both works of inserting non-narrative material deemed to be of considerable significance for the reader, but hardly relevant within the framework of the narrative itself, at appropriate places of the story.

Whereas there are many potential points of attachment for ethnographic matters in a broad narrative such as Herodotus's, which deals with the history of widely different lands and nations, there are only a few landmarks in the history of the Exodus, the journey through the Wilderness and the entry

27. See especially D. Damrosch, *The Narrative Covenant: Transformations of Genre in the Growth of Biblical Literature* (Ithaca, NY: Cornell University Press, 1991 [1987]), and various other publications by the same author. Inserting a piece in a different literary genre was also a common procedure in Akkadian literature: see Benjamin R. Foster, *Before the Muses: An Anthology of Akkadian Literature* (Bethesda: CDL Press, 1993), I, pp. 23-24.

into the Promised Land that easily lend themselves to the insertion of longer stretches of legal and ritual discourse, while the accounts of later history are clearly less suitable for this purpose. For this reason these passages cluster around the giving of the Law on Mt Sinai, some stations in the Wilderness and the last phase of Moses' life, near the border of the Promised Land, and we need not be surprised that such extended insertion of non-narrative material is thus limited to a few places only.

As we attempt to read Primary History as a whole, it may be useful to add a few words about the literary genre of the entire Primary History, not in order to provide a systematic treatment or to take issue with the implicit or explicit opinion of others, but with the intention to show that the view of its origin as set forth here can provide us with some insights about these issues that cannot easily be gained in any other way, and to provide material for further discussion. I therefore merely offer some of my thoughts on this important subject, as I think the time has not yet come for a full treatment.

We have seen that, while the narrator often speaks with an authoritative voice, telling his readers what happens in closed places such as inner rooms and even giving insight into the workings of God's mind, so to say, at other places the information provided seems to be contradictory or trivial. To the conscientious reader, Primary History indeed shows a re-markably hybrid character, which appears to provide considerable support for theories supposing a gradual process of growth and putting together of various texts. The Bible text looks like a mosaic of texts of various types, which have been put one beside the other, and sometimes even one inside another, while at times the information provided in one appears to con-tradict what is said in another one.

It has often been noted that there are also signs that point in a com-pletely different direction. It can be observed firstly that the texts follow an almost completely linear course in time from the Creation to the fall of Jerusalem in 587 BCE, with hardly any gaps worth speaking about, and secondly that many texts appear to exhibit close connections with one another. There seems to be a curious contradiction here, and one can fully understand why Spinoza (and after him many others) supposed that the work was left unfinished: on this view, a great redactional work on various texts was only partially completed, leaving all kinds of contradictions and inconsistencies between the original texts. In this model, uniformity can be ascribed to the final redaction, variety to its not having been completed. Though it cannot be used to prove anything, it is capable of explaining the irregular form of Primary History very well. Still, it seems worth while to try to describe and, if possible, also explain the form of Primary History as we see it before us now. Indeed, it is essential for the theory about the origin of Primary History set forth above that its final form was intended to be as it is. The problem is not so much, of course, what this literary form looks like, as we see it before our eyes, but why it looks the way it does and how we can describe it in terms of conventional qualifications.

Let us start with the construction of a historical model, and go on to a synchronic description afterwards. I would say that this highly unusual literary form can be easily understood if we assume that the author of Primary History had more or less the same literary ambition as Herodotus, while wishing to abstain from the most characteristic literary technique of his work, namely the presence of a voice that is claimed to be identical with the author's, with everything this entails for estimation of certainty of the information, various versions, personal notes, etc. The absence of this personal character of the narrator's voice thus causes a number of problems, of which I shall discuss the four that seem most important to me.

First, variant versions of one story, or alternative scenarios for certain courses of events, cannot be presented with a phrase such as 'I heard two different stories, and do not know which one is the right one', or 'the second one is more likely, in my view'. Secondly, non-narrative texts such as lists, which are for some reason considered to be relevant for the course of the narration, cannot be presented by the persona of the author, as with Herodotus's famous description of the Persian army and navy in *Histories* VII, 61-99. Likewise, summaries of what has happened and announcements of what is going to be told at the end and the beginning of larger units of text cannot be given in the conventional manner. Finally, explicit references in the narration to what has already been told or what is still to follow can no longer be made any more.

For the last problem our author applied his characteristic method of intertextual links through the use of identical or similar words, expressions and situations . He could evidently not say something along the lines of 'Well, in the period of the Judges things finally had got so far out of hand that Israelites behaved fully as badly as the people of Sodom in Abraham's days, and look what came from it', and go on with the stories of Judges 19–21. What he did was to formulate the story of the cruel reception of the Levite and his wife in Gibeah in such a way that no reader could escape the congruence with the boundless immorality of the Sodomites in Genesis 19.[28]

---

28. See also below, Chapter 4, Section 1, for the significance of the place of this episode at the end of the book of Judges.

The author of Primary History has expanded the use of poetry within his prose account to include the possibility of announcing what is still to come. Thus Genesis 49 proves to be a perfect pivot between the history of the patriarchs and the twelve ancestors of the Israelite tribes on one side, and the national history of Israel in its land from the book of Joshua onwards. Exodus 15, the Song of the Sea, likewise looks back to the Exodus and the death of the persecutors, and forward to the conquest of the Promised Land. There are several other subtle methods of working into the narrative evaluation of what has already been said and announcement of what is still to come; see below for the especially striking instance at the beginning of 1 Samuel.

Thus we see that the consequences of the third and fourth problems do not affect the course of the narrative or its general shape, but only its literary structure; for the first and second types this is entirely different. The choice to use these elements in spite of the limitations of authorial presence causes blocks of text to fall out of the framework of the continuous narration.

This causes a particular problem in the first case, as the reader suddenly finds variant versions standing as anonymous pieces of narrative between what is to be attributed to the narrator's normally authoritative and infallible insight into the events he tells his readers about. This creates an enormous dilemma for the reader, who is at times wondering whether the text he or she is reading is or is not of the authoritative character normally attributed to this work.

The author or redactor of Primary History has apparently not chosen to solve the dilemma himself, but instead left it to his readers to discern between the various layers of his account. In a way, this is another type of intertextuality, completely different from the one we have just discussed. From the presence of alternative versions of one story the reader is to conclude that in this particular case he or she is not dealing with an authoritative text, and to start comparing the two versions. In order to make this work not unduly difficult, the author has often connected the two versions by the use of the same key-words or narrative elements. One of the nicest instances of two such versions that the reader is almost invited to inspect is the case of the first meeting of Saul and David as discussed below in Chapter 4, Section 4.

From these examples it becomes clear again that the author of Primary History seems to have had little choice but to develop to the highest degree of perfection the method of intertextual links through the use of the same or comparable names, words and situations. This made his own work, as well as the readers', more difficult than it would otherwise have been, but it also created new opportunities. The interaction between different parts of the discourse can be much more subtle than in Herodotus's more or less conventional approach. The information provided in the lists at times contradicts what is told in the stories and the question of which version is to be preferred can be left undecided much more easily than in the Hero-dotean approach. Additionally, the juxtaposition of two versions can be used to achieve an entirely new effect, namely to stress what the two versions have in common. It can even be maintained that the presence of the two creation accounts at the beginning of Genesis amounts to a state-ment, firstly about part of the method that this work is going to use (in fact another instance of the use of literary means to introduce the book of Genesis or even the entire biblical history), and secondly about what is optional and what is certain in the narrator's view. Perhaps one could rephrase the message of the first two chapters of the Bible as something like: 'It is not entirely clear to us how the world was created, nor how humankind acquired a special stature therein, but it is certain that our God himself, by whatever name one prefers to call him, created everything and gave human beings an especial position among his creatures, in fact made them almost divine'; but I may be drifting across the border of theology with this, so I had better leave further speculation to others.[29]

All this led to the curious situation, which may have originated by accident but probably finished with being intentional, that Primary History has a number of characteristics usually associated especially with the genre of the dossier, which contains various texts about one subject. This type of text or texts is well known, though it is rarely recognized that in not a few cases it constitutes a literary genre in its own right. There are, of course, natural dossiers or archives, that which have been collected together for some practical purpose, such as tax-collecting, guaranteeing one's per-sonal rights or keeping an archive of important events. In such instances it is evidently not very useful to regard such a dossier as a literary collection or composition. There are also, by contrast, literary dossiers, where the message to be conveyed or the story to be told is put in the form of a

29. Note, by the way, that Herodotus also begins his work with different versions of one episode. This may have the same background of putting the author's method before the reader right at the beginning of the work. It seems very likely, in any case, that the author of Primary History read the beginning of the *Histories* in this way, and derived his own method of beginning the work from there, though it appears to fit even better in his own work than in Herodotus's.

collection of supposedly independent texts, whether of a literary or of an administrative nature. For modern scholarship, it is at times very difficult to determine whether certain texts were composed as a literary dossier, or are mere collections of originally separate documents, or are some sort of mixture of the two. This is especially clear with a book such as Ezra, supposedly a collection of various documents about the rebuilding of Jerusalem and the Temple and the re-establishing of the Jewish religion in the time after the captivity, but in the view of many at least in part worked over by one or more redactors. Elsewhere I tried to demonstrate that the book of Daniel, seemingly a loose collection of various court stories about Daniel and visions told by him, some instances of these two categories in Hebrew and others in Aramaic, is also such a dossier (made partly after the example of Ezra) and was probably composed as a whole, whether or not its elements once circulated independently.[30] Good terms to describe such a work may be 'unitary dossier', 'composed dossier', or 'linear literary dossier': a work that is formally a dossier, but exhibits continuity of action and contents under this guise. In view of the observations presented above, it would seem very likely now that the same characterization is valid for the much longer and more complicated Primary History: supposedly a work consisting of nine books, most of which contain a variety of different material, but in reality a well-composed unity with only occasional lapses from the master plan of its author.

The Land of Canaan

We have seen how important the matter of the ownership of the Promised Land was to the author of Primary History. While writing his history, he apparently refrained from using certain designations which he considered as in a way anachronistic, because they would expose the course of his narrative too soon. Thus, as is well known, we find only some allusions to the city of Jerusalem in the Pentateuch, but not a single explicit reference. Similarly, he could hardly refer to something called 'the land of Israel' in his work, at least not in the parts dealing with earlier history. When he wanted to assign another name to this land, however, our author must have been confronted with a problem experienced by many ancient and modern writers and rulers wishing to describe it: this land, on the crossroads between various nations, tongues and cultures, inhabited by people with

30. See my 'The Writing of Daniel', in J.J. Collins and P.W. Flint (eds.), *The Book of Daniel: Composition and Reception* (Leiden: E.J. Brill, 2001), pp. 291-310.

greatly varying linguistic, ethnic and religious backgrounds, simply did not have one encompassing name accepted by everyone, which is one of the reasons why the indication 'Palestine' (from 'Philistines' or 'Philistea', so really a *pars pro toto*) was used from early times onwards by some authors (Herodotus himself uses it several times), and 'Judaea' probably served more or less the same purpose with others.[31] It seems rather likely that our author likewise chose a name that originally had a more limited application in order to describe the entire land, which resulted in the curious situation that in the prophetical books 'Canaan' and 'Canaanites' have somewhat different meanings from those in Primary History.[32]

Egypt: Real and Literary Geography

Up to now the Egypt of Primary History that we have dealt with here is not the real country straddling the Nile, but what we could call a mirrored variant of Lydia and its capital Sardis. We have not yet considered the fact that the real Egypt is dealt with at length by Herodotus, mainly, though by no means exclusively, in his second book, which is devoted almost entirely to the history and culture of Egypt. It would be truly amazing if the description of this country, which took up so much of Herodotus's attention, had not influenced the structure and contents of Primary History. One naturally tends to look for parallels for those instances where Egypt is mentioned in Primary History, especially in relation with Palestine, and there are indeed a number of instances where influence from Herodotus cannot be excluded, though none where this connection is certain. The purpose of the following enumeration of possible parallels is not to attempt to prove dependence on the work of Herodotus, but to show the mere possibility that the details in these stories ultimately derive from Herodotus.

31. This seems to be the most likely explanation of the material collected and discussed in L.H. Feldman, 'Some Observations on the Name of Palestine', *HUCA* 61 (1990), pp. 1-23; Feldman himself opts for the universal application of 'Judaea' for this purpose, but he occasionally stretches the arguments too much in order to fit them into his theory.

32. On the name Canaan and its use in Primary History, and elsewhere in the Hebrew Bible, see especially N.P. Lemche, *The Canaanites and their Land: The Tradition of the Canaanites* (Sheffield: JSOT Press, 1991), and his 'City-Dwellers or Administrators; Further Light on the Canaanites', in A. Lemaire and B. Otzen (eds.), *History and Traditions of Early Israel: Studies Presented to Eduard Nielsen* (Leiden: E.J. Brill, 1993), pp. 76-89.

When Cambyses is poised to invade Egypt at the beginning of Herodotus's third book, and hesitates about the right way to take, the difficulties of the coastal road between Palestine and Egypt are described at some length.

> The only entrance into Egypt is through this desert. From Phoenicia to the boundaries of Cadytis [probably Gaza] the country belongs to the Syrians known as 'Palestinian': from Cadytis, a town, I should say, not much smaller than Sardis, the seaports as far as Ienysus [perhaps identical with modern El-Arish] belong to the king of Arabia; from there as far as Lake Serbonis, near which Mt Casius runs down to the sea, it is once more Syrian territory; and after Lake Serbonis (where Typhon is supposed to be buried) Egypt begins. The whole area between Ienysus on the one side, and Mt Casius and the Lake on the other—and it is of considerable extent, not less than three days' journey—is desert and completely without water (Her. III, 5).

It has hardly received any attention that this description bears a striking resemblance to the beginning of the Israelites' journey from Egypt to the Promised Land, namely their arrival at the Red Sea and their departure from there.

> Then the Lord said to Moses, 'Tell the people of Israel to turn back and encamp in front of Pihahiroth, between Migdol and the sea, in front of Baalzephon; you shall encamp over against it, by the sea' (Exod. 14.1).

> Then Moses led Israel onward from the Red Sea, and they went into the wilderness of Shur; they went three days in the wilderness and found no water (Exod. 15.22).

Though one cannot exclude the possibility that the accounts, both mentioning the lake (or 'sea'), the mountain and the three days' journey without water, depend on a stereotypical description current in antiquity, in the light of the other aspects of the relation between Herodotus and Primary History it seems rather likely that the start of the Israelites' itinerary was borrowed from Herodotus, and that Baal Zephon is indeed to be identified with the Casius mountains near Pelusium (see above), and that the Red Sea of the Exodus account should therefore be identified with the Sirbonian lake.

Herodotus and Primary History preserve remarkably similar stories about the Assyrian king Sennacherib undertaking a campaign against the Egyptian king, which was apparently foiled before reaching the country proper. In the Bible, the ultimate purpose of this campaign is not mentioned, but the 'Ethiopian' Pharaoh Taharqa is mentioned. Sennacherib is said to have invested Jerusalem also, somewhat surprisingly after the readers have been told that Hezekiah gave him the tribute he required of him. There are two exchanges between the Assyrians besieging the city and the defenders, in which the Assyrians taunt Hezekiah and his god, the prophet Isaiah predicts an Assyrian defeat and Hezekiah himself presents a letter from the Assyrian king in the Temple, in which his trust in God is mocked. God then intervenes himself and strikes down a tremendous number of men among the Assyrians.

> [2 Kgs 18.13] In the fourteenth year of King Hezekiah Sennacherib king of Assyria came up against all the fortified cities of Judah and took them. [14] And Hezekiah king of Judah sent to the king of Assyria at Lachish, saying, 'I have done wrong; withdraw from me; whatever you impose on me I will bear.' And the king of Assyria required of Hezekiah king of Judah three hundred talents of silver and thirty talents of gold. [15] And Hezekiah gave him all the silver that was found in the house of the Lord, and in the treasuries of the king's house. [16] At that time Hezekiah stripped the gold from the doors of the temple of the Lord, and from the doorposts which Hezekiah king of Judah had overlaid and gave it to the king of Assyria. [17] And the king of Assyria sent the Tartan, the Rabsaris, and the Rabshakeh with a great army from Lachish to King Hezekiah at Jerusalem. And they went up and came to Jerusalem.
>
> [2 Kgs 19.8] The Rabshakeh returned, and found the king of Assyria fighting against Libnah; for he heard that the king had left Lachish. [9] And when the king heard concerning Tirhakah king of Ethiopia, 'Behold, he has set out to fight against you', he sent messengers again to Hezekiah, saying, [10] 'Thus shall you speak to Hezekiah king of Judah: "Do not let your God on whom you rely deceive you by promising that Jerusalem will not be given into the hand of the king of Assyria…"'
>
> [2 Kgs 19.35] And that night the angel of the Lord went forth, and slew a hundred and eighty-five thousand in the camp of the Assyrians; and when men arose early in the morning, behold, these were all dead bodies. [36] Then Sennacherib king of Assyria departed, and went home, and dwelt at Nineveh.

In the work of Herodotus, by contrast, Sennacherib's opponent is not the historical figure Taharqa, but the enigmatic priest-Pharaoh Sethos.

> Next on the throne after Anysis was Sethos, the high priest of Hephaestus. He is said to have neglected the warrior class of the Egyptians… As a result, when Egypt was invaded by a strong force under Sennacherib, the king of Arabia and Assyria, not one of them was willing to fight. The situation was grave; not knowing what else to do, the priest-king entered the shrine and, before the image of the god, complained bitterly of the peril which threatened him. In the midst of his lamentations he fell asleep, and

dreamt that the god stood by him and urged him not to lose heart; for if he marched boldly out to meet the Arabian army, he would come to no harm, as the god himself would send him helpers.

By this dream the king's confidence was restored; and with such men as were willing to follow him—not a single one of the warrior class, but a mixed company of shopkeepers, artisans, and market-people—he marched to Pelusium, which guards the approaches to Egypt, and there took up his position. As he lay here facing the Assyrians, thousands of field-mice swarmed over them during the night, and ate their quivers, their bowstrings, and the leather handles of their shields, so that on the following day, having no arms to fight with, they abandoned their position and suffered severe losses during their retreat. There is still a stone statue of Sethos in the temple of Hephaestus; the figure is represented with a mouse in its hand, and the inscription: 'Look upon me and learn reverence' (Her. II, 141).

A great deal has been written about the relation between these two accounts, and opinions are divided about this, though few commentators assume that they are completely independent from each other. I shall not enter into the details of this discussion, but shall merely consider whether it is thinkable or even likely that the biblical account derives from Herodotus, and may even be meant to be reconciled with it.

Through the juxtaposition of Hezekiah's prayer (2 Kgs 19.14-19), Isaiah's prophecy of deliverance (vv. 20-34) and the action of the Angel of the Lord (vv. 35-37), a unity of place is suggested which, though tacitly assumed by many commentators, is not confirmed by a precise reading of the text. In Primary History, Sennacherib is said to have been at several places in Palestine, but never near Jerusalem. Instead, he sends his emissaries with an army from Lachish (2 Kgs 18.17), and a second mission with a letter for Hezekiah from Libnah (2 Kgs 19.8-13). We are not told where he is when disaster strikes, but it seems highly unlikely even within the confines of this story that he would encamp his army under the walls of besieged Jerusalem. On the other hand, Herodotus does say unequivocally that Sennacherib reached or came close to Pelusium, where the Egyptian army in its depleted state was waiting for him. It seems at least possible that the author of Primary History incorporated this story into his account, changing evidently incorrect or possibly offensive details such as the name of the Pharaoh or the plague of the mice, which he will surely have understood as an oblique reference to Apollo, the god of mice and of the pest. The episode of Hezekiah entering the Temple to put his case before God himself may also owe much to the comparable account of Sethos: in the biblical account Hezekiah has taken the place of Sethos, asking the god to come to his rescue and being answered by him—the only time in Primary History a monarch appears before God in the Temple to ask for deliverance from the enemy. Finally, it may be observed that the account in 2 Kings, even though it partly duplicates Herodotus's story, may still be read as another account of the same episode, with only the naturalistic explanation of Sennacherib's defeat being replaced by a miraculous divine intervention.[33]

A further instance of a campaign passing through Palestine in the period common to Herodotus's account of Egyptian history and Primary History may be found in what both books say about Pharaoh Neco. Herodotus tells that he campaigned against the 'Syrians', unfortunately not specifying them in any way: '...and in addition he attacked the Syrians by land and defeated them at Magdolus, afterwards taking Cadytis [again, probably Gaza], a large town in Syria' (Her. II, 158). In Primary History, by contrast, we only have a brief mention of an encounter between Neco and King Josiah of Judah:

> In his days Pharaoh Neco king of Egypt went up to the king of Assyria to the river Euphrates. King Josiah went to meet him; and Pharaoh Neco slew him at Megiddo, when he saw him. [30] And his servants carried him dead in a chariot from Megiddo, and brought him to Jerusalem, and buried him in his own tomb. And the people of the land took Jehoahaz the son of Josiah, and anointed him, and made him king in his father's stead (2 Kgs 23.29-30).

Here also, commentators have pondered about the relation between the two episodes, as even the places where the action takes place (Magdolus versus Megiddo) look very similar; there are, however, alternative identifications possible for Herodotus's Magdolus. The main difference between the stories is that Herodotus only mentions the fight with the 'Syrians', whereas Primary History correctly states that Neco was on his way to fight the Assyrians. Here, as in the preceding example, it is entirely possible that the author of Primary History established a point of contact between Herodotus and his own work by providing this information; in view of Herodotus's often unusual transliteration of Semitic toponyms the identification of Magdolus with Megiddo would not pose especial difficulties. Still, in both accounts of the campaign of Neco in Palestine the information provided is so limited that we can hardly advance beyond educated speculation.[34]

33. Cf. the discussion of the entire episode in Cogan and Tadmor, *II Kings*, pp. 223-51.

34. See also Cogan and Tadmor, *II Kings*, pp. 300-302.

The only cycle of stories in the Bible that is almost entirely located in Egypt and provides information about this country in some detail is the series of chapters describing events after Joseph arrives in Egypt in Genesis 39, until his death in Genesis 50. The Egyptian parallels have been the subjects of several studies, in which the evidence of Herodotus is also included.[35] Here I would like to point out only one parallel, which is so characteristic that it provides a direct connection between the time-frames of Primary History and of Herodotus once we accept that they are indeed describing the same event. In Genesis 47, Joseph makes clever use of the hunger of the population to buy their land and make them all into tenants of Pharaoh.

> [Gen. 47.18] And when that year was ended, they came to him the following year, and said to him, 'We will not hide from my lord that our money is all spent; and the herds of cattle are my lord's; there is nothing left in the sight of my lord but our bodies and our lands. [19] Why should we die before your eyes, both we and our land? Buy us and our land for food, and we with our land will be slaves to Pharaoh; and give us seed, that we may live, and not die, and that the land may not be desolate.' [20] So Joseph bought all the land of Egypt for Pharaoh; for all the Egyptians sold their fields, because the famine was severe upon them. The land became Pharaoh's; [21] and as for the people, he made slaves of them from one end of Egypt to the other. [22] Only the land of the priests he did not buy; for the priests had a fixed allowance from Pharaoh, and lived on the allowance which Pharaoh gave them; therefore they did not sell their land. [23] Then Joseph said to the people, 'Behold, I have this day bought you and your land for Pharaoh. Now here is seed for you, and you shall sow the land. [24] And at the harvests you shall give a fifth to Pharaoh, and four fifths shall be your own, as seed for the field and as food for yourselves and your households, and as food for your little ones.' [25] And they said, 'You have saved our lives; may it please my lord, we will be slaves to Pharaoh.' [26] So Joseph made it a statute concerning the land of Egypt, and it stands to this day, that Pharaoh should have the fifth; the land of the priests alone did not become Pharaoh's.

The first Pharaoh to be mentioned in some detail by Herodotus is Sesostris, among whose achievements Herodotus recounts: 'It was this king, moreover, who divided the land into lots and gave everyone a square piece of equal size, from the produce of which he exacted an annual tax' (Her. II, 109). As this is the only Pharaoh of whom Herodotus tells something comparable, he would be the prime candidate for being identified

---

35. See the classic study by J. Vergote, *Joseph en Egypte: Génèse chap. 37–50 à la lumière des études égyptologiques récentes* (Leuven: Publications Universitaires, 1959).

with the Pharaoh of the Joseph cycle. If this identification of the Pharaoh of Joseph is correct—and it should be realized that it hangs only by the thread of Sesostris's policy with regard to the land—the Pharaoh who issued the edict ordering the killing of the Hebrew boys must be his son and successor Pheros, likewise mentioned by Herodotus, unfortunately without relevant details (Her. II, 111), and the Pharaoh of the Exodus must be his successor Proteus (Her. II, 112-20). There may be an indication that this conclusion is indeed correct. Herodotus tells his readers that this Proteus received the Trojan prince Paris together with Menelaus's wife Helen, whose abduction provoked the Trojan war. After investigating the affair, Proteus chased away Paris and retained Helen as a guest until Menelaus came to Egypt after the conclusion of the war and the fall of Troy to take her back to Greece; Helen would in this version of the history never have been to Troy herself. The interesting consequence of this line of thought would be that the time of the Exodus from Egypt would coincide with that of the Trojan war, which may well have been an attractive thought for the author of Primary History with his lively interest in Greek history. Our author cannot have failed to observe that already for Herodotus the Persian campaigns against Greece mirrored the Trojan war, to such a degree in fact that the beginning and end of his work refer to it, albeit indirectly (see above).

Herodotus's 'Syria', 'Palestinian Syria' and the Jews

It would seem that all the instances where Herodotus speaks about or hints at Palestine or the road to it, as well as most cases in which he relates something about the 'Syrians' living there, are to be found in some form in Primary History; it may not be superfluous to add that this work contains a considerable amount of additional material dealing with the history of the Near East and Egypt not found, or in a less correct form, in the work of Herodotus. Still, it would seem that the author of Primary History deliberately employed almost every opportunity to establish a parallel with the *Histories*. Unless this is purely coincidence—which is rather unlikely in view of the theory unfolded here about the relation between Herodotus and Primary History—this must mean that the author of Primary History assimilated the entire text of Herodotus's *Histories*, not merely the parts that were interesting for the structure of his own historical account (books I and VII–IX), noted the places where Herodotus appears to refer to Palestine or its inhabitants, and incorporated a connection to these references in his own work. Sometimes this connection is of a literary nature only, as in the parallel between the Scythians of Her. I, 103-106 and the kings of the east of Genesis 14, or between the road connecting Palestine and Egypt used by Cambyses in one direction, and by the Israelites leaving Egypt in the other, but often the event mentioned by Herodotus is to be found in a modified form in Primary History, as in the case of Pharaoh Neco's campaign or Sennacherib's spectacular defeat. This does not mean that our author did not have independent information about these events (he indeed often enlarges or corrects Herodotus's account), but that he apparently strove to include each one of these episodes in his own work. The reason for this procedure may lie in the fact noted above, that at first glance the Jews are apparently never deemed worthy of mention in the *Histories*: in this way a number of contacts between the two great works would be established, which would also furnish the perceptive reader with a good reason to suppose that the 'Syrians' or 'Palestinian Syrians' of Herodotus should usually be identified with the Jews.

At two places in his work, Herodotus refers to the original home-country of the people inhabiting Syria-Palestine. Right at the beginning of his work (I, 1) he notes that the 'Phoenicians', the inhabitants of the sea-coast of this country, originate from the coast of the 'Red Sea' (*epi tei Eruthrei thalassei*), by which name he probably designates the present-day Persian Gulf, whereas in VII, 89, the beginning of the catalogue of the number of ships contributed by various nations of the Persian empire to Xerxes' fleet, he tells his readers that the inhabitants of 'Phoenicia and the Syrian part of Palestine' themselves trace their origins to this location. It is enticing to compare this with the origin of Abraham's family in Ur of the Chaldees as told in Genesis 11, as ancient Ur is nearer to the Persian Gulf than any other of the major cities of ancient Mesopotamia. Of course it is impossible to draw conclusions from this parallel (and note that Herodotus appears to mean especially the Phoenicians), but it fits very well in the general picture of deliberate connection of Primary History with the work of Herodotus with regard to locations and events connected with Palestine.

Preliminary Conclusions

My observations about the relationship between Herodotus's work and Primary History, and about the contrast between the two, have far-reaching consequences, which can only be mentioned very briefly here, summarized in a number of preliminary conclusions. First and foremost, we now perceive that Primary History in its present form is a historical work that was written or composed in deliberate contrast with the *Histories* of Herodotus, in order to stress both the parallels with that work and the contrast between the history of Israel and Herodotus's account of the wars between Greeks and Persians. The author of Primary History appears to have improved upon his example in several respects. His erudite and many-sided work, with its wonderful stories and deeply thought-out intertextuality, indeed ranks among the most impressive historical works of antiquity.

It is in a way amazing that its dependence on Herodotus has never been noticed before, as it is in a way so evident that it proves almost impossible to ignore it once one becomes aware of it, the crossing of the sea between two continents in order to conquer the country on the other side being the most striking, but by no means the only, close parallel. The reason must be the remarkable mastery of the biblical narrator, who transformed the stories in such a subtle way that they no longer really look or feel like the original episodes, though they have, in fact, often remained quite close to them. The descriptions of Xerxes' triumphant army at the crossing of the Hellespont and of the Israelites fleeing before their Egyptian oppressors through the sea simply do not feel the same, whatever the formal agreements between them. Certain episodes of Primary History can indeed be read very well in contrast with Herodotus: whereas Xerxes has the Hellespont punished symbolically by branding it and throwing manacles into its waters, thus acting against nature itself, and makes great exertions to cross it, Moses parts the waters with a single gesture; whereas only the eldest son of Pythios is killed, in Egypt all the first-born, both human and animal, die; the conquest of Greece fails and the land of Canaan finally falls to the Israelites (though they are to lose it again many centuries later).

From this fundamental observation several secondary conclusions can be inferred. The date of the final redaction of Primary History is the late fifth or early fourth century BCE (maybe even a little later), and it was probably written both to establish a history of the people of Israel, which may until then have only existed in bits and pieces, and to impose a normative view of Israelite religion on the Jewish world of the time. Whether or not it was written for the purpose, one can observe that it subsequently served to enhance tremendously the prestige of Judaism in the ancient world. In its present shape it is largely a unitary work, though earlier material had probably been employed. Of course, there is a possibility that after the great work was completed, subsequent editing added, removed or modified material. It would seem preferable, however, to assume the basic unity of the work first, and to have recourse to such conjectures of secondary developments only after new criteria have been developed for determining which would be the hallmarks of later change in the text of

Primary History. Thus there is probably no real break between this work and later Jewish traditions—which means that the rabbinical idea of Written Torah and Oral Torah complementing each other may be more correct than is generally assumed (note, for example, that even with the date proposed above there would not be much more than a century between the publication of Primary History and its translation into Greek, usually dated to the third century BCE, which evidently incorporates certain extra-biblical traditions), and well-known omissions such as the details of Sabbath law and dietary laws may have to be ascribed largely to deliberate choice, rather than to the development of Israelite law or the vicissitudes of legal tradition. The connection of some characteristic Jewish habits with certain momentous events in the history of the world or of the people of Israel, on the other hand, may have been intended to parry anti-Jewish polemics.

By contrast, the distance of this work from the social, political and religious realities of the earlier period is not easily to be gauged; though the suggestion that the concept of 'Ancient Israel' as evinced in Primary History is a comparatively recent invention of Jewish groups in the Persian period[36] should not be rejected out of hand, there is a distinct possibility that this historical account made ample and accurate use of earlier sources for at least part of the work. In any case, the problems encountered when attempting to analyse its account of earlier history are comparable to those faced by all students of ancient historical works. Blatant incorrectness in one case does not exclude reliability in another, nor does the fact that history can be made to fit into a certain pattern by itself provide an argument against or in favour of its reliability.

An interesting side-effect of my observations is that the critical approaches based directly or indirectly on the Graf–Wellhausen theory will probably have to be modified considerably in view of these observations. Finally, it is notable that Primary History is indeed simply the work that it always implicitly purported to be, but as which it has rarely been regarded by later readers: a continuous account of the history of the people of Israel from the creation of the world to the Babylonian Exile as observed from the point of view of a pious Jew living at least some time after the last

36. See, for example, Thompson, *Early History of the Israelite People*, and Davies, *In Search of 'Ancient Israel'*, and the discussion in a recent issue of the *Journal of Biblical Literature*: I. Provan, 'Ideologies, Literary and Critical: Reflections on Recent Writing on the History of Israel', *JBL* 114 (1995), pp. 585-606; T.L. Thompson, 'A Neo-Albrightean School in History and Biblical Scholarship?', pp. 683-98; P.R. Davies, 'Method and Madness: Some Remarks on Doing History with the Bible', pp. 699-705.

event described in it, the release of King Jehoiachin by the Babylonian king Evil-Merodach around 560 BCE.

It need hardly be said that all this will make it necessary to rethink many of the established assumptions concerning the literary genesis of this historical work and the view of the history and the religion of Israel based on these assumptions. It also seems likely that on closer scrutiny more contacts between the History of Israel and Greek authors will be found. Finally, it may be worth while to attempt to apply the method of literary congruence proposed here to other Jewish and non-Jewish literary works from antiquity. This way to let one literary work generate another one may have been more common than we realize at the moment. The consequences are certainly very far-reaching, and it is somewhat ironic that the work that appears to be most capable of furthering our insight into the History of Israel as related in Primary History has been around since antiquity without ever having been used for the purpose.

For the study of the work of Herodotus an important result of my investigations would seem to be that we now realize that the background of Primary History is an early integrated reading of the *Histories*. I have mainly discussed the consequences of the parallels between the *Histories* and Primary History for the determination of the origin and nature of the second work, but of course the dependence between the two as assumed here also provides information about the way in which the author of Primary History read and interpreted Herodotus's work. In due time, the admittedly rather limited information provided by Primary History on this subject will have to be integrated in the general reception history of the *Histories*. For the time being I shall therefore limit my survey to a few observations only.

It would seem that the author of Primary History, who as noted above must have written his work either in the last decades of the fifth or in the fourth century BCE, had access to the *Histories* in more or less the same form in which we have them now, especially since he apparently even copied the number of its books and since his borrowing of various elements spans the entire series.

He had a good eye for some of the details of the narrative as well as for the structure of the entire work. Note, for example, that just as Herodotus suggested (but did not state or discuss) that Pythios was the grandson of Croesus, so Primary History suggests that the Pharaoh of Joseph is the grandfather of the Pharaoh of the Exodus, again without making this relationship explicit. The author of Primary History often added to a literary effect already intended in the *Histories*, as in the case of the 'double dream' of Astyages, possibly an innovation of Herodotus on the basis of the material available to him, elaborated into three double dreams in Genesis, the reason for which is stated explicitly in Gen. 41.32.

In some instances it is not clear whether he recognized an intended literary feature in the *Histories*, or transformed an accidental phenomenon for his own use, or perhaps did both at the same time. At first sight, the way in which he combined elements of the crossing of the Hellespont and the Pallene affair seems not directly based on the intention of Herodotus, whereas the parallel he noted between the Hellespont and Salamis was probably intended, but the situation in Herodotus may be more complicated than a *prima facie* glance would suggest; further research is needed here. The same goes for the series of deceptions in Herodotus's first book. Above I noted that there seems to be no direct causal connection between the first group of two and the remaining three deceptions, whereas the series of five cases of deception is unbroken in Genesis. In such cases it is not clear whether the author of Primary History thought that his account was based on the correct interpretation of the *Histories*, probably assuming that Herodotus sometimes suggested causal relations without mentioning them explicitly, or whether he simply intended to improve on what he found in his source.

Whatever value is to be attached to his analysis of Herodotus's work, it is entirely clear that the author of Primary History had an intimate knowledge of the *Histories*, and had profoundly contemplated their structure and contents. His is the earliest integral reading of this great historian's work, and the first and probably also the best of the long series of its imitations.

Whatever our final conclusion about each one of these issues may be, it would seem very likely now that Cicero, when he called Herodotus the 'Father of History' (*De legibus* 1.1.5), was more right than he could have realized, and that Herodotus, if not the father of biblical history, was certainly its foster father. The author of Primary History, in fact, carried Herodotus's concept to far greater religious, cultural and psychological depths, not content with imitating the *Histories*, but convincingly surpassing his great example. Therefore, it is hardly surprising that, though the *Histories* of Herodotus are still read and studied intensively nowadays, the work created by the author of Primary History is at the basis of the Jewish, Christian and Islamic civilizations and has thus become the most influential literary work of world history.

Chapter 4

CONSEQUENCES FOR THE STUDY OF BIBLICAL LITERATURE

During the last two decades, the literary study of the Hebrew Bible in general, and of Primary History in particular, has undergone a remarkable acceleration and transformation. Hallmarks of the early stages of this development have been, to mention only a few works, Robert Alter's *The Art of Biblical Narrative* (1981) and Shimon Bar-Efrat's *Narrative Art in the Bible* (first edition of English translation 1989, original Hebrew 1979). One of the notable characteristics of this movement has been a remarkable degree of respect for the traditional Hebrew text in its Masoretic form as it has been handed down to us. All this started when various types of critical study still reigned supreme, and these basically contradictory views of the text of Primary History have now coexisted for a number of years, with advocates of the literary approach often recognizing the merit of methods such as historical criticism or redactional criticism, without actually giving them a place in their own studies. In fact, the supposed results of the critical approaches, which look upon the present-day Hebrew text as the result of a process of amalgamation and redaction of a number of originally separate texts, were recognized in name, though usually not in fact, as literary researchers simply could not put them to any significant use within the framework of their own studies. One could argue that with the receding interest in critical studies of the Hebrew text, the literary people have won the day simply through the gradual retreat of the other party, but this view obscures the fact that historical criticism was not only the antipode, but to a degree, and at least for some of the literary researchers, also the legitimation for studying the Hebrew Bible as literature: namely as the final result, through one or several redactional processes, of the crystallization of the literature of ancient Israel. If for some reason we find the hypothesis of this process of growth underlying the Hebrew text as we now have it unconvincing, the questions of what we are studying and whose work we are subjecting to our scrutiny no longer have any answer. The question why Primary History lends itself so well to a literary analysis becomes even more pressing than before. If we are studying an originally unitary text, it ought to be possible to say at least something about its origin. If, conversely, we are dealing with a heavily redacted series of originally independent texts, we should at least attempt to understand why this redaction was so extremely successful in literary terms. In other words: while studying the books of Primary History as literature one can abstain from asking historical questions for a long time, but in the long run one will have to give some sort of answer, minimally a working definition of the nature and origin of the collection.

Having in the previous chapter formulated the theory that the entire Primary History as we now have it was the deliberate creation of one historian or a group of historians living in late Persian or early Greek times, we can attempt to give a preliminary survey of the changes this may effect in its literary study. For this purpose a number of case studies are presented below, all taken from the history of the beginning of the monarchy in Israel as found in the books of Samuel and the first two chapters of the book of 1 Kings.[1]

In the first study the way in which our author or authors managed to preface major episodes of Primary History with information about its contents and purpose is discussed, as exemplified by the beginning of the books of Samuel. After that, I shall study some aspects of the underlying patterns of these stories, and also discuss their character as being partly of the literary genre of the unitary dossier; a few interesting cases of intertextual links will also be discussed there. Intertextuality as a literary means for indicating the larger inner structure of the history that is being described and as an instrument for understanding the passages that have been linked in this way, i.e. as an invitation to the reader to study two episodes or passages together, is the subject of the third case study, 'two wise women'. Finally, the well-known problem of contradictory duplicate stories is tackled in a

1. A very brief list of some of the literature dealing with these chapters, in which much further literature is discussed: J.S. Ackerman, 'Knowing Good and Evil: A Literary Analysis of the Court History in 2 Samuel 9–20 and 1 Kings 1–2', *JBL* 109 (1990), pp. 41-64; C. Conroy, *Absalom Absalom! Narrative and Language in 2 Sam. 13–20* (Rome: Biblical Institute Press, 1978); J.P. Fokkelman, *Narrative Art and Poetry in the Books of Samuel*. I. *King David* (Assen: Van Gorcum, 1981); D.M. Gunn, *The Story of King David: Genre and Interpretation* (Sheffield: JSOT Press, 1978); P. Kyle McCarter, *I Samuel: A New Translation with Introduction and Commentary* (AB, 8; Garden City, NY: Doubleday, 1980); *idem*, *II Samuel: A New Translation with Introduction and Commentary* (AB, 9; Garden City, NY: Doubleday, 1984); J.-W. Wesselius, 'Joab's Death'.

new study of the two different accounts of the way in which David came to know his predecessor King Saul. In all of these studies I shall also give especial attention to the function of the repetition of words, phrases, passages and situations to provide links with other places in Primary History and the various effects attained by this procedure.

It is not my intention to prove that my view of the issues taken up in these case studies is the correct one, or even that it is markedly superior to others. For this reason these studies do not pretend to be all-encompassing treatments of the problems they are dealing with. What I want to do here is merely to show that certain features of these stories can be connected quite naturally with what I established to be important characteristics of the style and literary nature of Primary History. In other words, I shall attempt to show that one can deal successfully with certain literary problems on the basis of the overall view of Primary History set forth above. The comparison with the work of Herodotus will again prove quite enlightening, this time not for the structure of the work, but in order to sketch (in addition to what has been said) a profile of the possible ambitions of the author or authors of Primary History, the way these were curbed by the apparently self-imposed limitations on the presence of the narrator in this history, and the methods that were developed to work around these limitations. Again it must be said that the diachronic approach, describing the ties between Herodotus's *Histories* and Primary History, is certainly not the only way to look at the authorial methods and approaches of Primary History as described here, but the explanations proposed here appear to function very effectively on the synchronic level also, and have the merit of being the first attempt to find the origin of a number of these characteristic features of Primary History.

1. *The Narrator's Programme: Samuel and Eli in 1 Samuel 2 and 3*

One of the most serious consequences of the choice of a non-identified, partly depersonalized narrator for the various episodes of Primary History must have been, as I noted above, that it would be very difficult to indicate the contents of the entire work or of parts of it at the beginning. One possible choice would have been to omit such headers, announcements or summaries entirely, but the author has apparently chosen a completely different approach. At the beginning of most of the nine books that traditionally constitute Primary History, namely Genesis, Exodus, Leviticus, Numbers, Deuteronomy, Joshua, Judges, Samuel and Kings, we find verses or chapters that on closer scrutiny serve very well as an introduction, not merely to the episodes at the beginning of the book, but to the book in its entirety. This introduction usually refers back to the last part of the previous book in some way, either to the death of the great leader described there (Joseph in Exodus, Moses in Joshua, Joshua in Judges), or to the location of the action (Egypt in Exodus, the tent of meeting in Leviticus and Numbers, the land of Moab in Deuteronomy, Shiloh in Samuel), or it is part of a continuous series of stories (the Succession History in Kings). It should be noted, by the way, that these observations lend further support to the idea discussed above that the division of Primary History into nine books is indeed original, and make a derivation of this number from the work of Herodotus even more likely.

In this section I shall study one of these cases in some detail, namely the beginning of the book of Samuel (nowadays divided into the books 1 Samuel and 2 Samuel, but originally one book), in which the lives of Samuel, Saul and David, and with that the early history of the monarchy in Israel, are narrated. Particular attention will be given to its function as a statement of the narrator's programme for the book of Samuel and the first two chapters of Kings. Although I shall not study all details of the transition between Judges and Samuel here, some preliminary observations are in order. The separation of the action of the two books is, in fact, somewhat more marked than in the case of the other books. Judges ends with a number of stories that take their point of departure from the cruel episode of the Levite who persuades his estranged concubine to come home with him again, and is received hospitably by an Ephraimite who is living in the town of Gibeah, which itself belongs to the tribe of Benjamin. During the night, the men of the town gather outside the house and ask for the stranger to be delivered to him, so that they may do their will with him. The cowardly men offer to deliver their daughter and their concubine, respectively, to the mob, and the concubine is indeed pushed out of the house. She is raped and dies as a consequence, and the Levite cuts her dead body to pieces and sends a part to each of the twelve tribes of Israel. Benjamin stands behind its own men of Gibeah, and the others campaign against Benjamin and kill all the females and a large part of the males. The book of Judges ends with the attempts to find new wives for the remaining Benjaminites.

Samuel starts with the story of the childless Hannah, the birth of her son Samuel and his education in the sanctuary of Shiloh. No continuity of action is found here, nor do we see persons figuring on both sides of the separation between Judges and Samuel. Still, the final chapters of the book of Judges seem to form a prelude, though a very unusual one, to the events

of the books of Samuel. The remarkable series of stories about the consequences of the abomination at Gibeah, itself representing a partial
resumption of the story about sinful Sodom in Genesis 19, are mainly
located in and around places that are also the location of important actions
in the books of Samuel: Gibeah is Saul's capital, Shiloh the place of the
ancient Israelite shrine, Bethlehem the birthplace of King David, and
Jerusalem the originally non-Israelite city which under David was to take
over the position as the seat of both worldly and religious authority. One
place of lesser importance, Jabesh in Gilead, plays an important part in
King Saul's life, as his first act of liberation for the people of Israel was on
behalf of Jabesh (1 Sam. 11), and its inhabitants finally took away his dead
body from the city wall of Beth Shean, where the Philistines had hung it
after his defeat and death, and gave it a worthy burial (1 Sam. 31.8-13).
Thus this series of stories provides a good point of departure for the books
of Samuel, both because of the stories' location and because they depict
the total state of lawlessness and wantonness reigning in Israel at the end
of the time of the Judges, when it was acutely felt that 'there was no king
in Israel; every man did what was right in his own eyes' (Judg. 21.25).

At first glance, the books of Samuel do not start with offering the most
important facts of what is to follow in them, or a summary of what the
readers are to be told, but with a seemingly anecdotal and unimportant
series of events. Readers are told of the childlessness of Hannah, the wife
of a certain Elkanah from the tribe of Ephraim; of her being baited by
Elkanah's other wife Peninnah, less loved by her husband but in the
possession of a number of children; of Hannah's desperate prayer in the
sanctuary in Shiloh, for which Eli the priest berates her; of her vow to dedi-
cate her offspring to the service of God, the answering of Hannah's prayer
and the fulfilment of her vow. None of this leads the reader to expect
something that transcends the incidental and anecdotial sphere; this is
especially remarkable because the book of Judges, as we have seen, ended
with a very momentous event, namely the near-destruction of the tribe of
Benjamin. With the prayer or song that Hannah is said to have uttered in 1
Sam. 2.1-8,[2] however, the perspective undergoes a radical change. While on
the one hand the song, as was only to be expected, stresses the power of
God to give or withhold children (1 Sam. 2.5), on the other hand it contains
expressions and sentences that can hardly be fitted into the hitherto prevalent framework of the themes of childlessness and motherhood, such as the
power of God to elevate the humble one to a royal status (vv. 7-8), his

---

2.   The exact term used is 'she prayed' (*wattitpallel*; 2.1).

protection for those who rely on him (v. 9) and the punishment for his enemies (vv. 9-10), culminating, at the end of the song, with an explicit reference to the anointed king (v. 10), who at that moment in the history of the people of Israel has not yet appeared on the stage.[3]

After Hannah's song the story seems to return to matters of limited interest, even though we understand that the transgressions said to have been committed by Eli's sons bode evil for the future: Hophni and Phinehas are said to have taken from the offerings near the tabernacle at will, not merely the part that by right belonged to them, thus showing their contempt for regular sacrifice service (2.12-17).[4] After that we see a short reappearance of Hannah and her husband, who bring the little Samuel a coat every year, and are blessed by Eli, after which Hannah bears five more children (2.19-21); we also see Eli admonishing his sons, apparently with very limited success (2.22-25). Following this a 'man of God' appears, who confronts Eli with the grave consequences of his sons' acts and of the fact that he has not been able to keep them from committing them: the priesthood will be taken away from his family, and his descendants will beg those who will take their place to be allowed to perform small services for some bread (2.27-36). After that, again something unusual happens, at least something unexpected within the ordinary framework of these biblical stories: one night God himself calls the young Samuel and tells him the verdict of the house of Eli. Because of the behaviour of Eli's sons and his inability to restrain them, Eli's house will be severely punished, according to the things that have been announced; this probably refers back to the words of the 'man of God' in ch. 2 (3.1-14).

Looking at the entire range of stories in the books of Samuel and the first two chapters of 1 Kings, that is to say the episodes dealing with the activities of Samuel, Saul and David, which are of such vital importance for the history of the people of Israel, one sees a small number of constant factors, themes that keep recurring throughout these stories, and whose significance clearly transcends their importance within the individual stories. The first one is, not unexpectedly, the early history of kingship in Israel: Samuel makes at first Saul and, after his rejection by God, David king of the people of Israel. The function of this, which transcends the

3.   On the function of this chapter within the books of Samuel see especially W. Brueggemann, 'I Samuel 1: A Sense of a Beginning', *ZAW* 102 (1990), pp. 33-48.

4.   Another sin of the men is mentioned only in 2.22, where Eli hears of his sons' licentiousness with the women who visited the tabernacle.

story itself, is evidently to make it clear to the reader how this kingship came into the possession of David and his descendants in a legitimate manner. The second subject that keeps returning is the story of how the priesthood was taken away from Aaron's direct descendant Eli and his offspring, and was given to Zadok son of Ahitub, who had been a relative outsider before, even if apparently also a descendant of Aaron; this theme is explicitly mentioned at the end of this cycle of stories, when King Solomon chases Eli's descendant Abiathar away as high priest (1 Kgs 2.27) and instates Zadok instead (v. 35). This story also has wider significance: according to this story Zadok's line is to be regarded as the legitimate family of high priests in Israel.[5]

A remarkable trait of these stories is that their contents are in many instances supported and reinforced by their formal structure: the narrator's priorities and the state of mind that he wants to inspire in his reader have often been expressed in his story through formal literary means. This observation, by itself easily made but rarely stated explicitly, has two important consequences. First, our options in determining the purpose for which a story has been written are strongly curtailed and steered in a certain direction. Leaving aside the possibility that certain stories used to circulate independently before being incorporated into the cycle that they are in now, we have in my opinion no choice but to accept that the formal structure of the so-called Succession History (2 Sam. 9–1 Kgs 2), to mention only one striking example, strongly confirms the traditional view that David's sin against Uriah and Bathsheba takes a central position in these chapters, as expressed in the remark in 1 Kgs 15.5, 'because David did what was right in the eyes of the Lord, and did not turn aside from anything that he commanded him all the days of his life, except in the matter of Uriah the Hittite', so that on the one hand there is little reason to regard that verse as secondary, and on the other hand no discussion of the description of David's rule can be complete unless it takes this idea into account.

I shall attempt to demonstrate that the two main themes of this series of stories, which have been briefly discussed above, are introduced in close connection with each other directly after its beginning, partly through the

5.   For a discussion of these themes and their incorporation in 1 Sam. 1–15, see J.S. Ackerman, 'Who Can Stand before YHWH, This Holy God? A Reading of 1 Samuel 1–15', *Prooftexts* 11 (1991), pp. 1-24. The theme of the first-born child or the first-chosen person being rejected for some reason in favour of another one is of course very popular throughout the Hebrew Bible; for example the cases of Cain, Esau, Reuben and Saul.

formal structure of the chapters where they first come to the fore. In 1 Samuel 2 and 3, after the persons of Samuel and Eli (with his sons Hophni and Phinehas) have been introduced in the first chapter, in the story about Hannah, the rise of Samuel and the decline of the house of Eli are described in parallel and closely related episodes, in a way announcing the exchange between king and priest, which is more or less prominently present in many of these stories. I also want to point out that the presence of this structure shows that these chapters belong together with regard to both their literary nature and their substance, and that for that reason there is little reason to assume that larger portions of the text are secondary insertions.

At first sight the two chapters under discussion look somewhat untidy. Among the various subjects, seemingly only loosely connected, that are dealt with in these chapters, we find Hannah's joy, the crimes of Eli's sons, the blessing received by Hannah and Elkanah, and finally the reproach of Eli for his sons and the announcement of the grave consequences of their sin for the house of Eli, first through a 'man of God' to Eli himself and then through direct divine revelation to Samuel. It is hardly surprising that many commentators wanted to regard these chapters as a more or less random collection of traditions.[6]

An exception has been a short article by Yehudith Ilan, who proposed to recognize a chiastic structure in 2.11-26. In her opinion the statements about Samuel's family in vv. 19-21 are in a central position, and around them are placed references to Samuel (vv. 18 and 21), to Eli's sons (vv. 17 and 22), to their behaviour and their reproach (vv. 13-16 and 23-25), again the sons of Eli (vv. 12 and 25), and finally references to Samuel again (vv. 11 and 26). Apart from a number of minor points (I hesitate about her proposal to divide the passages about the sons of Eli into two neutral references separated by their deeds and their rebuking by Eli) one can only say that it is hardly possible that her results are accidental. An important objection against Ilan's proposals, however, is that she does not make it clear why exactly Samuel's family should be in the middle of the structure and with that in the middle of the attention, for it cannot be easily seen why this should rank as more important than the other matters touched upon in this chapter. I am also inclined—but this does not by itself invalidate what Ilan wrote about the structure of the episode—to think that she is somewhat hasty in proposing on the basis of her structural observations that the story about the 'man of God' was added secondarily, because it

---

6.   See the literature mentioned in McCarter, *I Samuel*, p. 67-101 *passim*.

would not fit within the original structure.[7] For these reasons, in spite of the likeliness of her observations about the parallel nature of certain passages, I remain skeptical about the conclusions that she draws from them.

It would seem to be necessary to look once more very carefully to see whether there are elements that can lead us to an encompassing thought behind the structure of the episode under discussion here. Such an element is found surprisingly easily: between the longer episodes of these two chapters we find a number of relatively short sentences relating the growing up of young Samuel. They often repeat the same expressions, apparently in order to connect them together and thus to structure the section they are in. Three of them (2.11, 18; 3.1) contain statements that 'the boy' (Samuel) serves (*šrt*) God; three others (2.21, 26; 3.9) describe his growing (*gdl*) while he is 'with' God, or while God is 'with him'; in all six we find the four-letter name of God YHWH to the exclusion of any other indication. It may be useful to present these six sentences together here, in Hebrew and in English translation:[8]

(2.11)   *wᵉhanna'ar hāyā mᵉšāret 'et YHWH 'et pᵉne 'elī hakkohen*
         And the boy ministered to the Lord, in the presence of Eli the priest.
(2.18)   *ušᵉmu'el mᵉšāret 'et pᵉne YHWH na'ar ḥāgur 'epod bad*
         Samuel was ministering before the Lord, a boy girded with a linen ephod.
(2.21)   *wayyigdal hanna'ar šᵉmu'el 'im YHWH*
         And the boy Samuel grew in the presence of the Lord.
(2.26)   *hanna'ar šᵉmu'el hālak wᵉgādal waṭob gam 'im YHWH wᵉgam 'im ᵃnāšīm*
         Now the boy Samuel continued to grow both in stature and in favour with the Lord and with men.
(3.1)   *wᵉhanna'ar šᵉmu'el mᵉšāret 'et YHWH lipne 'elī*
         Now the boy Samuel was ministering to the Lord under Eli.
(3.19)   *wayyigdal šᵉmu'el waYHWH hāyā 'immo wᵉlo hippīl mikkol dᵉbārāw 'arṣā*
         And Samuel grew, and the Lord was with him and let none of his words fall to the ground.

If we look at the six parts into which these chapters are divided through these six sentences, we see that three of them mainly deal with Eli and his

---

    7. Yehudith Ilan, 'The Literary Structure of 1 Samuel 2.11-26', *Beth Mikra* 31 (1985–86), pp. 268-70 [Hebrew].
    8. The place of these sentences within the structure of 1 Sam. 2 and 3 has also been studied, though from a different angle, by Michael Fishbane, 'I Samuel 3: Historical Narrative and Narrative Poetics', in K.R.R. Gros Louis (ed.), *Literary Interpretations of Biblical Narratives*, II (Nashville: Abingdon Press, 1982), pp. 191-203.

house (2.12-17, 22-25, 2.27-36) and that the other three have the family of
Samuel and his rise as their subject (2.1-10, 19-21; 3.2-18); in this way
these chapters can easily be divided into two distinct groups, though there
are clear connections between the two. The two main themes of the books
of Samuel are thus found one beside the other in these chapters. The
connection of Eli with the priesthood will need no further comment; the
fact that the function of Samuel is in particular that of precursor of the
monarchy, if it needs any proof at all, is confirmed by the way in which
the transfer of authority from Samuel to Saul in 1 Samuel 12 is described.
If we look more closely, we see that throughout 1 Samuel 2 and 3 one
aspect of the theme of royalty has been placed beside a corresponding
aspect of the theme of priesthood, so that we have three pairs of the
treatment of those aspects. The order of the main themes is briefly told:
Samuel–Eli–Samuel–Eli–Eli–Samuel; of the three different aspects: behaviour of persons (Hannah and Elkanah on the one hand, Eli's sons on the
other)—Eli's reaction to this behaviour—the consequences of Eli's reaction for his own family. With this in mind, we can make a table of these
two chapters, in which corresponding passages can easily be seen (Table
4.1).

Table 4.1 *Main Themes in 1 Samuel 2 and 3.*

Hannah (Elkanah vs. 11)	2.1-10	
n'r + šrt	11	
		Behaviour
Sons of Eli	12-17	
n'r + šrt	18	
Hannah (and Elkanah)	19-21	
n'r + gdl	21	
		Reactions of Eli to behaviour
Sons of Eli	22-25	
n'r + gdl	26	
Man of God	27-36	
n'r + šrt	3.1	
		Consequences for Eli's house
God to Samuel in dream	2-18	
[*n'r*] + *gdl*	19 (and 3.19–4.1)	

Now that we have recognized this structure it is certainly useful to take
a closer look at the sentences referring to the young Samuel. It becomes
apparent that small changes in formulation have the function of letting

them connect smoothly with the passages before and after them, which often do not refer to Samuel themselves. In nearly all the instances such a connection is evident, and I shall only mention a few very striking cases. Thus we see in 2.11 on the one hand the opposition between Elkanah returning home and Samuel, who remains in Shiloh, and on the other hand through the mention of Eli a transition to the episode of his sons' sins. In 2.18 the repetition of the words *'et p^{e}ne YHWH*, 'before the Lord', of the preceding verse indicates the contrast between the godless behaviour of Eli's sons and Samuel's piety, while the mention of his clothes anticipates the coat that his mother brings to him every year in Shiloh. In 2.21 Samuel's growing *'im YHWH*, 'with the Lord' (RSV with a free translation: 'in the presence of the Lord') has the function of a contrast with the growing up at home of his brothers and sisters (2.21), in 2.26 of a contrast with the sons of Eli, who are definitely not 'with the Lord and with men' (*'im YHWH w^{e}gam 'im ^{,a}nāšīm*), while the formulation also prefigures the connection 'man of God' directly after it, because the plural of the word *'iš*, 'man', is used beside the Tetragram.

It now appears quite clearly, by the way, why the observations of Yehudith Ilan in her article are so accurate: she identified a clearly recognizable structure in the verses 2.11-26, which we now perceive to be part of the pattern I have discerned throughout ch. 2 and 3.

The observation that both narrative lines, the one of Eli and the one of Samuel, anticipate what is to happen later on in the books of Samuel, is confirmed by the fact that in both the Anointed of God is mentioned once; this Anointed can hardly be anyone but the king of Israel, a function that at the time of the action described was as yet non-existent! These references have symmetrical places within the structure of these chapters: the first one is in 2.10, at the end of the Song of Hannah, in the first Samuel episode of these chapters; the second one in 3.35, near the end of the last Eli episode. It should also be noted that the narrative lines of the main themes are connected through the place where everything happens, namely the sanctuary in Shiloh, and the person of the priest Eli, who plays a more or less prominent role in all six of the episodes. In view of this last observation it is hardly surprising that at the end of the entire cycle of stories, in 1 Kings 2, when David's house has indeed been continued through the succession of his son Solomon, there is an explicit reference to the rejection of the house of Eli in Solomon's banishing of Eli's descendant Abiathar from Jerusalem and the high priesthood.

Thus we see that an implicit and in a way almost hidden introduction was given to the cycle of stories in the books of Samuel, which is probably to be explained from the above-mentioned practical problems connected with the way in which the author of Primary History perceived his task. As we have seen, in all the books of Primary History the person of the author is completely absent from the work that he composed, though his ordering hand can be recognized in nearly every passage. Such a narrator encounters tremendous problems if he wants to announce or briefly review his work or a larger part of it. Unlike the great Greek historians, he is unable to start with telling who he is and what important theme underlies his work. We also noted that if he still wants to make some sort of announcement and to draw attention to the importance of what is going to be told in his work or in a major section of it, he has no choice but to work such an announcement into the story itself by incorporating it into his text, for which poetical and prophetical sections lend themselves especially well. This is exactly what our narrator did here: throughout the story about the growing up of Samuel in the sanctuary of Shiloh he has woven the strands of the introduction to his entire work, or at least of the part that stretches until the end of 1 Kings 2. Some parts of this introduction also have a clear function within the story itself; others, especially in the Song of Hannah, gain unambiguous significance for the reader only as the stories in the books of Samuel unfold.

As a conclusion we can say that in 1 Samuel 2 and 3 the narrator of the books of Samuel (and probably of the entire Primary History), after having captured the reader's attention with the intriguing and moving story of the childless Hannah in 1 Samuel 1, briefly indicates the programme and range of his work: what this work is about is the way in which the royal house of the Israelites, in the person of David and his descendants, came into being, and he makes it clear that this development does not rest on human power, but solely on the divine will. Beside this he announces a second narrative line about the way in which the high priesthood came into the hands of Zadok and his descendants. The preliminary end of these developments appears to be indicated, as far as its literary aspect is concerned, by David's resumption of the themes of Hannah's song in 2 Samuel 22–23,[9] and as far as the substance is concerned through David's succession as king by his legitimate heir Solomon, of whom it is said that 'the Lord loved him' (2 Sam. 12.24), who carries out the verdict against the house of Eli, as the narrator explicitly tells us (1 Kgs 2.26-27).

The key function of the chapters 1 Samuel 2–3 is formally indicated because both great themes of the books of Samuel, of the worldly power

9. See Brueggemann, 'I Samuel 1'.

of Samuel, Saul and David on one side, and of the high priesthood on the other, have been juxtaposed as pairs in three corresponding parts of their structure, and because both contain a reference to the anointed king, in a poetical section in one and in a prophetic statement in the other. The six-fold repetition with functional variations of one sentence serves to separate these six parts, and thus to structure these chapters formally. Through these remarkable literary means the author overcame the problems facing him when he wanted to introduce a major section of his work, and succeeded in giving an impressive introduction and a programme for this essential part of Primary History.

2. *God, Man and Fellow-Man*

One of the characteristics of the biblical literature that has always fascinated scholars and lay readers alike is its mixture of various literary genres. The main action is usually described in simple narrative prose, but interspersed we find poetry, legal and ritual texts, prescriptions for religious service in the Temple and elsewhere, and lists of various kinds, usually genealogies or administrative texts. This is hardly a unique trait of the Hebrew Bible, as various authors in the Greek and Latin cultural sphere do the same, and Herodotus's work constitutes once again one of the closest parallels. Still, the author of Primary History experienced some problems not encountered by authors of comparable works, as he did not have the opportunity to embed all of these genres in the continuous narrative. True, the poetry and the prescriptive texts could usually be introduced in the appropriate places of the Bible text, but this goes for only part of the administrative texts. It should perhaps be stressed that the term 'administrative text' applies to its formal appearance only; whether such texts ever functioned within an administrative system is far from certain, in most cases even rather unlikely. This problem was discussed above in a fairly general way, and here I shall attempt to study one of these cases in depth; another one is to be discussed in section 4 of this chapter.

A second point to which I shall give attention in this chapter in some detail is the lack of the narrator's explicitly pronounced personal opinion and of the persona of the narrator as recipient of varying and conflicting pieces of information about the reason or motivation for certain actions, as treated in general terms above. We will see that certain features of these stories can be explained as resulting from a desire to remedy this situation by providing information through various manners, each with a different degree of reliability, which often cannot be gauged with complete certainty, so that it becomes possible to let them come into conflict. This achieves the apparently desired result of conveying in an indirect and implicit way the uncertainty that could not be imparted directly on the reader.

There are few biblical passages that have elicited a larger number of literary reflections than the series of stories around King David in the books of Samuel and the beginning of 1 Kings. One of the most striking properties of this large literature is the fact, obvious even to the reader who has absorbed only a small part of it, that there are relatively few elements in these stories about which the authors agree even in outline. In particular the accounts of the reasons why the main characters are supposed to perform certain acts vary greatly from one work to another. This can hardly be attributed only to their own preferences, but is to be ascribed largely to their use of the liberty left them by the original texts, which provide us with very limited information about these motives. Only rarely we are told anything about the inner life of the main characters. If their thoughts or emotions come to external expression in their words or deeds we may be informed about them, but even then this is not always the case. It may be added that there are not a few instances where it would appear that the text gives ample opportunity to suspect other motives than those given by the characters of the story, and that one even gets the impression that this may have been done intentionally.

Among scholars dealing with the same material there is, perhaps not surprisingly, not less disagreement about vital subjects such as the character of King David, and closely intertwined with this the intention of the stories about him in the books of Samuel. In the view of some researchers he is an ambitious and ruthless person, who comes to power and stays there by killing all potential opponents, while cynically invoking all kinds of excuses for the crimes perpetrated by himself or by his subordinates, usually that it all happened while he was unaware of it. In the opinion of others he is the God-given sovereign who commits hardly any untoward acts during his entire career. Between these extremes there is an entire spectrum of varying views about the matter, but it needs to be said that there are surprisingly numerous indications for the two extremes in the stories themselves. On the one hand the innocence and virtuousness of David are continually confirmed by explicit statements in the text of the Bible; on the other hand it is pointed out so clearly that David derives great advantage from all sort of crimes that it would almost seem that the text that nominally praises him stains his reputation by associating him very directly with various crimes. Most students have dealt with this exe-getical dilemma by combining arguments for both views and arriving at a mixed evaluation of King David and his character, according to their scholarly view and personal preferences. The overall result, however, can never be very satisfactory, because it would seem possible that on the basis of exactly the same texts greatly varying views can be defended.

While the problem of the motives of King David, the main character of most of these episodes, is most pressing, the same problem certainly exists for the other persons in the stories, and for them there is also a wide variety of opinions as to why they act as they do.

In general it can be observed that if there is so much difference of opinion among serious researchers, it seems rather likely that the problem is in for-mulating the question, rather than in finding an answer straight away. In this case it would seem that the question should not be something like: 'What is the best explanation for David's behaviour?' (or for the behaviour of any other person figuring in these stories), or, connected with this, 'What is the real reason for writing down various episodes of the history of David?', but rather: 'How is it possible that there can be so much difference of opinion about each and every one of these issues?' Unless, which seems quite unlikely, many scholars understand the texts completely wrongly, the back-ground of this variety of opinions has to be in the nature of these texts.

In order to attempt to discern some general patterns in the motives that we can assume behind human acts in these stories, I shall discuss four cases, all well known and treated very often in the secondary literature. I shall first make an inventory of the expression of various motives within the stories; afterwards I shall attempt to treat these motives systematically. We will see that not a few of these motives have apparently been hidden in the text of the Bible; I shall dwell at some length on the phenomenon of hidden information and shall consider the possible consequences for the tradition of the biblical texts. Finally I shall briefly discuss the reason why the stories around David are formulated the way they are.

Joab's Death

The violent death of David's army-commander Joab, desired by David himself in the 'testament' that he addresses to his son Solomon in 1 Kgs 2.5-7, and brought about by Solomon in 1 Kgs 2.28-34, I have discussed at some length elsewhere, and it will therefore receive only some brief remarks here.[10] David and Solomon appear to agree wholeheartedly about

---

10. Wesselius, 'Joab's Death'.

the reason why Joab must die: he treacherously killed two rival command-
ers, namely Abner (2 Sam. 3.27) and Amasa (2 Sam. 20.8-10). Although
this accusation appears to be well founded and Joab's guilt established
beyond any reasonable doubt, many readers will automatically think that
these acts are very far in the past when David and Solomon speak about
them at the beginning of 1 Kings, and that, moreover, David himself has
left them unpunished ever since. It is not at once clear why there should be
a punishment for Joab exactly at this time, and it takes little effort to
suspect secondary motives for both monarchs on this issue; it should be
said that the story itself provides considerable assistance for this.

In the passage under discussion David and Solomon both discuss the
fate of three persons,[11] and it is hardly accidental that for both of them
these three can be connected with an important episode in their lives. In
the case of David we find Joab, Barzillai and Shimei, who played parts in
the revolt of Absalom. With Solomon we find Adonijah, Abiathar and Joab
again; all three were involved in the attempt of Solomon's half-brother
Adonijah to claim the throne in 1 Kings 1. Through this structural feature
certain other motives of both are presented to us, which could have been
imagined readily in any case: David wanted to kill the man who did his
son Absalom to death against his express wishes, Solomon wanted to
eliminate a dangerous adversary.

Even this intellectually plausible reason for Joab's death leaves the
reader in a way unsatisfied, because no clear moral grounds have been
given for his violent death. It would seem, however, that such a morally
satisfactory reason can be found in the only instance in these stories where
Joab causes an evidently innocent person to be killed. In 2 Samuel 12
Uriah the Hittite's wife Bathsheba is impregnated by David while Uriah
himself is out at the siege of Rabbat Ammon, after David saw her take a
bath after her period from the roof of his palace. David fears the consequences of her pregnancy and tries to make her husband sleep with her in
order to cover it up. Whether through Uriah's moral scruples or through
his suspiciousness, the scheme does not succeed, and David sends Uriah
back to Joab with a letter in which he is asked to settle the affair by assign-
ing Uriah to a very dangerous place in battle. Thus it happens, Uriah is
killed and David takes Bathsheba into his palace.[12] Once a small amount

---

11. See my 'Joab's Death', especially p. 342, for the reasons to see the decision
about Shimei and the subsequent events in 1 Kgs 2.36-46 as separate from the preceding three verdicts pronounced by Solomon.

12. An episode that received a masterly treatment at the hands of Meir Sternberg in

of fantasy has led us to this connection between Joab's guilt and punishment, it becomes apparent that there are clear references to this motive
within the biblical text itself, especially in its literary structure. First, the
story of the succession to David's throne in 1 Kings 1 and 2 is the first in
which Bathsheba figures again after the subsequent episodes of Uriah, of
the birth of her first child and of the birth of Solomon; secondly, the so-
called Succession History of David (2 Sam. 9–1 Kgs 2) exhibits a con-
centric structure, in which the passage containing the death of Joab
corresponds with the story of Uriah's death.[13]

Summarizing, we can say that there are motives for Joab's violent death
on three different levels: first, there is the public reason why he deserved
this verdict, secondly the personal motives behind it, and finally, on the
deepest level, real justice is done and the divine plan is executed. We shall
see that this pattern is not exclusive to this case, but that for most actions
in the stories around King David such a threefold motivation can be discerned, which is indicated every time by means of various formal literary
patterns.

Ahithophel's Counsel
In 2 Samuel 16 David has fled from Jerusalem after the revolt of his son
Absalom, but has left ten of his concubines in order to take care of his
affairs in the city while he is absent. David's counsellor Ahithophel from
the town of Giloh, who has gone over to Absalom's side, advises Absalom
in 2 Sam. 16.21 to have a tent set up on the roof of the palace and to have
sexual intercourse with his father's concubines there. Ahithophel gives a
reasonable motivation for his counsel: 'and all Israel will hear that you
have made yourself odious to your father, and the hands of all who are
with you will be strengthened'.

Of course the reason that Ahithophel adduces in front of Absalom is
reasonable and adequate to the situation: by taking possession of his
father's harem Absalom on the one hand makes it clear that the rift
between him and his father will certainly not be bridged, and on the other
hand he announces plainly that he is the one who sits on the royal throne
and has assumed the royal prerogatives; in this way all those who have

his study *The Poetics of Biblical Narrative: Ideological Literature and the Drama of
Reading* (Bloomington: Indiana University Press, 1985), pp. 199-213 (an earlier version of the chapter dealing with the story of David and Bathsheba appeared in *Hasifrut*
1 [1968], pp. 263-92 [Sternberg with Menakhem Perry]).
    13. Wesselius, 'Joab's Death', pp. 344-45; see also below.

even the slightest sympathy for Absalom are forced to side actively with him. It needs to be said, however, that one would expect that at this moment, which is evidently regarded as critical for the success of the revolt, even more by Ahithophel than by the others who are present, as would seem apparent from his urging to action in 2 Sam. 17.1-3, he would have other priorities more closely related to the power struggle going on. It would indeed seem that his advice was not entirely unprejudiced.

Behind the evident reasons for Ahithophel's counsel a much more personal motive lurks, which is not directly visible to the superficial reader, but which, once noted, makes clear a great deal about certain aspects of the Succession History. By a combination of the first reference to Bathsheba in 2 Sam. 11.3 ('that is Bathsheba, the daughter of Eliam, the wife of the Hittite Uriah') and the designation of one of David's valiant men in a list of those heroes in 2 Sam. 23.34 ('Eliam, the son of the Gilonite Ahithophel') it becomes very likely that Ahithophel is represented as Bathsheba's grandfather.[14] Realizing this, we understand his adherence to Absalom's party much better: it is apparently suggested to the perceptive reader that he ineffectively tendered his grudge against David about the way in which he treated his granddaughter, and in this situation suddenly perceives an opportunity to take his revenge on the king. It would seem that the David of our story has the same view of Ahithophel's change of allegiance, as appears from his reaction to the news of Ahithophel's defection in 2 Sam. 15.31. David then addresses a prayer to God, but surprisingly does not ask him for salvation or for Absalom's defeat, but only for annulling Ahithophel's counsel. In our story, for David it is apparently completely clear that Ahithophel's enmity proceeds from David's own crime against Uriah and Bathsheba, according to the note in 1 Kgs 15.5 the only real crime that David has ever committed. And the point is even made clearer than that: the only instance in the entire Succession History in which it is said of God that he directly intervenes in human affairs is when he annuls the effect of Ahithophel's counsel (2 Sam. 17.14: '...the Lord had ordained to defeat the good counsel of Ahithophel, so that the Lord might bring evil upon Absalom'), through which God fulfils the promise made by way of the prophet Nathan in 2 Sam. 12.13, in which he revoked the verdict of death for David himself.

It could correctly be remarked that it is highly surprising that such a very personal motive for Ahithophel's actions would have been deeply

---

14. Wesselius, 'Joab's Death', pp. 346 and 349-50, and the literature quoted there.

hidden, waiting for an exceptionally perceptive reader, while on the other hand the reader's moral feelings would hardly be satisfied by the fact that this deed would be done to David only because of the hurt feelings of someone else. In the last resort, however, the course of action suggested by Ahithophel is part of David's punishment for taking away Bathsheba and killing her husband, which was announced by God to David through the prophet Nathan. He had already clearly announced David's punishment in 2 Sam. 12.11-12: 'Behold, I will raise up evil against you out of your own house; and I will take your wives before your eyes, and give them to your neighbour, and he shall lie with your wives in the sight of this sun.[12] For you did it secretly; but I will do this thing before all Israel, and before the sun.' This statement naturally arouses the perceptive reader's curiosity, so that when told about Ahithophel's counsel he or she knows that with this the divine punishment is indeed executed.

Apparently in order to point out the motives, both personal and divine, for the behaviour of Ahithophel to the attentive reader, one very special detail has been ingeniously inserted into the narrative: the tent in which Absalom is to come together with David's wives is on the advice of Ahithophel set up on the roof of the royal palace. This advice is functional within the framework of Absalom's purposes, as Ahitophel hastens to point out to him, because it will make it publicly known that there can be no more reconciliation between father and son, as the son has assumed all the father's prerogatives. That there is a hidden agenda on both the personal and the divine level appears only from the fact—known to the readers but probably not to most personages of the story—that this is the very place from which David saw Bathsheba for the first time (in 2 Sam. 12.2), and decided not to worry about the fact that she was already married![15]

The Death of the Amalekite
The third case to be treated here will also be discussed only briefly, with only those aspects being treated that are of importance for our survey here. In 2 Samuel 1 David is told about the death of his predecessor Saul by an young Amalekite man. David is at a disadvantage compared to the readers of the story, as he is unaware that the Amalekite's story is at best only partially true, whereas the readers have been informed about the exact circumstances of King Saul's death in the preceding chapter, 1 Samuel 31.

15. On this last detail see, for example, Fokkelman, *King David*, p. 210.

Saul asked his armour-bearer to kill him when the situation in his fight with the Philistines seemed thoroughly hopeless, and when the man steadfastly refused to kill the 'Anointed of the Lord', Saul had thrust himself onto his own sword; his armour-bearer then followed his example. The Amalekite, however, appears to project himself in the position of Saul's armour-bearer, with the essential difference that in his story he does not refuse Saul's request, kills him and returns from the battle alive in order to inform David.

It is almost certain that of these two stories about the death of Saul the first one is the correct one, as it is told by the narrator himself, and the second one a fabrication of the Amalekite, as convincingly demonstrated by Fokkelman.[16] He correctly noted that the Amalekite's real actions can only be reconstructed from a comparison of the two stories. Something that he did not comment upon, but which is very important in my opinion, is that these two accounts themselves invite such a comparison through the parallelism of the description of the situation at Saul's death: in 1 Sam. 31.4 Saul's sword is specifically mentioned as his weapon, in 2 Sam. 1.6 his spear figures instead; in 1 Sam. 31.3 Saul is threatened by archers, whereas in 2 Sam. 1.6 the Amalekite speaks about chariots and horsemen. Note also the use of the verb *dābaq* in 1 Sam. 31.2 (qal *wayyidbᵉqu*, 'and [the Philistines] overtook') and in 2 Sam. 1.6 (hiphil *hidbīquhu*, '[the chariots and the horsemen] were close upon him'). Of course both Saul and the Philistines would have possessed a variety of weapons, but here their mention clearly has the function of linking these passages.

After David has listened to the Amalekite's story he may be supposed to be in a very difficult situation, whether or not he actually believes the details of his report: on the one hand he realizes that the kingship of Israel is offered him for free, so to say, by the Amalekite's action; on the other hand he cannot let this deed go unpunished, both for moral and for practical reasons, whereas the Amalekite, not being an Israelite, has properly speaking not committed a crime by killing Saul at his own request. David's next question, however, elicits a response that offers him a way out. When the man answers that he is the son of an Amalekite foreigner (*ger*) living with the Israelites, David pronounces the verdict of death upon the man, who, in his function of resident foreigner, would have to respect the religious taboo on killing the Anointed of the Lord just like the Israelites themselves. On the surface everything is legal and correct now,

16. See Fokkelman, 'A Lie, Born of Truth'.

but the secondary motives of David, readily to be suspected already, are stressed once more further on, because he mentions this case again in the context of the murder of Saul's son Ishbosheth by two of his servants (2 Sam. 4.9-11), from which the reader can easily conclude that David saw the Amalekite's case as a danger to his reputation and legitimacy. Finally, however, it becomes clear to the reader that the Amalekite did not die through a juridical artifice or because of David's hidden ambitions, but because he mercilessly roamed over the battlefield in search of booty, as appears from a comparison of his story with what has been told us by the narrator himself in the preceding chapter. The fact that in this respect he is a 'real Amalekite', as they are described in Exod. 17.8-16 and Deut. 25.17-19, has received additional stress by the agreement in the description of Amalek's behaviour in Deut. 25.18 and the unnamed Amalekite's account of his own actions in 2 Samuel 1: both approach their victim treacherously 'from behind' (*'aḥar*: 2 Sam. 1.7), after first 'having met' (*qārā*: 2 Sam. 1.6) him, and do not 'fear' (*yāre*: the attitude of Saul's armour-bearer in 1 Sam. 31.4, in contrast with the Amalekite's lack of scruples in 2 Sam. 1.10) God or his Anointed One.[17]

Ziba and Mephibosheth

Above we noticed that in the case of Joab's death, behind more or less identical public motives various personal motives may be hidden, while on the divine level the motivation is one and the same again. There is also a case in which the personal motives of two people are mutually exclusive. In order to compensate for this, they ascribe different personal motives to each other in the presence of David, and interestingly David does not choose between these personal motives, but appears to attach equal value (or lack of it) to both.

When David has to flee because Absalom marches on Jerusalem, Ziba, who had been appointed by David in 2 Sam. 9.9-11 to serve the disabled

---

17. The words uttered by the Amalekite in this episode have always caused surprise among commentators (e.g. McCarter, *II Samuel*, pp. 56-64 *passim*), but are completely unproblematic once one realizes that they link this passage with Deut. 25.17-19. On Amalek in biblical and later literature see for example J. Maier, 'Amalek in the Writings of Josephus', in F. Parente and J. Silvers (eds.), *Josephus and the History of the Greco-Roman Period: Essays in Memory of Morton Smith* (Leiden: E.J. Brill, 1994), pp. 109-26, and the literature listed there, to which can be added A. Schuil, *Amalek: Onderzoek naar oorsprong en ontwikkeling van Amaleks rol in het Oude Testament* (Zoetermeer: Boekencentrum, 1997).

Mephibosheth, Jonathan's son and Saul's grandson, and to care for him, meets David with provisions. Being asked why Mephibosheth was not with him, Ziba answers that he had stayed at home in the hope of seeing the kingship returned to his family as a result of the present events (2 Sam. 16.1-4). David on the spot gives all Mephibosheth's possessions to Ziba. When David returns, however, Mephibosheth comes out to meet him, stating that Ziba deceived and unjustly denounced him, implying that at least one of the asses on which Ziba brought the provisions was meant for him to ride on in order to join the king in his flight, because he could not walk as a result of his handicap (2 Sam. 19.24-30). He has lent particular credence to his story by abstaining from washing and shaving from the day David left Jerusalem. Finally, somewhat to our surprise, David does not choose between the two accounts, but orders that Ziba and Mephibosheth are to divide the possessions between them.

Evidently, the public declarations made by the two about their own and the other's behaviour and its explanation, that is to say their personal motives, are mutually exclusive. As usual, for both certain points of attachment can be found in the text, without a clear preference of the narrator for one or the other emerging. It should be noted that, whatever the precise motives of these two people may have been, the result has been that Ziba appeared with his asses with provisions at the moment when David was in a desperate situation, fleeing in haste from Jerusalem, thus allowing him to reach a safe place from where he could rally his own forces. Ziba can in fact be said to have contributed considerably both to saving King David's life and to preserving the kingship for him and his house.

That is not yet the end, however, of our survey of human motives for actions which finally seem to fit in the divine plan with the appearance of Ziba in 2 Sam. 16.1-4. David himself has been involved in the series of causes for this encounter, and there are certain different reasons to be discerned for his decision with regard to Mephibosheth in 2 Samuel 9. First, David himself indicates that he wants to show his loyalty to his beloved friend Jonathan's son by letting him sit at the royal table in Jerusalem. There is no reason to doubt this motive itself, but it has often been noted that by treating Mephibosheth well in Jerusalem, David would pre-empt attempts to concentrate forces loyal to Saul around Mephibosheth or other members of his family. The final reason within the series of stories appears only during Absalom's revolt: had David not taken the decision of 2 Samuel 9, there would have been no reason that, right after David's prayer for the annulment of Ahithophel's counsel and the appearance of Hushai the Archite, who was to effect this, Ziba would appear with the provisions that enabled David to flee without any delay from the victorious Absalom. It is hardly accidental that these two encounters take place on both sides of the place 'where David used to bow down for God' (2 Sam. 15.32 and 16.1). We are indeed dealing with a threefold motivation on the personal and public levels, which turns out to fit seamlessly within only one divine plan.

Motives on Three Levels
In Table 4.2 I put the result of our survey in a systematic form. It is interesting to see how, by means of various literary devices, a threefold motivation has apparently been incorporated into all the passages discussed above.[18]

Table 4.2 *Threefold motivation in the stories of David.*

	Public	*Personal*	*Divine*
Joab	text (2×)	structure of context (2×)	structure of Succession History
Ahithophel	text	genealogy (list)	prophecy of Nathan
Amalekite	text	association with other case	comparison with preceding chapter; implicit reference to Deut. 25
Ziba, Mephibosheth	text	Mephibosheth in Jerusalem	Ziba with provisions near holy place

Once we have established that it was apparently deemed important to achieve this threefold motivation, we are faced by the questions why this was considered important on the one hand, and why this evidently desired structure was tucked away so deeply that few have been able to recognize it on the other. It would seem that the only reasonable answer is that the author, by means of this procedure, attempted to render human experience of reality in an adequate manner. In the reality outside public literature the motives acknowledged by people themselves, usually reasonably understandable and coherent, are readily available. It is more difficult with personal motives, which may not be pronounced openly: they are only revealed indirectly. Least visible of all is how the perplexing reality around us fits within God's plans and intentions (for those who do not

18. In the last case I only presented David's point of view; the same observations about the triple motivations are valid for Ziba and Mephibosheth.

reject such a notion): this can only be observed from long experience, or because certain people are consciously or unconsciously involved in the realisation of these plans. One of the particular characteristics of biblical Hebrew prose is that certain vicissitudes of human sensory and emotional experience are mirrored in the texts. In this case this means that the hidden nature of certain things in reality, apart from certain intimations, is reflected in the texts: with the hidden indications in the texts both what is hidden and the fact that it is hidden are imparted to the perceptive reader.

It is interesting in this connection that the divine reasons for human acts are more or less deeply hidden in three out of the four cases discussed above, whereas in one instance they are revealed to the reader very clearly through the words of the prophet Nathan. Unsurprisingly, the prophet acts here as an intermediary, enabling contact between divine and human spheres in this matter.

Within the framework described here it seems rather likely that personal and public motives are offered to the reader with the intention of letting him or her be undecided and uncertain about them. The reader is not provided with the means to make certain that one or the other is to be chosen, except in the case of King David himself, who is often said by the narrator to have been guiltless and pious, so that his public statements are indeed confirmed. The reason why, if one abstracts from the narrator's assurances to the contrary, the uncertainty about David's motives is maintained all the same is probably that in this way the impression of the described actions on the people around him is rendered very effectively: the readers know that David was the man of God's heart and did not commit crimes, apart from one conspicuous and far-reaching case, whereas for the contemporaries all this must have been somewhat less apparent, at least in the representation of the story.

The phenomenon of the deliberate hiding of information in biblical Hebrew prose texts has never been the subject of a separate investigation, though once one gives attention to the matter it appears to be quite common. It may be maintained that the continuing relevance of rabbinical exegesis for modern biblical research is especially clear for this subject. Not a few of the phenomena described here are only revealed through a very thorough reading of the texts involved, with attention to every detail and the conviction that the text is much richer than it appears on a superficial reading—precisely the strong points of rabbinical interpretation. I hope to return to this elsewhere, but will merely give a brief discussion of two kinds of instance of hidden information.

Studies discussing hidden chronology in biblical texts have been published by, among others, J.P. Fokkelman, who showed that the time of death of King Saul exactly coincides with David's victory over the Amalekites.[19] I wrote myself about the book of Jonah, showing the simultaneity of the acts of Jonah 1 and 2 on the one hand, and Jonah 3 and 4 on the other, for both of which probably an interval of three days is to be assumed.[20]

It seems a reasonable assumption that, especially in Primary History of Genesis–2 Kings, but probably also in other pieces of biblical Hebrew prose, precise chronological information is always intended to make the reader compare what is narrated with another element in the narration, or alternatively to let it fit into a larger chronological framework.

Hidden Information and Lists

We saw that part of the information needed to evaluate the attitude of the counsellor Ahithophel could only be obtained from one of the lists of persons at the end of the book 2 Samuel. This interesting phenomenon merits closer consideration here.

A curious development within recent Hebrew Bible scholarship is that through the advances made by the literary approach to its texts the respect for the text as we now have it has grown significantly, and that many scholars refrain from proposals for changing it, unless they think they have absolutely no alternative. In this roundabout way scholarship appears to return to the situation that prevailed before modern critical movements arose, when it became usual to attempt to reconstruct the prehistory of the text rather than to try to understand it in its present form.

There is one area in which this return has hardly taken place as yet, and I would like to propose that it should. Students of the Hebrew Bible as literature quite naturally tend to concentrate on texts of the type of literature in which they are interested, and to leave alone those elements that appear to disturb their unity. In a way this is a re-emergence, but this time in a more subtle form, of the tendency prevalent in historical-critical studies of relying on the researcher's verdict to regard certain parts of the text as secondary. This led many literary researchers of David's Succession History (2 Sam. 9–1 Kgs 2), to mention only one striking example, to

19. J.P. Fokkelman, 'Structural Reading on the Fracture between Synchrony and Diachrony', *JEOL* 30 (1987–88), pp. 123-36.

20. J.-W. Wesselius, 'The Message of the Book of Jonah' (forthcoming).

disregard the stories, psalms and lists found at the end of 2 Samuel (chs. 21–24) when studying it.[21]

Of course we might find it sufficient to point out that a case such as Ahithophel's makes it abundantly clear that such information provided outside of the regular course of the narrative is at times essential for understanding it, but it may still be useful to ponder on this problem a little longer, particularly in view of D.M. Gunn's interesting observations about the last chapters of 2 Samuel. Gunn supposes that they have been put in the spot where they are now in order to undermine the reader's confidence in the text that he or she has been reading up to that point, and to provide an entirely new view of its contents.[22] He rightly notes that the information provided in these chapters often contradicts what is said earlier on in the history of David, not in the form of casual differences between one traditional text and another, but in close connection with those earlier stories. His observations fit very well in the framework of the view of Primary History set forth above and the function of the so-called 'contradictions' therein.

One of the most important functions of the insertion of lists in the narrative parts of the Hebrew Bible appears to be providing the hidden information discussed above. Lists are usually not simple enumerations that have been accidentally preserved, so to say, from the administrations of, for example, Moses or David, and have not been incorporated in their present context more or less haphazardly or even accidentally, but form an essential part of the stories into which they have been inserted. A careful reading of these lists brings the reader back to the strictly narrative parts and often elucidates their contents.

I shall give only one additional example of the use of lists for providing the reader with 'hidden' information. J.C. Siebert-Hommes has shown the

21. Compare, for example, the subtitle of Fokkelman's book, *Narrative Art and Poetry*: 'II Sam. 9–20 and I Kings 1–2'; see also the purely literary verdict of Sternberg, *The Poetics of Biblical Narrative*, p. 42: 'a sorry stretch of discourse'.

22. D.M. Gunn, 'Reading Right: Reliable and Omniscient Narrator, Omniscient God, and Foolproof Composition in the Hebrew Bible', in: D.J.A. Clines *et al.* (eds.), *The Bible in Three Dimensions: Essays in Celebration of Forty Years of Biblical Studies in the University of Sheffield* (Sheffield: JSOT Press, 1990), pp. 53-64, especially p. 57 n. 1: 'the levelling of the narrator and a summary ironic treatment of David'; see also his remark in his 'New Directions in the Study of Biblical Hebrew Narrative', *JSOT* 39 (1987), pp. 65-75 (p. 71): 'an engineered collapse of reader confidence'; compare also Walter Brueggemann, '2 Samuel 21–24: An Appendix of Deconstruction?', *CBQ* 50 (1988), pp. 383-97.

importance in the story about the birth of Moses in Exodus 2 of the omission of nearly all the names of the persons who play a part in it.[23] One could add to her observation that the fact that even the names of Moses' parents have been intentionally left unmentioned is driven home to the reader by the passage Exod. 6.13-24, where the offspring of the patriarchs Ruben, Simeon and Levi is enumerated, from which it appears that the parents of Moses, Aaron and Miriam are by no means insignificant people: Jochebed, a daughter of Levi himself, and her nephew Amram, a grandson of Levi.[24] Only when we read this we can be sure that the omission of their names in Exodus 2 was not the result of their being unknown, but that the names of these direct descendants of Levi had deliberately been left out of the story in order to stress that Moses' origins had completely shifted to the background.

As a conclusion we can state that, whereas from a purely stylistic and literary point of view it can be defended to leave lists and comparable enumerative passages out of consideration when studying biblical narrative, they are an essential part of the message that is to be conveyed by the text and cannot be missed when studying the text as a whole, unless the sole purpose is a purely formal study of narrative prose. One of the striking characteristics of most biblical texts is the integration of prose, poetry and lists into a coherent pattern, and discussing them separately is consequently useful only to a limited degree.

Literature as a Mirror of Reality

It may be useful to give some further illustration of the idea set forth above, namely that the visible or invisible presence of certain emotions, thoughts or motives within a story is often rendered through literary effects aimed at the reader's personal experience when reading the text, without any additional explicit indications. One additional example must suffice here, this time from the same group of stories around King David.

After David's crime against Uriah and Bathsheba, and the subsequent reproach and announcement of punishment by the prophet Nathan in 2 Samuel 11–12, which first culminates in the death of the first child issuing from the union of David and Bathsheba, there is no more reference to the theme of David's misbehaviour. The mere fact, however, of the recurrence

23. J.C. Siebert-Hommes, 'Twelve Women in Exodus 1 and 2: The Role of Daughters and Sons in the Stories Concerning Moses', *Amsterdamse Cahiers voor Exegese en Bijbelse Theologie* 9 (1988), pp. 47-58.

24. See Chapter 1 on the origin and function of this genealogy.

of David's punishment in the form of the death of his sons and the taking away of his wives throughout the description of the later part of his reign at least suggests that this affair has commanded his attention right to the end of his life. Its not being mentioned there, in contrast with an unexpected reference to it in 1 Kgs 15.5, seems to be a deliberate strategy to indicate that we are dealing with a subject that could not be discussed. The silence about the affair of Uriah, combined with its likely presence in David's head, is expressed in the text through a stylistic device which, though aimed especially at the reader, tells us a lot about the protagonist, King David himself.

In at least three instances the wording of the story clearly makes the readers expect that the matter of Uriah is going to be mentioned, but in every one of these cases the reader is deceived, so to say: the text continues in an unexpected direction. During her conversation with David, the wise woman from Tekoa suddenly addresses him with the words (2 Sam. 14.13): 'Why then have you planned such a thing against the people of God as a guilty one (*k^e'āšem*)' (RSV differently); we, the readers, know that David is indeed guilty, but expect something different from what really follows, where the woman only berates him for not letting Absalom return.[25] When David has to flee from Absalom, he is cursed by Shimei with the words (2 Sam. 15.7): 'Begone, begone, you man of blood, you worthless fellow!'; the reader automatically thinks of the only case in the Succession History where David is said to have sinned greatly, but from the sequel of Shimei's words it turns out that he is merely thinking of the death of Saul's relatives, in which David had no share according to the story. Finally, we are led astray one last time by the beginning of the text about Joab in David's 'testament', which he pronounces to Solomon in 1 Kings 2: 'Now you know what Joab the son of Zeruiah did for me...'. Most modern translations give for Hebrew *'āśā lī* in 1 Kgs 2.5 something like the RSV: '...what Joab the son of Zeruiah did *to* me' (italics mine), but it has often been noted that David's words are at least ambiguous. Once more, our patterns of expectation are shattered through a literary device that reflects the ominous and fearful silence about Uriah's affair very adequately by impressing King David's state of mind on the reader to a surprising degree.

Concealedness and the Care for a Correct Text
It is well known that the main textual tradition of the Hebrew Bible, unlike deviating text types such as those of the Dead Sea Scrolls, of the Samari-

---

25. On this episode see Section 3 below.

tans and those supposedly underlying certain ancient translations, is
unusually reliable and precise. This is usually ascribed to its character as a
sacred text, which was to be transmitted as precisely as possible. While
this explanation by itself is doubtlessly right, it would seem that there may
be a little more to this reliability than mere religious scruples. I shall
engage in a little speculation about another reason why it might have been
considered essential that the text be transmitted completely unchanged.

It has been pointed out by many authors, especially clearly by Meir
Sternberg, that the texts of the Hebrew Bible on the whole do not contain
redundant information.[26] While tendencies towards harmonization and the
possibility of making errors are inextricably bound up with every form of
transmission of texts, such texts will certainly be highly sensitive to the
vicissitudes of manuscript tradition and extra precautions are at least very
useful, if not indispensable. This does not yet, however, by itself enforce
the extreme care that is characteristic of the Jewish tradition of the text of
the Hebrew Bible, because harmonizations and small errors can corrupt
the aesthetics and contents of the text to some degree, but will generally
leave its message more or less undamaged. With the hidden information
that we are discussing here the situation is completely different. Here even
very small changes in seemingly unimportant numbers or seemingly isolated personal names may make retrieval of this information virtually
impossible. For such a text a method of transmission as secure as that
found in the main tradition of the Hebrew Bible is indispensable: it is the
only way to allow the message of the text to survive throughout the centuries largely intact, and it seems rather likely that originally considerations
based on this realization have contributed to the inauguration of methods
for ensuring the purity and reliability of the text of the Hebrew Bible.
Conversely, the fact that this hidden information has been preserved even
in cases where the text clearly invites any conscientious redactor to make a
change that would render it more comprehensible, but would eliminate the
hidden information, indicates that it has hardly been tampered with in a
systematic manner. Some of the contradictions between the last chapters
of 2 Samuel and earlier parts of the books of Samuel virtually cry out to
the reader to be modified, and many modern and ancient translators could
not resist this call.

It can moreover be assumed that texts in which this kind of information
has been preserved are far superior to those from which it has disappeared.

26. Sternberg, *The Poetics of Biblical Narrative*, pp. 365-440 *passim*.

The latter texts cannot be used as an equally valuable source, because they have clearly been subject to the activities of redactors who did not understand the text's original meaning; this does not, of course, exclude the possibility that they preserve superior readings in isolated cases.

One of the consequences of this observation is that in the case of a comparison of the Masoretic text with other textual witnesses, for example the text underlying the Septuagint, the degree to which hidden information has been preserved should be a major criterion for determining their status, attempting to discern in every case whether systematic changes have been effected in this information, or whether all changes are to be attributed to corruption and viewed as arbitrary.[27]

What is the Intention of these Stories?

The most important result of these considerations for the questions about the origin and use of the stories discussed here is in my view the realization that the most important person is the one who is only rarely mentioned explicitly, namely the God of Israel. For this reason it is not very important whether the David described in the Bible indeed has the selfish intentions suggested in these stories. Time and again the text tells its readers through the information found in it, often in a deeply hidden form, that the actions of human beings, whether they like it or not, fit perfectly into God's plans. For this reason it is not particularly useful to characterize these stories as 'pro-Davidic', 'contra-Davidic', 'pro-Solomonic', as a purely literary composition, or whatever one wants to see in them.[28] Here also a return to the traditional view, albeit in a modified form, seems advisable. The story is intended to tell the reader how God's plan for his people Israel and his chosen king David and his descendants was realized in history. This does not, however, make David and the people around him into the true protagonists of the story; equally, the high aesthetic value of the texts and their function as valuable accounts of history, though certainly very important, are completely secondary to their religious intention.

3. *Two Wise Women*

It has long been recognized that the chapters 2 Samuel 9–1 Kings 2 in fact form one long series of stories dealing with the history of the succession of

27. This point of view may also be relevant for complicated situations such as that centring around the Masoretic text and ancient versions of the story of David and Goliath in 1 Sam. 17; see Section 4 below.

28. See the survey in Ackerman, 'Knowing Good and Evil'.

King David. The basic reason for discerning this cycle as a unitary composition, from which the chapters 2 Samuel 21–24 (which contain clearly
different material) are usually excluded, is one of content: beginning with
David's dealings with the person who appears to be the only surviving
grandson of his predecessor Saul, Mephibosheth the son of Jonathan, it
describes his sin against Bathsheba and her husband, Uriah the Hittite, and
the sad and often bloody events in the royal family, which are largely the
result of this evil deed, and which finally lead to Solomon's accession at
the beginning of the book of 1 Kings.[29] Far less attention has been given to
the fact that the literary structure of these chapters appears to delimit the
Succession History in exactly the same way through being composed of
comparable stories in parallel places, with the defeat in battle of Absalom's army against his father's experienced soldiers exactly in the middle.

The Succession History begins and ends with the introduction and the
demise, respectively, of some of the leading characters of the story of
David's flight from Absalom and the battle between their soldiers in the
centre. In 2 Sam. 9.1-13 a certain Ziba and Jonathan's son Mephibosheth
are introduced and forcibly linked together by David; in 2 Sam. 16.1
(before the battle) and 2 Sam. 19.21-30 (after it) their behaviour towards
each other and towards David is described. In 1 Kgs 2.36-46 the end of
Shimei is described, who had scolded and cursed David when he was
fleeing in 2 Sam. 16.5-13, but received mercy on his return in 2 Sam.
19.18-23. It should not pass unnoticed that Shimei, like Mephibosheth,
belonged to Saul's family: the Succession Narrative begins and ends with
a reference to one of Saul's relatives. Leaving these episodes behind us we
come to the story of David and Bathsheba and the prophet Nathan's
announcement of divine retribution in 2 Samuel 11 and 12, which ought to
correspond to another passage involving an intervention by Nathan,
namely the succession of David by Solomon and its aftermath in 1 Kings
1–2.[30] At this point the symmetry seems to be interrupted by the insertion
of a kind of summary of David's reign in 2 Samuel 22–24, with poetical
passages, lists of David's heroes and the story of his census of the
Israelites.[31] The symmetrical structure is clearly resumed with the accounts

29. See the literature mentioned at the begining of this chapter.

30. It can be maintained that these passages can be subdivided still further, the
story of Uriah's murder in 2 Sam. 11, which corresponds to the enthronement of his
wife's son in 1 Kgs 2, being detached from Nathan's interventions in 2 Sam. 12 and 1
Kgs 1.

31. This is not the right place to deal at length with the intricate problem of the

of the battles against other nations, Ammonites and Philistines respectively, in 2 Sam. 12.26-31 and 2 Sam. 21.15-22. Two stories about women who come into conflict with a harsh and hard reality follow, namely, that of Tamar's rape by her half-brother Amnon (2 Sam. 13) and Rizpah's months-long watch at the dead bodies of her sons (2 Sam. 22.1-14). The cycle of stories around Absalom's bid for power begins and ends with the appearance of two 'wise women', both of whom interact with Joab, and one of whom sets the events in motion by causing Absalom to return from the exile in to which he had fled after murdering Amnon (2 Sam. 14), whereas the other puts a final end to the revolt and its consequences by convincing the people of Abel of Beth-maacah that they should kill Sheba, the son of Bichri, who more or less continued Absalom's revolt (2 Sam. 20). In the centre, as noted, we find the elaborate description of the course of Absalom's revolt.

It is notable that the story of Shimei's confinement to Jerusalem and subsequent death may have to be detached from the other verdicts about certain persons by Solomon in 1 Kings 2 (Adonijah, Abiathar and Joab), as its position seems to have been determined by the macro-structure of the Succession Narrative. It must more or less have presented what one could call a subject of opportunity for the narrator when he composed the micro-structure of 1 Kings 2, as it connects very naturally with the actions taken by Solomon against several other persons.[32]

As I have noted elsewhere, the second story of an intervention by Nathan ought to be read in the light of the first.[33] The most evident

---

origin and function of 2 Sam. 22–24, but it is worthy of note that within the basic framework of the Succession Narrative the place of this summary of David's reign corresponds with Solomon's birth and the giving of this name in 2 Sam. 22.24-25: the placement of 2 Sam. 22–24 is thus probably not accidental. On the problem of the function of these chapters see Section 2 above. Note also that Bathsheba's genealogy, which is of prime significance for understanding some important aspects of the Succession Narrative, can be derived only from 2 Sam. 23.34.

32. The series of the three former verdicts and Shimei's death is highly functional, because each of the three death-sentences involved (Abiathar is only banished) ends one of the narrative lines of the story about King David: his last son (apart from Solomon, who was born after Nathan's prediction), the army-commander who during his entire career did his dirty work (especially in the case of Uriah) and the last member of Saul's family who was worthy of mention. After the conclusion of David's physical life, what the narrator perceived to be the basic elements of his career are removed from the stage.

33. On this, and the structure of the Succession History in general, see my 'Joab's Death', *passim*.

common denominator of the two stories is the position of women as sexual and marriage partners. In 1 Samuel 11–12 David took a woman from another man, thereby setting in motion the entire set of causal relationships which finally led to Solomon's accession. In 1 Kings 1–2 it is, besides Bathsheba's return in a prominent role (the only other time she figures in these stories), the position of Abishag the Shunammite that figures prominently, as a witness to the events of David's succession by Solomon and as a potential candidate for transference from King David's 'lap' to that of Adonijah. It is indeed the terminology connected with '(to lie in the) lap' which virtually ensures that the parallel between these passages is not in any way accidental (*šākab b^eḥeq*: 2 Sam. 12.3; 1 Kgs 1.2; *nātan b^eḥeq*: 2 Sam. 12.8). As noted above, this parallel also provides us with additional information about the way to interpret the events of the second episode.

It would seem, in fact, that in a number of other places the interpretation can benefit from studying the parallel stories together. Here I shall examine the case of the two interventions by 'wise women' mentioned above. Although there are a large number of instances in the narrative points of the Hebrew Bible where women are depicted as clever and capable, only in these two chapters do we find an explicit mention of a 'wise woman'.

The first is 2 Samuel 14, where David's army-commander Joab sends for such a 'wise woman' from the town of Tekoa in order to present a fake judicial case before David, with the intention of causing him to let his son Absalom return to Jerusalem. At the time Absalom was in exile in his mother's town of Geshur, because he feared retribution for the fact that he had killed his half-brother Amnon, avenging Amnon's rape of Absalom's full sister (and Amnon's half-sister) Tamar; for some reason David had left Amnon's crime unpunished, though it was hardly a secret that it had happened, as Tamar herself had lamented publicly about it. After having been instructed by Joab, the woman dons mourning clothes and asks for an audience with King David. She tells him that after her husband's death she was left with two sons, and that one of them has now killed his brother during a quarrel. The family, she continues, now puts her under pressure to allow the remaining son to be executed as a murderer. She insists on clemency for her son repeatedly, until David assures her with an oath that he will not be harmed. Then the woman suddenly changes her tone. She accuses David of saying this while he is at the same time guilty of refusing to let a 'banished one'—it is clear that Absalom must be meant—return home. Although she continues with her own case after that, David understands that something unusual is going on here. He asks the woman, still unexpectedly for the reader, whether Joab is behind all this. She acknowledges this, and David sends for Joab and orders him to let Absalom return. Absalom indeed comes back to Jerusalem, is at first not allowed to see the king, but puts Joab under pressure to effect a reconciliation (2 Sam. 14.25-33). Afterwards Absalom develops his plans for assuming power, resulting in his abortive revolt and his death (2 Sam. 15–18).

The second mention of a 'wise woman', in 2 Samuel 20, shows us Joab in an entirely different situation. After Absalom's death in the fight against David's soldiers, a rift has arisen between the northern and the southern tribes, which appears to foreshadow the division of the kingdom into Judah and Israel under Solomon's son and successor Rehoboam. This disagreement is used by a Benjaminite, Sheba, son of Bichri, who tries to assemble the Israelites behind himself. Joab pursues Sheba until he has to seek refuge in the northern town of Abel of Beth-maacah. The town is invested by Joab's men and seems likely to fall to them, with all the usual consequences for its inhabitants. At that moment a 'wise woman' who lives there mediates between the inhabitants of Abel of Beth-maacah and Joab: Sheba will be killed by the town's inhabitants and his head will be thrown over the wall to Joab. Thus it happens and Joab leaves the town alone.

Recognizing a close connection between these storiesis not only based on the portrayal of a woman who is called 'wise' in both instances, the fact that they are not very far apart, and a number of expressions common to both chapters.[34] As noted above, within the structure of the entire Succession History of David (2 Sam. 9–1 Kgs 2) they are clearly located in parallel places; in the use of certain Hebrew stems in *Stichwörter* and geographical names they also exhibit a striking resemblance, which has surprisingly never been commented upon. In 2 Samuel 20 the main action is framed by the 'blowing of the horn' (*tāqā' ba-šopār*, vv. 1–22), in 2 Samuel 14 the characteristic act is the supposed 'mourning' of the woman from Tekoa (*'ābal*: three derivations of this stem in v. 2; compare also *ʾᵃbal*, 'alas!', in v. 5). The Hebrew stems *tq'* and *'bl* strikingly and hardly accidentally recur in the places where the two women live: Tekoa (*tᵉqoa'*) and Abel (*'ābel*), respectively. This makes it once more clear how cautious one should be with historical and geographical conclusions from these stories: was the story adapted to these geographical names, was it the other

34. Conroy, *Absalom Absalom!*, p. 142 n. 99, mentions the following words and expressions: *mwt* + *šmd* (14.7) against *mwt* (hiphil) + *'bl* (20.19); *šḥt* (14.11 and 20.15.20); *naḥᵃlat ʾᵉlohīm* (14.16) in contrast with *naḥᵃlat YHWH* (20.19).

way round, or did the author of the story profit from a very happy coincidence? It seems hardly likely that an answer can ever be given to questions such as these. What can be observed, however, is that these agreements furnish additional links between the two chapters.

We shall put these stories beside each other, on the one hand in order to examine the characterization of the women as 'wise', on the other hand in attempting to throw some new light on a few very difficult passages in the chapters in which they are found. In particular, 2 Sam. 14.1-20 has been the object of many discussions already, which have not yet solved all of its problems.[35] As the passage in 2 Samuel 20 appears to be far less beset with exegetical problems than the one in ch. 14, I shall examine it first, comparing it with certain aspects of the story in 2 Samuel 14, and afterwards I shall use the results obtained for subjecting the other chapter to a thorough fresh examination.

The Wise Woman in 2 Samuel 20
Without any doubt, the most conspicuous sentences in 2 Samuel 20 are those addressed to Joab by the woman of Abel of Beth-maacah, after asking him who he is and whether he is ready to listen to her (vv. 18-19): 'They were wont to say in old time, "Let them but ask counsel at Abel"; and so they settled a matter. I am one of those who are peaceable and faithful in Israel; you seek to destroy a city which is a mother in Israel; why will you swallow up the heritage of the Lord?' The words that the woman is said to speak here are completely different in literary character from the simple prose used in the rest of the story, including the dialogues between the main personages: they even deviate from the rest of the woman's words in this passage and from Joab's answer.

The woman employs an elevated style of prose—one could hesitate whether it should perhaps be called poetry—in which we find some peculiar constructions with the absolute infinitive, as well as expressions that are quite uncommon elsewhere. Thus, to mention only one striking example, the well-known expression 'a city [which is] a mother in Israel' (*'ir we'em be yiśra'el*) has been derived from this passage, the only place in which it appears in the Hebrew Bible.

Of the special literary characteristics of this passage I want to note in

---

35. See beginning of this chapter above for literature on the Succession History. Specifically about 2 Sam. 14, see J. Hoftijzer, 'David and the Tekoite Woman', *VT* 20 (1970), pp. 419-44; K. Jongeling, 'Joab and the Tekoite Woman', *JEOL* 30 (1987-88), pp. 116-22.

particular the indignant question at the end, introduced by the word *lāmmā*, 'why?', and the use of the literary figure of *totum pro parte* in it: Joab is not, of course, destroying the entire heritage of God, but only a small part of it, namely the town of Abel. Another notable feature is the contrast that the woman makes between the ideal situation, which she considers to have originated in a remote past, and the threat of the present, now that the person being addressed by her plans to infringe on this situation: through comparison with a positively experienced past the present is characterized as especially negative. Finally it can be noted that this passage can quite naturally be divided into two groups of three short clauses or sentences, which are given here in transliteration of the Hebrew text and in translation:

They were wont to say in old time,	*dabber y^edabb^eru bārīšonā lemor*
'Let them but ask counsel at Abel';	*ša'ol y^ešā'^alu b^e 'ābel*
and so they settled a matter.	*w^eken hetammu*
I am one of those who are peaceable and faithful in Israel;	*'ānokī š^elume '^emune yiśrā'el*
you seek to destroy a city which is a mother in Israel;	*'atta m^ebaqqeš l^ehamīt 'ir w^e 'em b^eyiśrā'el*
why will you swallow up the heritage of the Lord?	*lāmmā t^eballa' 'et naḥ^alat YHWH*

We shall see that in 2 Samuel 14 there is a comparable contrast between a positive and a negative situation.

The Wise Woman in 2 Samuel 14
By contrast, in the passage in which the woman of 2 Samuel 14 is represented as speaking we do not find such a difference in style from the rest of the chapter, with the significant exception of her words in vv. 13-14, which are also semi-poetical and are also different from their context with regard to substance: in these two verses the woman does not speak about her fictitious case, but reproaches the king directly for his supposed shortcomings in a case that she does not specify very clearly, but which is easily recognizable as Absalom's.

If we put the woman's words here beside those of the woman from Abel, we see firstly a striking agreement in style, and secondly a congruence in structure, in that both contain a sentence introduced by the word *lāmmā*, 'why?' This indignant question to the person whose behaviour with regard to something that is God's own (in the first case, his people, in

the second, his heritage) is severely criticized is found at the beginning of
the woman's words in 2 Samuel 14, at the end in 2 Samuel 20, something
that can hardly be accidental. This observation fits in very well with the
way in which we saw that the actions of the wise women enclose the
episode of Absalom's revolt, with regard both to content and to formal
literary structure. As has been noted above, we also have here a contrast
between the present situation, which is experienced as bad, and an ideal
situation, which is not projected in the past, but is indicated with a reference to God's actions.[36] Finally, the words that the woman pronounces in
vv. 13-14 can easily be divided into units of three short clauses or sentences, this time not two but three units:[37]

Why then have you planned such a thing against the people of God?	*wᵉlāmā ḥāšabtā kāzot ʿal ʿam ᵉlohim*
For in giving this decision the king convicts himself, inasmuch as the king does not bring his banished one home again.	*umiddabber hammelek haddābār hazze lᵉbiltī kᵉ'āšem hāšib hammelek 'et niddᵉho*
[14] Though we must all die, we are like water spilt on the ground, which cannot be gathered up again;	[14] *kī mot nāmut wᵉkammayim hanniggārīm 'ārṣā ᵃšer lo ye'āsepu*
will not God make plans and devise means not to keep his banished one an outcast?	*wᵉlo yiśśā ᵉlohīm nepeš wᵉḥašab maḥᵃšābot lᵉbiltī yiddaḥ mimmennu niddāḥ*

Now that we have arranged the words of the wise women in 2 Samuel
14 and in 2 Samuel 20 according to poetical clauses, we can observe even
more structural agreements between the passages than has been done
above. At the end of the ch. 14 passage and at the beginning in ch. 20,
there is a striking use of nouns and verbs deriving from the same stems:
the repetition of *ḥšb* and *ndḥ* in 2 Sam. 14.14 can be contrasted with that
of *dbr* and in *š'l* 2 Sam. 20.18. We also see the repetition of the crucial
noun *hammelek*, 'the king', directly after the question introduced by *lāmmā*
in 2 Samuel 14, in contrast with the two instances of the word *yiśrā'el* just
before the question in 2 Samuel 20. Maybe it could even be maintained
that the use of the indication *ᵉlohīm*, 'God', in the passage in 2 Samuel 14
renders it parallel with and complementary to the 2 Samuel 20 episode,

36. See below for the possibility that the indicated action of God is thought to have
occurred in a distinct and identifiable situation in the past.
37. The translation occasionally pre-empts what will be stated below.

where the divine name YHWH appears. Even without this last observation, however, it is clear that the two passages are in a parallel position, and that it is not only possible, but even desirable to compare them with each other in order to determine their meaning as completely as possible.

In marked contrast with the situation in 2 Samuel 20, where the exact explanation of the words is not easy, but the actual situation is entirely clear, the words spoken by the wise woman in 2 Samuel 14 have caused many problems to ancient and modern exegetes. Numerous explanations, many of them quite subtle, have been given for the woman's words. It seems preferable not to search too much behind the woman's words: most important for understanding the story is not the meaning that the words spoken by the woman could ultimately have had, but rather the effect that they were undoubtedly expected by Joab to have on King David. In a way, this will be a serious type of heresy for students of literature: on the basis of what the narrator tells us, we are going to reconstruct the inner life of one of the main persons, in this case King David, with his expectations, fears and obsessions, as well as the knowledge that one of the other characters, in this case Joab, has of these feelings.[38]

It is difficult to determine what 'this word' in v. 13 refers to. Does it indicate the king's preceding declaration of his intentions in the woman's fictitious case, or what follows: 'that the king does not bring his banished one home again'? In the latter case we would have a nice parallelism between 'thinking' and 'saying', with the same object ('thinking' can hardly refer to anything but the sentence about not letting a banished one return), whereas in the first case the connection with what precedes would be clearer. Perhaps we must assume that 'thinking' and 'saying' are used in opposition here: the king is thinking of something bad, and thus saying something good while being in a situation of guilt. We shall see, however, that the difference between these two translations is not essential for the interpretation of the passage as a whole.

The 'we' in v. 14 can hardly be anything but the nation of Israel, because naturally they are the people who are under the special protection of Israel's God. Of course Hoftijzer is right in stating that it is not very likely that human mortality in general is hinted at here, but his suggestion that we are dealing here with the consequences of the king's guilt, which would ultimately endanger the entire people, seems somewhat far-fetched.[39] The

38. Compare the way in which David's state of mind after Nathan's first intervention is mirrored in the narrative.
39. Hoftijzer, 'Tekoite Woman', p. 433.

idea expressed here is probably that God, even if the members of his people are mortal and are as nothing compared to him, will make them return from exile. The particle *ki* must be translated as concessive (as 'though, whereas'), which is hardly unusual.[40]

The expression *nāśā nepeš* is, as Hoftijzer correctly noted, the usual way of saying 'to strive for', 'to long for'. The only thing that is really unusual is that the suffix after *nepeš*, which is found in all other attestations of this idiom, seems to be missing here. The explanation for this may well be that it was left out in order to avoid an explicit, albeit unintentional, reference to human characteristics of God (*napšo*, lit. 'his soul').[41]

Before starting a detailed discussion of the story of the woman from Tekoa, we shall first take a closer look at the circumstances of her appearance, as described in 2 Sam. 13.39–14.1.

David as King and Father
In the RSV the last verse of 2 Samuel 13 and the first of 2 Samuel 14 are rendered as follows: 'And the spirit of the king longed to go forth to Absalom; for he was comforted about Amnon, seeing he was dead. Now Joab the son of Zeruiah perceived that the king's heart went out to Absalom...'. K. Jongeling demonstrated[42] that the expressions in these verses that are usually translated in a positive vein, as expressing David's desire to see his son Absalom again, may also be translated as a description of David's wish to take Absalom by force from Geshur, the land of his mother, whence he had taken refuge after he killed Amnon. Jongeling astutely points out that the expression *watt°kal dāwīd hammelek lāṣet 'el 'abšālom*, translated by the RSV as 'And the spirit of the king longed to go forth to Absalom'[43], probably should rather be translated as 'And King

---

40. P. Joüon and T. Muraoka, *A Grammar of Biblical Hebrew* (2 vols.; Rome: Pontificio Istituto Biblico, 1991), § 171 b.

41. Compare, for example, the well-known instance in Zech. 2.12, rendered by the RSV as: 'For thus said the Lord of Hosts...for he who touches you touches the apple of his eye', of which it is said in rabbinical literature that the original form of the text must be something like: 'for he who touches you touches the apple of *my* eye'. On this famous case see Carmel McCarthy, *The Tiqqune Sopherim and Other Theological Corrections in the Masoretic Text of the Old Testament* (Freiburg: Universitätsverlag, 1981), especially pp. 61-70.

42. Jongeling, 'Joab and the Tekoite Woman'.

43. With an emendation reading *rwḥ*, 'spirit', instead of the name *dwd*, 'David'.

David longed to start out against Absalom'.[44] He is also certainly right in stating that the Hebrew words *kī leb hammelek 'al 'abšālom* of 1 Sam. 14.1 may be translated as 'that the king was angry at Absalom', rather than as 'that the king's heart went out to Absalom' (RSV).[45] The third suggestion made by Jongeling, namely to translate *kī niham 'al 'amnon kī met*, usually rendered as something like 'for he was comforted about Amnon, seeing that he was dead' (RSV), as 'because he was sorry that Amnon was dead', seems far less likely. True, in numerous cases where the niphal of *nhm* appears with probably this meaning, one can also translate differently, but precisely in this passage such an explanation seems far-fetched. It may be added that stylistically speaking it would hardly be very efficient to note quite abruptly, after the announcement that David wants to fetch Absalom from his exile, with the preceding story still echoing in the reader's head, that all of this happens because of Amnon's death. Such a construction is foreign to the style of biblical Hebrew prose. Jongeling's other ideas merit serious consideration, though it must be said that there are good reasons for the traditional interpretation, as I hope to demonstrate.

If we assume that David's sole intention was to punish Absalom severely, probably with death, for the crime that he had committed, we encounter a problematic contradiction with the indulgence that he shows for the acts of his son (2 Sam. 15.1-6), with his request to Joab at the height of Absalom's revolt to spare him (2 Sam. 18.5), and with his intense grief after Absalom's death (2 Sam. 18.32). Explaining this apparent contradiction by appealing to our own intuitive ideas about the mutability or complexity of human characters does not seem the best explanation, because we are not dealing with reality here, but with literary texts in which such a contradiction must be explained, unless—and we have no indication that this is the case—this contradiction is proper to this type of literature. Within the framework of the picture that the texts present of King David's character, the traditional interpretation of these verses fits much better than the one proposed by Jongeling, though philologically speaking his proposals are indeed very likely. We are evidently faced with a problematic contradiction, which may, however, be resolved through some other observations on the nature of these stories.

44. The piel of *klh*, 'to cause to languish', imperfect in the third person feminine singular for the undetermined subject.
45. See the list given by Jongeling of instances of *leb... 'al,* 'the heart...against' = 'angry at'.

One issue is left unmentioned by Jongeling, though in my view it is of prime importance for our understanding of these two verses. The way in which King David is designated here should not go unnoticed. The first time he is called 'King David', the second time simply 'the king'. It is well known that in biblical Hebrew prose such designations are not simple multi-purpose epithets, but are used with a specific purpose in each particular case, in order to make them fit in the context. The fact that David is designated with his full function seems to indicate that these verses aim at describing his activities or thoughts as king, rather than as father of Tamar, Amnon and Absalom. What had happened within his family would have been considered a terrible and shameful event in every monarchy of the ancient Near East, indeed in every time and place. It had become generally known that the king had left unpunished a serious crime within the royal family, the rape of one of the king's daughters by her own half-brother,[46] and had subsequently been unable to prevent revenge for this through another crime, this time even a murder. The perpetrator had fled the country to his mother's home country, a place where extradition was apparently not seriously considered. Such an event must have been highly damaging to the dignity and power of the king, in the eyes of both his subjects and his fellow-kings. In order to save his face he could hardly refrain from making plans to enforce extradition of the criminal. The mere fact that it is expressly noted that he waited for three years before undertaking this may probably be taken as an indication that his personal enthusiasm for doing so was at most very limited. This is readily understandable if one considers David's personal situation as well as his family's.

To the commonly adduced argument that David's reaction to the possibility of Absalom's death (2 Sam. 18.5) and later to the actual message of his death (2 Sam. 18.33) shows that he had a deeply felt love for his son, another and in my view quite important argument can be added. Combining David's own words and Nathan's message in 2 Sam. 12.6 and 10, we see that the David who is depicted in these stories knows that he is going to lose a number of his sons to unnatural causes. Having already lost his newly born son by Bathsheba and his oldest son Amnon, it seems unlikely that he really wants to add to his misery by bringing Absalom to

46. One of the main functions within the story of Tamar going away from the house of Amnon, lamenting herself after having been raped by him (2 Sam. 13.19), is to make it clear to the reader that the events can hardly have remained a secret to anyone.

justice—which would probably result in a verdict of death according to ancient Israelite law. In other words: in his position as king, David feels the duty and the necessity to bring his son back and punish him severely, but as a father he quite naturally finds this idea very unappealing, and makes little haste with pursuing this undertaking. This results in a personal paralysis of his activities, while on the other hand the insult done to the king of Israel remains visible to all. Joab considers this state of affairs and attempts to reach an acceptable solution by giving the king an alibi based on a wise judicial decision, made in the presence of all the courtiers and subjects who would be present during the king's audience, to let Absalom return unpunished.

The Strategy of the Woman from Tekoa
After the woman has subtly pushed the king to the point of issuing a formal declaration in her case and confirming it with an oath (v. 11), she addresses the king for two entire verses (vv. 13-14) specifically about the fact that he, in marked contrast with the divine standard, does not allow a banished one to return; of course, only Absalom can be meant here. She stresses the contrast of the king's behaviour with God's: in comparable cases God strives to let the banished person return. In a way this is a very unusual comparison: why would she let God's way of acting in general contrast so emphatically with the king's acting in one concrete case? It seems at least possible that she is not, in fact, pointing out a general characteristic of God, but that her words, through both sound and substance, remind the conscientious reader, who started at Genesis 1 and has now arrived at 2 Samuel 14, of two parallels in other stories, where God indeed allowed a banished one to return to his country, and that this is an intentional effect.

Firstly, the comparison of the act of *hasab*, 'to think', with people and with God appears elsewhere in the Hebrew Bible only in Gen. 50.20. Joseph's brothers, fearing that after the death of their father Jacob Joseph will finally take his vengeance upon them for selling him to Egypt (in Gen. 37), have asked him for mercy. In his answer Joseph says to them: *wᵉʾattem ḥᵃšabtem ʿālay rāʿā ʾᵉlohīm ḥᵃšābāh lᵉṭobā*, 'As for you, you meant evil against me; but God meant it for good...'. Here also *ḥašab* is used for evil human acts as opposed to God's benevolent actions, and also in this case God restores the situation as it was before the evil human action. In this way David is placed in one category with Joseph's brothers, who had also driven a member of their family from his land. In view of this parallel and of the fact that in 2 Sam. 20.19 the woman also gives a sweeping summary of the consequences of Joab's intended destruction of the town of Abel of Beth-maacah ('why will you swallow up the heritage of the Lord?'), it seems promising to consider 2 Samuel 14 in more or less the same way. In that light it becomes very likely that the woman's question, 'Why then have you planned such a thing against the people of God?' (14.13), does not reflect a very deep consideration of the ultimate consequences of David's actions, which would finally threaten the existence of the entire people,[47] but indicates the *punctum saliens* of Absalom's being banished. Just as in ch. 20, so here there seems to be a *totum pro parte*: because Absalom, being one of the members of the 'people of God', is being kept from his land, he is also kept from exercising his own religion, and in that sense David acts against the 'people of God'.[48]

The comparison with Joseph can be pressed even further. Although he did not return to the Promised Land during his natural life, except in order to bury his father in Genesis 50, during the Exodus his bones are taken along by the Israelites (Exod. 13.19), in agreement with the wish uttered by him in Gen. 50.25, and are finally buried in Shechem (Josh. 24.32), the place from which he disappeared to Egypt (Gen. 37.13-14). Thus God took care that the exile caused by his brothers was finally undone. It would seem therefore that the passage we are discussing here can be added to the series of the numerous intertextual links between the description of the life of David and the history of Joseph in Genesis 37–50.

This brings us to the second point: the stress on the religious aspect of a case of being driven from one's own country at once reminds us of an earlier episode of David's life, in which he was chased by Saul, the consequences of which David himself described to Saul, speaking about the people who supposedly slandered him: '…for they have driven me out this day that I should have no share in the heritage of the Lord, saying, "Go, serve other gods"' (1 Sam. 26.19). David is well aware that God finally let him return and called him to his present power and dignity.

It seems rather likely, therefore, that the reference to God's actions on behalf of people who have been driven away is not intended merely to indicate one of his general characteristics, but refers to these two distinct

47. As supposed by Hoftijzer, 'Tekoite Woman', pp. 431-33, who is followed in his opinion by Fokkelman, *King David*, p. 136.

48. For this reason it is hardly surprising that further on in the story Absalom gives as a reason for wanting to go to Hebron, where he subsequently started his revolt, that he wants to fulfil a vow that he supposedly made during his exile, namely to adore God there (15.7-9).

situations of great importance for David himself and for the people of Israel, in which God has indeed let a banished one return.

At the moment the woman says this, David realizes that with her earlier story she must have alluded to Absalom's case also, the connecting element of the two being the extenuating circumstances in the case of murder of one brother by another, as well as the factor that the murderer profits from his deed, the fictitious son of the woman from Tekoa because he is the sole surviving heir,[49] Absalom because he is apparently the next in line for the succession to the throne.

Fokkelman correctly notes that the woman continues her fiction with regard to the supposed murder of one of her sons by the other right to the end of her speech. After speaking the words concerning the incorrect attitude of the king with regard to letting a banished one return or keeping him away, which are far more difficult to understand than the rest of her discourse, she returns to the request for help to the king for saving the only son left to her.[50]

It is true that if one leaves out vv. 13 and 14, one could read the woman's discourse as a remarkable petition. Still we do not feel entirely satisfied if we conclude that she apparently does not drop the fiction of the purported case of her two sons, for we are even more than before confronted by the question of what purpose is served by the words in vv. 13-14. If they make it clear that the woman's case is a fiction, there would be no more need to expand it even further, as the woman does in vv. 15-17. It

---

49. To stress this is apparently one of the functions of the words that the family is represented as uttering among themselves or to the woman: ' "that we may kill him for the life of his brother whom he slew"; and so (*gam*) they would destroy the heir also'. It does not seem very likely that, as has often been supposed, this sentence aims at describing the family's greediness; the word *gam*, 'also', sometimes has a shade of meaning 'even' (*HALAT*, p. 188). From the use of the cohortative *wnšmydh*, literally 'let us destroy', it may not be deduced that the members of the family actually like doing this, if only because the form is used consecutively here, after the verbal forms that precede (Joüon and Muraoka, *Grammar*, § 116 b). In a comparable way, the fear of the woman that they will 'quench my coal which is left' (*wᵉkibbu*) need not indicate a bad character for the members of her family: the third person plural is commonly used in biblical Hebrew for expressing the undetermined subject (Joüon and Muraoka, *Grammar*, § 155 b). I would seriously consider the translation: 'thus my coal will be quenched'. On *gam* see also C.H.J. van der Merwe, 'Pragmatics and the Translation Value of *gam*', *Journal for Semitics/Tydskrif vir Semitistiek* 4 (1992), pp. 181-99.

50. Fokkelman, *King David*, p. 131; differently Hoftijzer, 'Tekoite Woman', *passim*, especially pp. 438.

seems rather likely, therefore, that the woman's words in vv. 13-14 do not betray the fictitious character of her own case, but that the function of these verses is a reflection on what directly precedes them: the oath with which David confirms that in the case of the woman the man who killed his brother would remain unpunished.

Making use of the fact that David mentions in his oath the name of the God of Israel, the woman remarks that the king's position with regard to that God is not the natural and correct relationship it should be: the king keeps another person removed from the country, and with that from the worship of God. She does not give any explicit juridical analogy between her case and Absalom's, but merely points out to the king that his attitude while pronouncing his oath is not pure, leaving it to him to draw his conclusions and face the consequences of his attitude. At the moment the king considers these words his attention is focused on the matter of Absalom. Then he realizes that with his oath in the supposed widow's case a possibility has been handed to him to get rid of his problem with Absalom through a reference to the parallelism between the two cases of fratricide, at least as far as the foreign aspect is concerned. The analogy between the two cases is not mandatory, but possible,[51] and when it leads to the desired result, in this case the return of Absalom to Jerusalem without the king's reputation suffering as a consequence, it is accepted by David with a certain avidity. A clear indication to this effect is that the king is not said to ponder for a moment about how he is going to react, which one would certainly expect if the outcome had been unwelcome, but at once orders Joab to bring Absalom back.

Why are the Women Called 'Wise'?
On the basis of the preceding observations we can take a fresh look at the characterization of the women in 2 Samuel 14 and 20 as 'wise'. The function of the woman in the story in 2 Samuel 14, and especially of her 'wisdom', seems to lie less in the adroit manner in which she executes Joab's instructions[52] than in the freedom of speech that she appears to have even in the presence of an absolute monarch such as King David: deriving

51. For this reason the problem that Hoftijzer discussed at length, namely whether the king had to feel bound by such an analogy in the real world of ancient Israel ('Tekoite Woman', pp. 421-23), seems hardly very relevant for the case under discussion.
52. Thus, for example, Fokkelman, *King David*, p. 141; Hoftijzer, 'Tekoite Woman', p. 444.

legitimacy from her mention of traditional religious values she can afford a degree of freedom of speech in the presence of the mighty and powerful that we can otherwise observe in these stories only for prophets. Whereas the prophet can do this because of his direct contact with the divine sphere, the freedom of speech of the wise woman apparently results from her observations about certain traditional values: she assigns the special character of a situation within the framework of general religious and social values. On the literary side this freedom and its background are expressed by the solemn tone of her words, and by the use of the stylistic figure *totum pro parte*.

More or less the same observation is valid for the wise woman of Abel of Beth-maacah in 2 Samuel 20. She is characterized not so much by the advice that she gives, which is not very remarkable, but rather through the liberty of speech that she can afford towards Joab even in a difficult situation, through which the right background for the execution of this advice arises on both sides. It is hardly accidental, therefore, that there is a striking stylistic likeness between the sentences spoken by the women in these two episodes.

Was David Really Not Aware?

I noted above that it is unlikely that the events concerning the woman of Tekoa only involved a private interaction between King David and the woman, but that the presence of an unspecified group of others played an important part in the way events unfolded. A comparable case can be found in 1 Kgs 2.19-24: the irrevocable character of Solomon's promise to his mother Bathsheba, in combination with her request for David's last female companion, Abishag from Shunem, for Solomon's brother Adoni-jah, renders Adonijah's physical elimination inevitable just because this scene is set in public, which we are specifically reminded of because an extra chair is set up for Bathsheba (1 Kgs 2.19).[53] The possibility that Solomon knew of this event beforehand is left open by the story, and it even seems rather likely that it is indeed suggested to the reader that he was aware of Bathsheba's request before she made it. One could imagine that in the episode of the woman from Tekoa the story at least leaves open the possibility that those present at this scene may have wondered whether the entire scene might not have been concocted with David's connivance, in order to enable him to spare Absalom and allow him to return to Jerusalem without losing face.

53. See my 'Joab's Death', pp. 347-48.

Such considerations bring us once more to one of the central problems of the stories of the stories around King David, namely that according to a literal reading of the text he is presented as God-fearing, righteous and perhaps even somewhat naive in his uprightness, while the same stories miss hardly any opportunity to provide suspicions of cynicism and calculation, both for the reader and, perhaps to an even higher degree, for the people who figure in the stories. What we see in this scene is probably just an additional instance of this ambiguous portrayal of King David.

Conclusion

By a comparison of the sentences spoken by the two wise women in 2 Samuel 14 and 2 Samuel 20, respectively, we can considerably clarify their meaning, especially those in ch. 14. The resulting view of the events described in that chapter can be summarized as follows. King David is trapped between his fatherly love for Absalom and his anger about the crime that he has committed and the accompanying insult to his royal dignity. Joab looks with dismay at the resulting passivity and the king's damaged image, and tries to resolve the dilemma through the intervention of a wise woman, whom he fetches specifically for this purpose from the town of Tekoa.

The woman from Tekoa puts a fictitious juridical case before King David. After David pronounces an oath about the woman's affair, she draws the king's attention to the fact that through his own behaviour towards Absalom he is not in a pure and correct relation towards the same God by whom he has just sworn his oath, especially since in a number of critical situations this God himself took measures to ensure that certain banished persons could return to his land and his service. In order, as it were, not to put too much stress on these words, she continues with her own fictitious case after that. David himself, however, when he is reminded of Absalom's case through the woman's words, realizes that his oath can also provide a satisfactory solution to his dilemma in the matter of Absalom, whom as a king he cannot let escape unscathed, while as a father he is quite unwilling to harm him. In this way David seems to serve his own interests, while for us as readers it is clear, on the one hand, that his decision entails a great deal of misery for himself and influences the history of the people of Israel decisively, and on the other hand that the divine preference for David's young son Solomon, 'whom the Lord loved' (2 Sam. 12.24), will result, through a series of events following one from the other, in his inheriting his father David's throne.

4. *Who Killed Goliath? The Two Versions of the First Meeting of David and Saul*

Above I discussed the dossier character of at least part of Primary History, most clearly visible in the presence of supposed administrative texts interspersed among the narrative episodes, but also in evidence in certain stories that interrupt the normally linear course of events in time, especially those found at the end of the book of 2 Samuel. I noted that in these cases the otherwise prevalent idea of the omniscient narrator, who is always correct in what he tells his readers, suddenly does not apply, and one version of history may plainly contradict another found elsewhere in the same work. This clearly touches upon the well-known problem of doublet stories in Primary History, stories that more or less contradict each other even though they are found not very far apart, at times even with one immediately following the other. Famous examples are the two accounts of creation in Gen. 1-2.3 and Gen. 2.4-7 and the two stories about the first encounter of David and Saul in 1 Samuel 16 and 17. These cases must, of course, be distinguished from those instances where we have no more than apparent doublets, where for example one of the two versions is told by a human witness or where the two versions complement each other without any contradiction. A good example of the first phenomenon is the episode of the death of King Saul discussed above, where one version is told by the narrator, whereas the other one is related by an evidently unreliable Amalekite. The second phenomenon can be observed in the story about Jacob's obtaining the rights of the first-born and his subsequent flight to Mesopotamia: the elements of Esau selling his rights to Jacob for a bowl of soup and Jacob, inspired by his mother, deceiving his father Isaac into bestowing the blessing of the first-born on him are not really contradictory; nor are the reasons for his journey to Mesopotamia, to avoid taking a wife from among the Canaanites (lit. the Hittites: Gen. 27.46) and because of his fear of his brother Esau (Gen. 27.42-43), mutually exclusive. Although such cases have some traits in common with the phenomenon discussed here, the most important difference is that they do not affect the normal position of the narrator.

Here I shall concentrate on one of the cases where the two versions directly follow each other, and where each one excludes the state of affairs as described in the other. We will see that both are told by the narrator himself, while there is no real difference in position between the two, and even in the sequel evidence can be found for the correctness of either account.

The story of the first appearance of King David of Israel, relating how in his youth he makes the acquaintance of King Saul through his capabilities as a musician, is one of the best-known of the entire Bible. David is the youngest son of a man from the town of Bethlehem in the land of the tribe of Judah called Jesse, who has seven sons besides him. One day the prophet Samuel visits Bethlehem. The readers have been told that he received a divine assignment to anoint one of Jesse's sons secretly as the new king of Israel, destined to replace the present King Saul, who has been rejected by God. After all Jesse's older sons have been paraded before Samuel, David is brought in, and God tells Samuel that this will be the new king. Once David has been anointed, the Spirit of God comes to rest on him, and almost simultaneously it departs from Saul and an evil spirit is sent by God and torments him. Saul can only find relief through listening to music, and David is known, besides being a shepherd, as an accomplished cither-player. He is taken to the court and, after his music proves to be very successful against the king's illness, he is even appointed as his armour-bearer. This story is related in 1 Samuel 16. Directly afterwards, in ch. 17, there follows a completely different account of the first meeting of the two, in which there are few, if any, references to the first story.[54] According to the latter version, David is sent by his father to visit his brothers, who are in the Israelite army which is fighting the Philistines under King Saul, and to take them some provisions. The Israelites are taunted every day by a huge Philistine, Goliath from Gath, wielding a spear, the shaft of which is 'like a weaver's beam' (v. 7), who comes forth and challenges the Israelites to let one of them fight with him in a man-to-man combat. David boasts that he will make short shrift of this mighty opponent, and indeed kills the giant. The other Israelites are encouraged by his example and soundly beat the Philistines. David's reputation rises rapidly and he is allowed to marry the king's daughter, but the victories that he gains make Saul jealous, and their relationship turns sour. In the meantime, under the influence of the evil spirit Saul tries to kill his minstrel David a few times by means of his spear (which he apparently keeps ready at all times), and after one of these incidents Saul sends some soldiers to David's house, who are to arrest and kill him the next morning. Through a ruse of his wife Michal (Saul's daughter, who was given in marriage to David as a reward for his killing of Goliath

54. Note that the difficult verse 2 Sam. 17.12 *wᵉdāwīd ben 'iš 'epratī hazze mibbet leḥem yehudā ušᵉmo yišay*, 'Now David was the son of this [RSV: an] Ephrathite of Bethlehem in Judah, named Jesse', though it appears to refer back to an earlier mention of Jesse, cannot be used to connect the two chapters.

and other military feats against the Philistines), who puts $t^e r\bar{a}f\bar{i}m$ (probably a kind of image) in David's bed, thus suggesting that he is lying in it, he can escape and he flees to Samuel and reports what has happened. A long period of fleeing and hiding starts, which comes to an end with the death of King Saul in battle against the Philistines, resulting in the kingship of Israel being thrown into David's lap, so to speak. We will, for the time being, leave the rest of David's life alone, and concentrate on the episodes describing his coming into contact with King Saul, and the growth of the jealousy and enmity of Saul towards David.

Even bearing in mind the ideas about the importance of lists as set forward in Section 2 above, the reader is necessarily surprised to read in a list at the end of 2 Samuel of a number of Philistines who have been slain by David's heroes: 'And there was again war with the Philistines at Gob; and Elhanan the son of Jaare-oregim, the Bethlehemite, slew Goliath the Gittite, the shaft of whose spear was like a weaver's beam' (2 Sam. 21.19). After it has been made extremely clear to us that Goliath was killed by David, not only by the description of their fight, but also by David cutting off the giant's head and taking it with him (1 Sam. 17.51-54), we are now told that it was another inhabitant of David's native town who killed the giant.[55] Still, it seems very unlikely that we are dealing with a different person here: the name, place of origin and even the description of his spear match exactly. Traditional religious exegetes tried, and try, to harmonize by assuming that Elhanan is merely another designation for David (which is, of course, hardly likely in the context of a list of his heroes),[56] and the re-working in the book of Chronicles declares the victim to have been Goliath's brother (1 Chron. 20.5). In any case it is clear that the Hebrew text as we know it presents us with great problems.

The idea that the narrator of the stories centring around King David confronts his readers with a number of rather formidable knots and problems is hardly new. Especially when certain personages are introduced as speaking, thus giving their own version of the narrative reality, the reader may rightly be suspicious. Their story is often not very likely in itself, and we even see certain literary means used to suggest that they do not speak

55. Note that his patronym is problematic. In the present form it looks like the result of a scribal error, as the second part, *'or^e gīm*, is identical to the second part of the metaphor used for Goliath's spear, *m^e nor 'or^e gīm*, lit. 'beam of weavers'. Chron. 20.5 has Elhanan son of Jair. Compare also the figure of Elhanan son of Dodo, also from Bethlehem, in 2 Sam. 23.24.

56. For example in *Targum Jonathan* on this verse.

the truth, or at least not the entire truth, and what they say is sometimes in flat contradiction of what the narrator tells his readers. Note, for example, the case of Mephibosheth and Ziba discussed in Section 2 above, where their stories simply contradict each other, which contradiction is apparently recognized as insoluble by King David, who sees no option but to let them share the possessions they have between them. Another case that has often been discussed in the secondary literature concerns the death of King Saul. In the last chapter of 1 Samuel we are told how he runs into difficulties during a battle against the Philistines, is surrounded by them and sees no way out. He asks his armour-bearer to kill him to avoid being taken captive alive and suffering humiliation and maltreatment of some sort at their hands. His servant, however, refuses to do this. Saul then throws himself on his own sword, and the armour-bearer follows his example. The Philistines find Saul's body, chop off the head and hang the body on the city wall of Beth Shean. In the immediately following chapter an unknown young man from the nation of the Amalekites comes to David and claims credit for having killed Saul at his own request and having brought the royal insignia with him in order to present them to David. The exact state of affairs with regard to this story, discussed in the second section of this chapter, is of less interest to us here than the fact, duly noted by J.P. Fokkelman, that the only way to deal with this situation is to make a hypothesis of how things could have happened: a good explanation would be to suppose that the Amalekite heard the conversation of Saul and his armour-bearer, perhaps from a kind of hide-out, and used elements from it for his own story, in which he projected himself in the armour-bearer's role; he probably took the royal attributes after the death of both.[57] This is, of course, a nice solution to the problem of the complicated relationship between these two chapters, but that is not the end of it. In one of the stories at the end of the book of 2 Samuel we find a reference to what happened to King Saul's dead body, 'on the day the Philistines killed Saul on Gilboa' (2 Sam. 21.12); various modern translations have renderings such as 'beat' instead of 'killed' (e.g. NIV: 'they struck Saul down'), but that is really an attempt at harmonization: the Hebrew *hikkā* in such a context usually denotes killing in battle, whereas in the story about Saul's death we have been told that he had not even been wounded yet when he decided to kill himself. Thus this story is completely contradicted by the sentence in 2 Sam. 21.12. It is hardly accidental that this piece of infor-

---

57. Fokkelman, 'A Lie, Born of Truth'.

mation is also given at the end of 2 Samuel, where as noted above we find more disturbing information, upsetting our reading of earlier chapters.

Having noted that the mention of Goliath's demise in the list of 2 Samuel 21 flatly contradicts the story of 1 Samuel 17, we are easily led to reconsider the content of this story and its context. It has often been remarked that in 1 Samuel 16 and 17 we are, in fact, dealing with two independent stories explaining David's presence at the court of King Saul, which are difficult to reconcile. It is very likely that the makers of the Septuagint noted this problem, and for this reason harmonized the two by merging them into one episode. There are indeed a number of problems involved in reading 1 Samuel 16 and 17 together, not the least of which is that King Saul apparently does not recognize the man who plays music in front of him almost every day, and whom he has made into his armour-bearer (1 Sam. 16.21) when he is dealing with him in the Goliath episode (1 Sam. 17.31-39, 55-58).[58]

That is not all, however. Certain pieces of information that we see in one chapter, we meet again in the second one, in a slightly different form, but with almost exactly the same substance. Jesse is said to have eight sons: in ch. 17 the precise number is mentioned (v. 12). In ch. 16 we first have seven sons, and finally David is added to the number (vv. 10-11); David is specifically described as the youngest one both in 16.11 and in 17.14 and as herding his father's sheep in 16.11 and 17.15. The names of the three oldest brothers are Eliab, Abinadab and Samma: in ch. 16 Samuel looks at them expectantly, thinking successively of each one of the three that this must be the designated king (vv. 6-9); in ch. 17 these three are again mentioned by name as having gone to war with the Philistines together with King Saul (v. 13). In ch. 16 Jesse, who is introduced in both chapters as someone whose name has not been mentioned before, apparently belongs to the eldest of the town of Bethlehem (vv. 4-5); in ch. 17 the readers are once more notified that he was already old at the time of the story (v. 12)—a necessary prerequisite to belong to the group of the 'eldest', of course! (In Hebrew, there is no difference between what is translated here as 'old' and 'eldest': both render Hebrew *zaqen*.) Further-

---

58. See for example the studies by various authors in Barthélemy *et al.*, *The Story of David and Goliath*. Cf. also A. van der Kooij, 'The Story of David and Goliath: The Early History of its Text', *ETL* 68 (1992), pp. 118-31. This is not the right place to take issue with these learned contributions, though it is clear that the relationship between the Hebrew texts and ancient versions should be re-studied in the light of the observations made here.

more, David's appearance is described twice, in remarkably similar terms: 'Now he was ruddy, and had beautiful eyes, and was handsome' (*w^ehu 'admonī 'im y^epe 'enayim w^etob ro 'ī*; 16.12); and: '...for he was but a youth, ruddy and comely in appearance' (*kī hāyā na 'ar w^e'admonī 'im y^epe mar 'e*; 17.42).

It should be noted that such agreements between two contradictory stories can normally be explained in two ways. Firstly we could assume that both drew from a common reservoir of narrative material about King David, originally circulated separately, and were finally put beside each other by a redactor. Of course in that case one could hesitate as to whether this redactor was merely careless, for some reason not taking the trouble of harmonizing the two versions, or attached such value to each of the versions that he refrained from bringing them into agreement with each other, or, finally, liked the juxtaposition of these two versions for some reason (the second and third explanations are not mutually exclusive, of course). Whatever option one chooses, it would be difficult to account for the rather precise agreement in certain key words and phrases. The second explanation is somewhat more disturbing, namely that whatever the exact origin of either story, they were extensively tailored to resemble each other very closely in some respects when one was set after the other in what is now our book of 1 Samuel. This line of thought assumes not only that two mutually exclusive accounts could be put beside each other, but that the attention of the reader would even be deliberately drawn towards their contradictory nature. This touches upon the general problem of the origin and nature of these so-called 'contradictions' in the Hebrew Bible, which have drawn attention ever since antiquity. Robert Alter devoted a chapter of his classic work on biblical Hebrew narrative to this problem, adducing our case as one of his examples. Alter's exposition constitutes the result of an interesting intellectual *tour de force*. He could or would not do away with the idea of composite texts, and fully acknowledged the likelihood that in cases of evident contradictions between different versions each had a separate pre-existence, having been inserted in the present text by a redactor, with the significant addition that the redactor deliberately left these contradictions in the text in order to achieve a certain literary effect. Alter's position is indeed a striking example of the need, even among scholars who are exclusively concerned with the literary study of the Hebrew Bible, to have at least a working hypothesis for the origin of the texts they are occupied with (see the Preface).

It keeps nagging at the reader: the stories cannot be both true, and the doubling of information appears to indicate that we are dealing here with two different explanations of David's presence at the court of King Saul, which are deliberately presented to the reader as alternatives. Looking for confirmation for one or the other from the sequel in the following chapters, we note to our surprise that both of these narrative lines run on beside each other in the next two chapters, almost as two parallel realities: one can read the story as a unity if one is ready to disregard certain minor inconsistencies, but either of the two versions is sufficient to explain subsequent events, and then without problems of consistency. The 'evil spirit', which was the reason why David had to play before Saul on the lyre, also causes the king to make two unsuccessful attempts to kill David, who was playing for him 'as he did day by day', with his spear (1 Sam.18.10-11 and 19.9-10, respectively). At the same time Saul, jealous because of David's military successes and seeing that he has become more popular than the king himself, wants to remove this potential competitor permanently (1 Sam. 18.6-9; 18.19–19.8). These two motives are nowhere connected with each other in any way, and independently have the result that Saul wants to kill David.

As if to let this pair of narrative lines come together again, they both end with a description of David's flight from Saul with almost identical words: *wᵉdāwīd nās wayyimmālēṭ ballaylā hu*, 'And David fled and escaped that night' (1 Sam. 19.10);[59] and *wayyibraḥ wayyimmālēṭ*, 'and he fled away [during the night][60] and escaped' (1 Sam. 19.12), respectively. Almost the same words are found again when the story, this time in the normal unitary form, continues with David's arrival with the prophet Samuel: *wᵉdāwīd bāraḥ wayyimmālēṭ*, 'Now David fled and escaped, [and he came to Samuel at Ramah, and told him all that Saul had done to him]' (1 Sam. 19.18).

In the following chapters we come across two references to the episode of David and Goliath. The first one is found when David, fleeing from Saul, arrives at the sanctuary in the place called Nob. The priest Ahimelech gives him, among other things, a sword which he describes as 'The sword of Goliath the Philistine, whom you killed in the valley of Elah...' (1 Sam. 21.9; compare also in the report about this event, made to Saul by the informer Doeg [22.10], '...the sword of Goliath the Philistine'), which was apparently preserved in the sanctuary: 'behold, it is here wrapped in a cloth behind the ephod' (21.9). This mention of David's feat seems hardly

59. LXX takes 'that night' with the beginning of the next verse.
60. Cf. Michal's words: 'If you do not save your life tonight, tomorrow you will be killed' (v. 11).

necessary here. The second case is the one in the list in 2 Sam. 21.19, which seems to contradict the first one, ascribing Goliath's death to the otherwise unknown Elhanan, without making it clear when this is supposed to have happened (though the context appears to suggest some time in the later part of David's reign).

Briefly said, the reader is confronted with contradictory signals all the time, and there seems to be really no way to find out who killed Goliath. If David did not do it, he must have made the acquaintance of Saul in some other way, and the story of his music-making seems to make a nice replacement. As if to make it clear to us that a choice for this story does not solve our problems either, the priest Ahimelech is said to refer unambiguously to David's victory over Goliath. As if to disqualify the other version of the story again, in which a part is played by David's wife Michal, who is later said to have remained childless (2 Sam. 6.20-23), she reappears in 2 Sam. 21.8, married to a certain Adriel and mother of no less than five children (who meet a grisly fate further on in the same chapter).[61] When reading these chapters, we are walking through a labyrinth that the author of David's biography constructed for us, and as long as we stay within the confines of his story we will not be able to find the exit, simply because he chose not to provide his readers with one.

It would seem that, as with other aspects of the narrator's art in Primary History, the intention of the author has been to stress the outcome of his story, the beginning of the Davidic dynasty, in a unique way, namely by creating uncertainty for the reader about nearly everything that lies on the way to this, even about the bare facts of the biography of King David himself. Not only can we and must we doubt the motives for human acts, what people say about each other and the stories they tell about events, this doubt is in this case even extended to the narrator's way of describing events and the information he provides his readers with. Sometimes two or even more versions of the reality are found, without the reader being given the means to make a correct choice. In the famous case of the death of Saul we think we can reconstruct what has really happened from the story as told by the narrator in combination with a mendacious version of the same, but a number of chapters further on we are once again reduced to our role of powerless and uncertain reader when it is briefly related to have

61. The RSV follows LXX in changing the name into that of her sister Merab (destined to marry David, but instead given to Adriel according to 1 Sam. 18.19), but the Hebrew text is unequivocal.

happened completely differently again. There are even cases—and no one seems to have noticed this before—where two lengthy versions of a certain episode are presented to the reader which cannot both be true, but which are still offered to us without the benefit of uncertainty being signalled through representing one of them as a second- or third-hand story. As noted above, personal doubt cannot be expressed through the limitations on the authorial voice that the narrator of Primary History felt compelled to impose, but the procedure described here comes as close to expression of authorial uncertainty as one can ever get within these constraints.

Even within this framework, the case that we are studying here, the first acquaintance of Saul and David and their subsequent estrangement, looks very intriguing. Two basically irreconcilable stories have been juxtaposed and have even been intertwined. The close connection between the two is stressed by their structure and their use of the same key words and names. Both begin with David being the youngest son of the Bethlehemite Jesse, herding his father's sheep at first; both describe his coming to Saul's court and end with his fleeing from there in the night, but otherwise they are completely different, though it should be noted that they are in a way also complementary: each stresses one of the two conventional main aspects of David's personality, the first one his musicianship, the second one his military capabilities. They have been knitted together in such a masterly way that at first sight it seems we are dealing with one continuous story, and their fundamental contradiction only appears when we are told in a list at the end of the series of chapters about King David that the Philistine giant Goliath was killed by an otherwise unknown fellow townsman of David, from which we are to conclude that it is at least subject to some doubt whether David did this, and we are led to reconsider the stories about their first meeting also.

It turns out once more that one of the most important vehicles for expressing such fundamental doubt is constituted by the lists of David's civil servants, his opponents and his bravest soldiers: they provide information not found in the stories themselves and at times even contradict the information that is otherwise provided unambiguously, thus opening our eyes for other contradictions in David's unusual biography.

The chapters 2 Samuel 16 and 17 thus constitute one of the clearest instances of the literary form of the unitary dossier in the entire Primary History. Two narrative lines are pursued beside each other, with the two different stories told by the narrator and the information provided in his lists existing side by side in his text, without any clue given to the reader whether one set of narrated events is to be preferred over the other: they are simply two conflicting and competing versions of narrated reality found in the dossier of the history of Ancient Israel.

CONCLUSION:
THE AUTHOR'S ACHIEVEMENT

We have seen that behind the text of Primary History, the books Genesis–2 Kings at the beginning of the Hebrew Bible, as well as behind several other historical books of the Hebrew Bible, a literary reality can be observed which, though by itself not very deeply hidden, has remained unnoticed ever since its study seriously began around the beginning of the Christian era. These books, each on the one hand consciously set up as a more or less linear account of events in the past, and on the other hand looking like a dossier of various texts, find their closure and unity through structural derivation, that is the use of the structure of another work, usually one whose subject is related to the book to be written. The derivation of the structure of Daniel from Ezra and the story of Joseph in Genesis 37–50, and of Ezra from Nehemiah, are interesting enough, but the fact that a comparable literary relation can be observed between Primary History and the *Histories* of Herodotus of Halicarnassus, with the structure of Primary History derived from that of the *Histories*, is perplexing and has far-reaching consequences for our view on the origin of the books of the Hebrew Bible, the cultural environment in which they were written and the way in which they have served to carry the culture and traditions of ancient Israel into the modern world until today.

I have studied the phenomenon of structural derivation, its parallels inside and outside the Hebrew Bible and the consequences for studying Primary History, but there may be more to this use of the linear literary dossier in combination with the derivation of the overall structure of the work. Here I can only begin to look for the reason why the author chose this relatively involved type of composition for his work. As noted in Chapter 4, Primary History in a number of instances evinces a three-fold division of the narrative reality. On the basic level it is a linear account in which every piece of information is to be taken at face value by the person whom we could call the naïve reader. On the next level doubt is raised in the conscientious reader's mind about the information that has been provided, whereas on the third and highest level the doubt is shown to be irrelevant, because all the contradictory paths of narrative reality fit within the overall plan of God for his people Israel and his chosen king David, and within the framework of God's justice. This fit is usually indicated by means of information provided by the formal structure of the text. Application of the same threefold division to the structure of Primary History may well serve to clarify the reason why the work was composed in this unusual way. First, we have the linear story of the origin of the world and of humankind, and of the history of the people of Israel. On the second level most of this history, in fact nearly every episode apart from the history of the two Israelite kingdoms in the ninth to sixth centuries BCE, is placed in doubt and the reader is even made to doubt whether the account that he or she is reading is really a unitary work or merely a collection of variegated stories, lists and other literary and non-literary pieces. Finally, the structure of the entire work confirms its unity and with its unity stresses its main content, namely Israel's special relation with its God and his plans for his people. The congruence with the only great historical work that was known at the time, which likewise describes the origin and identity of the author's nation, besides showing the tremendous literary capabilities of the author, indicates and affirms this main theme of Primary History.

We do not know whether our author first introduced the literary technique of structural derivation into Israelite literature, but it is clear that his work was the starting point of the literature of the Hebrew Bible as we have it now (as distinguished from the literature of Ancient Israel before that), and that at least in the historical books Ezra and Daniel the same technique was applied, whether or not their authors recognized the link with the *Histories*. His peculiar way of indicating the uncertainty of his own narrative, by contrast, was not followed by the other works, and they systematically emended the contradictions produced in this way when they covered the same ground. We can now recognize that the formation of the canon of the Hebrew Bible was not the process of addition, selection and redaction that is usually supposed, but at least in part the production of separate works which were to look like collected dossiers, but were in reality composed as unitary literary works, most aptly described as composed literary dossiers. It clearly was not the intention to deceive the prospective readers, but to provide a narrated reality that could be read on different levels, and which has indeed been read on two of these levels for many centuries. We now perceive that, interestingly, the rise of historical criticism since the seventeenth century, and of modern literary study of the Hebrew Bible in the last few decades, to mention only two of the many different critical approaches, really only serve to expose different parts of this literary reality on the second level, instead of looking at the text from a higher level of understanding, as is understandably supposed by many of their practitioners.

The identification of the third level of understanding, which is provided by the structural resemblance to the only other major historical work of the time, the *Histories* of Herodotus of Halicarnassus, while almost certainly not the last major discovery to be made concerning this intriguing text of Primary History, thus finally allows us to evaluate the tremendous achievement of its author and to place research up to this point in the proper perspective, and may help to encourage future research in hitherto unexpected ways. It is interesting to think of modern scholarship in its various branches largely playing parts for which the script was written almost two and a half millennia ago , with the antagonism between schools at least partly reflecting the multi-level construction of Primary History.

A significant part of what is regarded as common memory in large parts of the world—the biblical stories about Joseph, Moses, David and other generally known personages, and the all-important episodes of oppression in Egypt, Exodus, journey through the wilderness and conquest of the Promised Land—probably originated in their present form in the mind of one person only, a highly talented author who most likely lived and worked among the intelligentsia of Nehemiah's Jerusalem, in the second half of the fifth century BCE. His masterful work with its threefold level of understanding, together with his choice for anonymous authorship, assured that the work rapidly became a tremendous success, and would be read, used and studied more intensely than any other work before or since. It formed the conceptual and historical framework for the rest of the books of the Hebrew Bible, and from there for the host of literature flourishing around the beginning of our era. From his work, in the final analysis, the great monotheistic religions of Judaism, Christianity and Islam took their point of departure. Our anonymous writer truly was the most successful author of all time.

BIBLIOGRAPHY

Ackerman, J.S., 'Knowing Good and Evil: A Literary Analysis of the Court History in 2 Samuel 9–20 and 1 Kings 1–2', *JBL* 109 (1990), pp. 41-64.
—'Who Can Stand before YHWH, This Holy God? A Reading of 1 Samuel 1–15', *Prooftexts* 11 (1991), pp. 1-24.
Alter, R., *The Art of Biblical Narrative* (New York: Basic Books, 1981).
—*The World of Biblical Literature* (New York: Basic Books, 1992).
Avery, H.C., 'Herodotus' Picture of Cyrus', *AJP* 93.4 (1972), pp. 529-46.
Bar-Efrat, S., *Narrative Art in the Bible* (Sheffield: Almond Press, 1989 [original Hebrew edition Tel Aviv: Sifriat Poalim, 1979]).
Barthélemy, D., *et al.*, *The Story of David and Goliath: Textual and Literary Criticism. Papers of a Joint Venture* (Freiburg: Editions Universitaires, 1986).
Blanco, W., and J.T. Roberts, *Herodotus. The Histories: New Translation, Selections, Backgrounds, Commentaries* (New York: Norton, 1992).
Boedecker, D., 'The Two Faces of Demaratus', *Arethusa* 20 (1987), pp. 185-201.
—'Protesilaus and the End of Herodotus' Histories', *Classical Antiquity* 7 (1988), pp. 30-48.
Brueggemann, W., '2 Samuel 21–24: An Appendix of Deconstruction?', *CBQ* 50 (1988), pp. 383-97.
—'I Samuel 1: A Sense of a Beginning', *ZAW* 102 (1990), pp. 33-48.
—'The Baruch Connection', *JBL* 113 (1994), pp. 405-20.
Cogan, M., and H. Tadmor, *II Kings* (AB; Garden City, NY: Doubleday, 1988).
Conroy, C., *Absalom Absalom! Narrative and Language in 2 Sam. 13–20* (Rome: Biblical Institute Press, 1978).
Damrosch, D., *The Narrative Covenant: Transformations of Genre in the Growth of Biblical Literature* (repr.; Ithaca, NY: Cornell University Press, 1991 [1987]).
Davies, P.R., *In Search of 'Ancient Israel'* (Sheffield: Sheffield Academic Press, 1992).
—'Method and Madness: Some Remarks on Doing History with the Bible', *JBL* 114 (1995), pp. 699-705.
—*Scribes and Schools: The Canonization of the Hebrew Scriptures* (Louisville, KY: Westminster/John Knox Press, 1998).
Déaut, R. le, and J. Robert, *Targum du Pentateuque* (4 vols.; Paris: Cerf, 1978).
Dewald, C., 'Narrative Surface and Authorial Voice in Herodotus' Histories', *Arethusa* 20 (1987), pp. 147-70.
Dimant, D., 'Use and Interpretation of Mikra in the Apocrypha and Pseudepigrapha', in M.J. Mulder and H. Sysling (eds.), *Mikra: Text, Translation, Reading and Interpretation of the Hebrew Bible in Ancient Judaism and Early Christianity* (Assen: Van Gorcum, 1988), pp. 379-419.
Drews, R. *The Greek Accounts of Eastern History* (Washington: Center for Hellenic Studies, 1973).

Feldman, L.H., 'Some Observations on the Name of Palestine', *HUCA* 61 (1990), pp. 1-23.

—*Jew and Gentile in the Ancient World* (Princeton: Princeton University Press, 1993).

Fishbane, M., 'I Samuel 3: Historical Narrative and Narrative Poetics', in K.R.R. Gros Louis (ed.), *Literary Interpretations of Biblical Narratives*, II (Nashville: Abingdon Press, 1982), pp. 191-203.

—*Biblical Interpretation in Ancient Israel* (Oxford: Clarendon Press, 1988).

Flory, S., 'Who Read Herodotus?', *AJP* 101 (1980) 12-28.

Fokkelman, J.P., *Narrative Art and Poetry in the Books of Samuel*. I. *King David* (Assen: Van Gorcum, 1981).

—'A Lie, Born of Truth, too Weak to Contain it', *OTS* 23 (1984), pp. 39-55.

—'Structural Reading on the Fracture between Synchrony and Diachrony', *JEOL* 30 (1987–88), pp. 123-36.

Foster, B.R., *Before the Muses: An Anthology of Akkadian Literature* (2 vols.; Bethesda: CDL Press, 1993).

Frei, P., and K. Koch, *Reichsidee und Reichsorganisation im Perserreich* (Freiburg: Universitätsverlag, 1996).

Friedman, R.E., *Who Wrote the Bible?* (New York: Summit Books, 1987).

Gabba, E., 'The Growth of Anti-Judaism or the Greek Attitude towards Jews', in W.D. Davies and L. Finkelstein (eds.), *The Cambridge History of Judaism* (Cambridge: Cambridge University Press, 1989), II, pp. 614-56.

Georges, P., *Barbarian Asia and the Greek Experience: From the Archaic Period to the Age of Xenophon* (Baltimore: The Johns Hopkins University Press, 1994).

Gera, D.L., 'Bereaved Fathers in Herodotus', *Scripta Classica Israelica* 12 (1993), pp. 36-50.

Gibson, J.C.L., *Canaanite Myths and Legends* (Edinburgh: T. & T. Clark, 1978).

Gnuse, R., 'The Jewish Dream Interpreter in a Foreign Court: The Recurrent Use of a Theme in Jewish Literature', *JSP* 7 (1990), pp. 29-53.

Godley, A.D., *Herodotus* (4 vols.; LCL; London: Heinemann, 1920–1924).

Gould, J., *Herodotus* (London: Weidenfeld and Nicolson, 1989).

Gransden, K.W., *Virgil's Iliad: An Essay on Epic Narrative* (Cambridge: Cambridge University Press, 1984).

Greenstein, E.L., 'The Formation of the Biblical Narrative Corpus', *AJS Review* 15 (1990), pp. 151-78.

Gunn, D.M., *The Story of King David: Genre and Interpretation* (Sheffield: JSOT Press, 1978).

—'New Directions in the Study of Biblical Hebrew Narrative', *JSOT* 39 (1987), pp. 65-75.

—'Reading Right: Reliable and Omniscient Narrator, Omniscient God, and Foolproof Composition in the Hebrew Bible', in D.J.A. Clines *et al.* (eds.), *The Bible in Three Dimensions: Essays in Celebration of Forty Years of Biblical Studies in the University of Sheffield* (Sheffield: JSOT Press, 1990), pp. 53-64.

Halpern, B., *The Emergence of Israel in Canaan* (Chico, CA: Scholars Press, 1983).

Hoftijzer, J., 'David and the Tekoite Woman', *VT* 20 (1970), pp. 419-44.

Houtman, C., *Exodus* (3 vols.; Kampen: Kok, 1986–1996) [in Dutch].

—*Der Pentateuch. Die Geschichte seiner Erforschung neben einer Auswertung* (Kampen: Kok Pharos, 1994).

Ilan, Y., 'The Literary Structure of 1 Samuel 2.11-26', in *Beth Mikra* 31 (1985–86), pp. 268-70 [Hebrew].

Jacob, B., *Das erste Buch der Tora. Genesis* (Berlin: Shocken, 1934).

Jongeling, K., 'Joab and the Tekoite Woman', *JEOL* 30 (1987–88), pp. 116-22.

Joüon, P., and T. Muraoka, *A Grammar of Biblical Hebrew* (2 vols.; Rome: Pontificio Istituto Biblico, 1991).

Knauer, G.N., 'Vergil's *Aeneid* and Homer', *GBRS* 5 (1964), pp. 61-84, reprinted in S.J. Harrison (ed.), *Oxford Readings in Vergil's* Aeneid (Oxford and New York: Oxford University Press, 1990), pp. 390-412.

—*Die Aeneis und Homer: Studien zur poetischen Technik Vergils mit Listen der Homerzitate in der Aeneis* (Göttingen: Vandenhoeck & Ruprecht, 1964).

Kooij, A. van der, 'The Story of David and Goliath: The Early History of its Text', *ETL* 68 (1992), pp. 118-31.

Lateiner, D., *The Historical Method of Herodotus* (Toronto: University of Toronto Press, 1989).

Lawee, E., 'From the Pages of Tradition. Don Isaac Abarbanel: Who Wrote the Books of the Bible?', *Tradition* 30.2 (1996), pp. 65-73.

Lemche, N.P., *The Canaanites and their Land: The Tradition of the Canaanites* (Sheffield: JSOT Press, 1991).

—'City-Dwellers or Administrators: Further Light on the Canaanites', in A. Lemaire and B. Otzen (eds.), *History and Traditions of Early Israel: Studies Presented to Eduard Nielsen* (Leiden: E.J. Brill, 1993), pp. 76-89.

—'The Old Testament: A Hellenistic Book?', *SJOT* 7 (1993), pp. 163-93.

Magonet, H., 'The Names of God in Biblical Narratives', in J. Davies *et al.* (eds.), *Words Remembered, Texts Renewed: Essays in Honour of John F.A. Sawyer* (Sheffield: Sheffield Academic Press, 1995), pp. 80-96.

Maier, J., 'Amalek in the Writings of Josephus', in F. Parente and J. Silvers (eds.), *Josephus and the History of the Greco-Roman Period: Essays in Memory of Morton Smith* (Leiden: E.J. Brill, 1994), pp. 109-26.

Mandell, S., and D.N. Freedman, *The Relationship between Herodotus' History and Primary History* (Atlanta: Scholars Press, 1993).

Marx, A., 'La généalogie d'Exode vi 14-25: sa forme, sa fonction', *VT* 45 (1995), pp. 318-36.

McCarter, P.K., *I Samuel: A New Translation with Introduction and Commentary* (AB, 8; Garden City, NY: Doubleday, 1980).

—*II Samuel: A New Translation with Introduction and Commentary* (AB, 9; Garden City, NY: Doubleday, 1984).

McCarthy, C., *The Tiqqune Sopherim and Other Theological Corrections in the Masoretic Text of the Old Testament* (Freiburg: Universitätsverlag, 1981).

Merwe, C.H.J. van der, 'Pragmatics and the Translation Value of *gam*', *Journal for Semitics/ Tydskrif vir Semitistiek* 4 (1992), pp. 181-99.

Momigliano, A., 'Die Juden und die griechische Kultur', in *Die Juden in der alten Welt* (Berlin: Wagenbach, 1988), pp. 28-48.

Nielsen, F.A.J., *The Tragedy in History: Herodotus and the Deuteronomistic History* (Sheffield: Sheffield Academic Press, 1997).

Olmstead, A.T., 'Persia and the Greek Frontier Problem', in Blanco and Roberts, *Herodotus. The Histories*, pp. 377-89 [*Classical Philology* 34 (1939), pp. 305-22].

Porten, B., *Archives from Elephantine* (Berkeley: University of California Press, 1968).

Provan, I., 'Ideologies, Literary and Critical: Reflections on Recent Writing on the History of Israel', *JBL* 114 (1995), pp. 585-606.

Redford, D.B., 'The Literary Motif of the Exposed Child (cf. Ex. ii 1-10)', *Numen* 14 (1967), pp. 209-28.

Schuil, A., *Amalek: Onderzoek naar oorsprong en ontwikkeling van Amaleks rol in het Oude Testament* (Zoetermeer: Boekencentrum, 1997).

Selincourt, A. de, *Herodotus: The Histories* (Harmondsworth: Penguin Books, 1954).

Siebert-Hommes, J.C., 'Twelve Women in Exodus 1 and 2: The Role of Daughters and Sons in the Stories Concerning Moses', *Amsterdamse Cahiers voor Exegese en Bijbelse Theologie* 9 (1988), pp. 47-58.

Spinoza, B. de, *Tractatus Theologico-Politicus* ([Amsterdam: J. Rieuwertsz], 1670).

Stern, M., *Greek and Latin Authors on Jews and Judaism* (2 vols.; Jerusalem: Israel Academy of Sciences and Humanitiess, 1974 and 1980).

Sternberg, M., *The Poetics of Biblical Narrative: Ideological Literature and the Drama of Reading* (Bloomington: Indiana University Press, 1985).

Strasburger, H., 'Herodots Zeitrechnung', in W. Schmitthenner and R. Zoepffel (eds.), *Studien zur Alten Geschichte* (Hildesheim: Olms, 1982 [1956]), pp. 627-75.

Thompson, T.L., *Early History of the Israelite People: From the Written and Archaeological Sources* (Leiden: E.J. Brill, 1992).

—'A Neo-Albrightean School in History and Biblical Scholarship?', *JBL* 114 (1995), pp. 683-98.

Tov, E., *Textual Criticism of the Hebrew Bible* (Assen: Van Gorcum, 1992).

Ulrich, E., *The Dead Sea Scrolls and the Origins of the Bible: Studies in the Dead Sea Scrolls and Related Literature* (Grand Rapids, MI: Eerdmanns, 1999).

Van Seters, J., *In Search of History* (New Haven: Yale University Press, 1992).

—*Prologue to History: The Yahwist as Historian in Genesis* (Louiseville, KY: Westminster/ John Knox Press, 1992).

—*The Life of Moses* (Kampen: Kok Pharos, 1994).

Vaggione, R.P., 'Over All Asia? The Extent of the Scythian Domination in Herodotus', *JBL* 92 (1973), pp. 523-30.

Vandiver, E., *Heroes in Herodotus: The Interaction of Myth and History* (Frankfurt: Lang, 1991).

Vergote, J., *Joseph en Egypte. Génèse chap. 37-50 à la lumière des études égyptologiques récentes* (Leuven: Publications Universitaires, 1959).

Wesselius, J.-W., 'Joab's Death and the Central Theme of the Succession Narrative (2 Samuel ix–1 Kings ii)', *VT* 40 (1990), pp. 336-51.

—'Openbare en verborgen motieven voor handelingen in de verhalen rondom koning David', *Amsterdamse Cahiers voor Exegese en Bijbelse Theologie* 11 (1992), pp. 42-64 [in Dutch].

—'Samuël en de zonen van Eli: De betekenis van de structuur van 1 Samuël 2 en 3', in E.G.L. Schrijver, N.A. van Uchelen and I.E. Zwiep (eds.), *The Literary Analysis of Hebrew Texts. Papers read at a Symposium held at the Juda Palache Institute, University of Amsterdam (5 February 1990)* (Amsterdam: Juda Palache Insituut, 1992), pp. 35-44 [in Dutch].

—*De eenheid van het boek Daniel: Openingscollege van de Faculteit der Godgeleerdheid UvA, 3 September 1993* (Amsterdam: [privately printed], 1993) [in Dutch, with an English summary].

—'De bedrogen bedrieger als oorsprong van het geschiedverhaal bij Herodotus en in het Oude Testament', in A.M. van Erp Taalman Kip and I.J.F. de Jong (eds.), *Schurken en schelmen. Cultuurhistorische verkenningen rond de Middelandse Zee* (Festschrift J.M. Bremer; Amsterdam: Amsterdam University Press, 1995), pp. 33-43 [in Dutch].

—'Herodotus, vader van de bijbelse geschiedenis?', *Amsterdamse Cahiers voor Exegese en Bijbelse Theologie* 14 (1995), pp. 9-61 [in Dutch, with an English summary].

—'In de bijbel is de pen van Herodotus zichtbaar', *Athenaeum Illustre* 4 (1995), pp. 36-39 [in Dutch].

—'Wie doodde Goliath? Onzekerheid in de bijbelse levensbeschrijving van koning David', *Biografie-bulletin* 6 (1996), pp. 49-58 [in Dutch].
—'De zoon van een vreemdeling, een Amalekiet. Observaties over 2 Samuel 1', in Jan-Wim Wesselius, Hanna Blok, Karel Deurloo, F.J. Hoogewoud and Piet van Midden (eds.), *Magister Morum: Opstellen voor Jan Sanders van leden van de Societas Hebraica Amstelodamensis* (Amsterdam: [privately printed], 1996), pp. 63-70 [in Dutch].
—'Analysis, Imitation and Emulation of Classical Texts in the Hebrew Bible', *Dutch Studies Published by the Near Eastern Languages and Literatures Foundation* 2 (1996), pp. 43-68.
—'The Language of the Hebrew Bible and the Language of Ben Sira and the Dead Sea Scrolls', in T. Muraoka and J. Elwolde (eds.), *Sirach, Scrolls and Sages: Proceedings of a Second International Symposium on the Hebrew of the Dead Sea Scrolls, Ben Sira, and the Mishnah, Held at Leiden University, 15–17 December 1997* (Leiden: E.J. Brill, 1999), pp. 338-45.
—'Discontinuity, Congruence and the Making of the Hebrew Bible', *SJOT* 13 (1999), pp. 24-77.
—'Towards a New History of Israel', *Journal of Hebrew Scriptures* [www.arts.ualberta.ca/JHS or www.purl.org/jhs] 3 (2000–2001), article 2; PDF version pp. 1-21.
—'The Road to Jezreel: Primary History and the Tel Dan Inscription', *SJOT* 15 (2001), pp. 83-103.
—'The Writing of Daniel', in J.J. Collins and P.W. Flint (eds.), *The Book of Daniel: Composition and Reception* (Leiden: E.J. Brill, 2001), pp. 291-310.
—*Language, Style and Structure in the Book of Daniel* (forthcoming).
—'The Message of the Book of Jonah' (forthcoming).
Younger, K.L., *Ancient Conquest Accounts: A Study in Ancient Near Eastern and Biblical History Writing* (Sheffield: JSOT Press, 1990).
Zadok, R., *The Jews in Babylonia During the Chaldean and Achaemenian Periods According to the Babylonian Sources* (Haifa: University of Haifa, 1979).

INDEX OF REFERENCES

OLD TESTAMENT

INDEX OF AUTHORS

JOURNAL FOR THE STUDY OF THE OLD TESTAMENT
SUPPLEMENT SERIES